WHOLE EARTH
JUSTICE

A STORY ABOUT CHANGING THE WORLD

To Terri Herb
Thanks
Gene

GENE TIERNEY

PAGE PUBLISHING, INC.
Conneaut Lake, PA

First originally published by Page Publishing 2020

www.wholeearthjustice.com

ISBN 978-1-64628-272-2 (pbk)
ISBN 978-1-64628-273-9 (digital)

Printed in the United States of America

A special thanks to the following people for their help
and encouragement in the writing of this book:

Dr. Glen Anderson
Kathryn Anderson
Barbara Arney
John Benda
Rob Dalton
Ann Manning
Marla Mullaney
Jim Tierney
JoAnne Tierney
Maura Tierney
Michael Tierney
Hobart Stocking
Jay Walljasper

INTRODUCTION

Apocalyptic messages about environmental and social problems ahead have become ubiquitous. We receive them from the media, they're talked about by friends and family, they've made it into the curriculum of our schools, and they're the subject of endless punditry. Often these messages are designed to make us fearful and, through that fear, build a consensus for change. This story is different from that. It's not about external or abstract threats; it's about us, humankind, our journey, and how the problems we face fit into that journey. It provides a context for the threats we face and a context for our response. In this story, human civilization is neither the villain, a complacent fool, or a selfish victim; we're the heroes, and we're on an epic journey of self-discovery and growth as we face the conditions, consequences, and opportunities presented along the path of our journey.

According to science, modern humans emerged two hundred thousand years ago in Africa. Based on our unique qualities and character, it was predictable that humanity would become the dominant species upon this planet. It was predictable that the human population would grow and flourish and consume greater and greater portions of the planet's bounty, placing increasing pressure on all other living species. So it's no surprise that our actions would someday tax the capability of Earth to provide for us, and our very existence would be threatened. This is a familiar story we've seen play out many times before. A new species enters an environment with few rivals. Its population increases until the environment is no longer able to sustain further growth and consumption. Eventually, the once-dominant species becomes vulnerable to new threats, and its population is diminished or extinguished altogether. Nature is a self-regulating system that balances itself through boom-and-bust cycles of growth and destruction.

So is the demise of humanity inevitable? Is there no way for us to alter this natural cycle of growth and destruction? And if there is another path, what would that look like? We explore those questions here.

Whole Earth Justice tempers the dark, threatening messages of environmental, social, and economic self-destruction, with a reminder of our collective capacity to generate transformative change. Contrary to dogmatic assertions, we have not been complacent and sitting motionless while disaster looms, but rather, we have been building toward this moment of transformation for a very long time. This manuscript presents the familiar development process of individual humans (from a dependent childhood to an independent adolescence, to an interdependent adulthood) as a pattern that can be seized upon to understand human history and navigate out of the crises we currently face. Lastly, we explore how our current situation challenges us to leave our tribal instincts behind, to learn how to speak with a communal voice, to become a more mature, interdependent humankind, and in the process create a more just civilization.

It's true that we live in perilous times. Times in which our very survival as a civilization and as a species are on the line. But we also have the comfort of knowing our past and what we're capable of, and perhaps that knowledge can help us understand our present and future? We are ready for the challenges this time in our journey presents. We have the tools and skills to grow and create a more sustainable inclusive world, and we are doing so every day.

> *It is from numberless diverse acts of courage and belief that human history is shaped. Each time a man stands up for an ideal, or acts to improve the lot of others, or strikes out against injustice, he sends forth a tiny ripple of hope; and crossing each other from a million different centers of energy and daring, those ripples build a current which can sweep down the mightiest walls of oppression and resistance.* (Robert F. Kennedy)

Chapter 1

THE BIRTH OF WHOLE EARTH JUSTICE

University of Minnesota Campus

As the police arrive at the rally, it's hard to distinguish between the protesters and the many onlookers who stopped to watch. The rally was strategically planned for four thirty to coincide with a meeting of the university regents, rush-hour traffic and to make the evening news. The traffic along Fourth Street, running in front of the administration building starts to slow as protesters march along the sidewalk, yelling slogans.

"DIVEST THE ENDOWMENT FROM PREDATORY COMPANIES!"

"TAKE BACK AMERICA!"

"STOP ECONOMIC INJUSTICE NOW!"

"RESPECT THE LIVING ENVIRONMENT OF PLANET EARTH!"

"END POVERTY! STOP HOMELESSNESS!"

The crowd is clearly with the protesters, and many show their support by pumping their fists and cheering. Honks of support also rise from the cars slowly passing by. The protest rally is indistinguishable from scores of other student protests that had happened on that same spot over the years except for one noticeable characteristic, many of the protesters are wearing a pair of underwear briefs on the outside of their pants.

A group of police officers gathers in an open space next to the administration building. One of them, a linebacker-sized man nervously tapping a thick baton against the palm of his hand, walks over to what looks like the core of the protest group and says, "It's time to leave. Anyone who stays will be arrested and forcibly removed."

"What are the charges, Officer?" a woman with a cyclist windbreaker and a backpack says.

"Who are you? Are you in charge here?" the policeman snaps.

"Professor Justice Miller," she replies.

The police officer doesn't respond, he walks away and then is seen talking to someone on the phone. Justice takes out her mobile phone and texts, "MIGUEL, MINNOW IN TROUBLE! PROTEST ON CAMPUS…LIKELY ARRESTED WITH OTHERS SOON. TRYING TO HOLD OUT UNTIL MEDIA ARRIVES."

Miguel is Justice's cousin and lifelong friend who is an attorney in Chicago. He reads the message while riding the L Train home after work. He reflexively frowns, pauses to think for a moment, then dials Jake Johnson an old friend from the days when they were both undergrads at the university and worked together at the campus newspaper. Jake now works for a Twin Cities TV station.

"Hey, how are you doing, Miguel, it's been a while," Jake says.

"Hi, Jake, yes, I'm looking forward to catching up, but I've got kind of a situation I'm hoping you can help me with."

"Sure, what's up?"

"Well, it's my cousin Justice."

"Oh yeah, the goalie from the Gophers women's hockey team a few years ago? She made that amazing save that put the Gophers into the Frozen Four NCAA semifinals, right? Yes, but that was almost a decade ago and she's an economics professor at the U now."

"Anyway, she's involved with a protest rally taking place at the university in front of the administration building and the police are getting ready to start arresting people."

"Right now?" Jake asks.

"Yes, as we're speaking, I just received a text from her!"

"Well, nothing came through the police channels, we monitor constantly," Jake says.

"Can you get a crew in there?" Miguel asks.

"Yep, on their way."

"Thanks, Jake. I'll call you back in a little bit."

Then Miguel texts Justice back, "CHANNEL 11 CAMERA CREW ON ITS WAY. I'M ON MY WAY AS WELL. I WILL CONTACT YOU AS SOON AS I ARRIVE. COOPERATE SO YOU DON'T GET HURT, BUT DON'T TALK."

Then Miguel calls his wife. "Hi, babe, sorry, but there's been a change of plans."

"What's up?" his wife, Alesha, says.

"I'm riding the train out to the airport, I've got to go to Minneapolis. Justice has been arrested and needs my help."

"Oh my god, what happened?" Alesha asks.

"I don't have details yet, but my understanding is that she's being arrested for participating in some kind of protest. I will keep you posted as I learn more. My guess is, I'll be home tomorrow some time."

"Hard not to appreciate the irony of someone named Justice being arrested for being a protester," Alesha adds.

"Yeah, well it could have serious repercussions for her, depending on what happens. Universities and colleges aren't very tolerant of this kind of thing."

"Don't you need to pack a bag or something?"

"I'm sure I can find what I need over at Mom and Dad's. They never throw anything away."

"Okay, well, good luck, let me know if there's anything I can do."

Back on campus, the top police officer blares through a megaphone, "Anyone who doesn't disperse now will be arrested! If you're a student or faculty member, you risk being suspended."

The police line up as if preparing to take an action to disperse them and the atmosphere intensifies. Shouts of instructions ring out through the crowd.

"Everybody, sit down!"

"Try to resist until the news media gets here!"

"Lock arms!"

Two hours later, and Miguel is seated at his gate at O'Hare waiting for his flight. Just as he's about to board the plane, a breaking news story flashes across the gate TV on the protest rally. He holds off boarding and calls Justice's phone. Voice mail.

He calls Jake.

"I saw the story in the airport," Miguel says.

"Yeah, we got a national exclusive, thanks to your tip."

"Has anyone been hurt? Any word on Justice?"

"No, but the police reported there was one faculty member involved, and yes, I know some batons came out and a few protesters got roughed up a little by the police. I believe several were taken to the university hospital with superficial wounds."

"Okay, thanks, Jake, I'll call you when I get in. It's close to mid-night by the time Miguel's plane arrives at MSP airport." As soon as the plane touches down, Miguel calls Jake.

"Any new information?" Miguel asks.

"I don't have anything new about Justice, but four protesters were sent to the university hospital with minor injuries."

"Man, how did it get so out of hand?"

"I don't know, but as I understand it, they were there because a regents meeting was taking place. Somebody at the university wanted them removed and the protesters sat down and refused to cooperate. There is one weird aspect to the story, however," Jake says.

"What's that?"

"Well, we got an exclusive because of your call."

"I'm not following," Miguel says.

"This was a major police action, but it never came across the police radio. None of the other media outlets got anything either."

"And that's unusual?" Miguel asks.

"Well, for this type of action it is…I mean, they do SWAT actions and other types of raids in secret for tactical or intelligence reasons, but not for this kind of thing."

"Well, maybe it was a spontaneous action," Miguel says.

"That's the thing, if it was a spontaneous action, they would have been all over the radio talking about it. No, this had to have been planned in advance and deliberately kept silent," Jake says.

"That means the police had to have known the protest was going to take place, and they carefully planned the intervention, so as to not be filmed by the press."

"That's interesting. Don't the protesters usually provide a notice to the media of events like this?"

"Yes, but we don't usually send a reporter unless it's going to be really big or the police are going to be involved. We just get too many groups looking for coverage."

"Sure, I see," Miguel responds.

"Thanks for your help, Jake, I'll talk to you tomorrow."

Miguel texts Justice's phone. No response. He then calls the phone, and it goes right to voice mail, and he leaves a message.

He then calls the police and identifies himself as Justice's attorney.

"Spell your full name please," the police operator says.

"M-I-G-U-E-L M-I-L-L-E-R."

"And a phone number, please."

He gives her his mobile phone number.

"Okay, I'll call you back in a few minutes," the operator says.

A couple of minutes later, the police call back.

"Okay, she had given us your name earlier," the operator says.

"Can I see her right now?" Miguel asks.

"No, you can see her at the courthouse in the morning."

"Has she been interviewed yet?"

"No, she requested her attorney be present, so the interview never happened."

"What are the charges?"

"Nothing yet, you'll have to go to the court in the morning."

He then calls Justice's parents. Both her parents pick up different extensions and say hello.

"Uncle Matt and Aunt Emma, this is Miguel, I've just arrived in town and I've spoken with the police. Justice is in custody for the night but is scheduled to go before Judge Anderson in the morning at the Hennepin County Government Center downtown. I'll be able to see her then."

"Thank you so much for coming, Miguel, we're worried she's injured. The TV showed her getting hit and being dragged off."

"I think she's probably okay. The police said they took several protesters to the hospital with superficial wounds, but she wasn't among the injured."

Miguel then calls his parents' house to tell them he's in town and asks if he can stay there.

"Of course, come over," his mother, Maria, says.

By the time he pulls up at his parents' house, both his mom and dad are up in their bathrobes, and they've got tea on the stove.

"I tried to call you, and then when I didn't get through, I called Alesha, and she told us you were on your way already. Matt and E are pretty upset and worried," Miguel's mother, Maria, says.

"Yeah, I just spoke with Uncle Matt and Aunt E a few minutes ago. I'm going to meet Justice at the courthouse in the morning."

"Did you see the news accounts on TV?" Miguel asks.

"Yes," his dad, John, says. "There's tape of Justice being struck with a baton and then being carried off by police. I hope she didn't get hurt."

Miguel arrives at the courthouse in downtown Minneapolis at 8:00 a.m. and identifies himself as Justice Miller's attorney to the clerk of the court. He's informed that Judge Anderson will be the presiding Judge and the arraignment will take place at 9:00 a.m. He's also told that he can see his client at eight forty-five in the conference room attached to Judge Anderson's courtroom. He's shown to the conference room to wait.

He contacts Jake and tells him what the schedule is.

"Yep, we've got a crew ready. We'd love to interview Justice if they release her this morning," Jake says.

"Okay, I'll talk to her about that."

"We'll have a reporter and camera crew set up on the steps of the courthouse if she decides to speak."

About twenty minutes later Justice arrives in the conference room, looking tired and disheveled.

She gives Miguel a big hug and looks like she's about to cry. "Thank you for coming!"

"Grampa taught us Minnows must stick together and help each other," Miguel responds. "Are you injured?" Miguel asks.

"I've got a bruise on my forearm, but other than that, I'm fine," she says as she twists her arm to reveal the bruise.

"I'm not sure what they're going to charge you with, so just let me do the talking and follow my instructions."

"Yes, well, why should this moment be any different?" she says with a smile and a sarcastic voice.

Miguel rolls his eyes and smiles.

"They're likely to file charges, then they will set bail if necessary, depending on the charges."

A few minutes later, they're both led into the courtroom.

The bailiff announces, "All rise, the Honorable Judge Anderson presiding."

The judge enters the courtroom and asks Justice if Miguel is her attorney.

She nods.

The judge says, "You must speak so the court reporter can record your answer."

"Oh, sorry, yes, Your Honor, Miguel Miller is my attorney."

Then the county attorney reads the charges: "Count one, obstruction and interfering with a police action. Count two, incitement."

"How do you plead?" Judge Anderson asks.

"Not guilty, Your Honor," Miguel says.

There is some discussion among the judge, the county attorneys, and Miguel about bail, but in the end, the judge releases her without bail. A short time later and she learns that the university administration is putting her and all the students who participated under administrative review for violations of the university's code of ethics. In her case, however, they also cited possible violations of her employment contract. This step is a precursor to any suspension or termination that would be handed down.

As she and Miguel are about to leave the courthouse, he cautions her, "I think there is likely to be some press out there. You can talk or not, it's up to you. If you decide not to speak, I may say a few words on your behalf," Miguel counsels her.

"Okay, I'm too tired and don't want to say anything," Justice responds.

When Justice and Miguel emerge onto the courthouse steps, several hundred students and her supporters are there to greet her. Their chants grow upon seeing her. "HELL NO, WE WON'T GO, TILL YOU LET JUSTICE GO!"

Reporters had set up a tangle of microphones at the bottom of the steps. Surprised to see the size of the crowd, Justice raises her arms and waves a peace sign, which set off thunderous cheering. Then she leaned forward into the mics and says, "SAVING THE EARTH IS THE ONLY WAY, THAT IS WHY WE'RE HERE TODAY!" The crowd chants the slogan back to her, but after a couple of rounds, replaces "saving the earth" with "Justice." "JUSTICE IS THE ONLY WAY, THAT IS WHY WE'RE HERE TODAY!" As two burly police officers move in to disassemble the makeshift podium, she steps away and is met by a young female reporter closely trailed by a CNN cameraman. The crowd continues chanting. "JUSTICE IS THE ONLY WAY, THAT IS WHY WE'RE HERE TODAY!"

"What was the protest about?" the reporter asks.

"We need to stand up now for the kind of world we want to live in."

The reporter continues, "Our understanding is that the demands being made by the protesters have to do with divesting university endowment funds from companies that you don't agree with?"

"We want to stop them from doing business with corporations whose actions endanger the future of our planet and the well-being of everyone who lives on it: fossil fuels, arms merchants, predatory financial institutions, and others."

"How did the protest get violent?"

"That's a good question. We were peacefully assembling in front of the administration building where the university's regents were meeting, when the police showed up and started arresting people. We continued to behave peacefully and then the police became very aggressive and started hitting people with their batons. It just spiraled out of control from there."

"Were you hit with a baton, Professor?"

"Yes, I was, in fact…" And Justice reveals a splotchy purple bruise on her forearm.

"We have film of some of the students wearing underwear over their pants. Do you know why they were doing that?"

"Yes, I do," she says with a chuckle. "It's to imitate a classic cartoon superhero outfit. They're expressing their commitment to be heroes for the cause."

"The cause of divestment?"

"No, it's bigger than that. Divestment is just one element. They're expressing solidarity and commitment to a movement focused on environmental sustainability and social justice."

"Justice for who?" the reporter asks.

Justice looks at the reporter and says, "The whole Earth needs justice. We're all in this together."

"And that's why they're wearing underwear on the outside?"

"Yes, exactly, and I think it makes the point very well."

The professor then looked straight into the camera and says, "Be a hero for social justice and environmental sustainability. Stand up and be counted now for Whole Earth Justice!"

It was a slow news day, so footage of the protest and the professor's interview played repeatedly over several hours on TV networks globally and stayed at the top of online news feeds. This made Justice into something of an international figure. For the next several days she fielded interview requests from around the country and across the globe. She continued to pop up regularly across the media in the following months, especially after similar protests erupted in other places. Justice had inadvertently become a spokesperson for what is being called Whole Earth Justice, an organic self-organizing movement centered on social and environmental justice.

Several days after the protest incident, the university terminated Justice's employment for cause, citing violations of her employment contract. But they neglected to remove the online MOOC (Massive Open Online Courses) version of her class Futurama 2.0 from the university's website. Enrollment in the class went through the roof in the wake of the media coverage. It quickly became the most popular class at the university and in a few weeks the most popular class in the country.

At this point the university began to rethink their position. Considering that Justice Miller was the granddaughter of the late Bill Miller a very popular professor of anthropology at the school. She was an alumnus of the university undergraduate and graduate schools. She was the goalie on several of the Gophers' most successful women's hockey teams and a popular professor of economics. Now she's got the most popular online class in school history, and she's starting to show up frequently on TV as a commentator on the social justice movement. The administration passed the issue of reinstating Professor Justice Miller to the board of regents for a vote. The body includes twelve regents and the school president makes thirteen. They voted to reinstate her, with probationary status, which means if she violates the terms of the probation, her termination will be reinstated. There were two no votes, one from the university president, Hogwood, and the other from Jack Dahl, a regent who owns a large medical technology company and who's name appears on several buildings around campus.

On the first day after the suspension was lifted, Justice was in her office for the first time, taking memorabilia back out of the box she had just packed up a short time earlier. A picture of her grandpa Bill sitting in a lawn chair on the dock and she and Miguel as children holding up small fish they had just caught. A picture of her parents at one of her graduations. A framed photograph from the newspaper of her making the save that sent the Gophers to the NCAA tournament that year. And a new picture of she and Miguel on the steps of the courthouse after being released from jail. The phone rings. "Miguel, thank you," Justice says as she answers the phone.

"Good morning and you're welcome. Are you back in your office yet?"

"I'm just unpacking stuff right now. By the way, there are as many pictures of you in here as there are me!"

"Ha, are you including the one of you and me on the dock with Grandpa and the fish?"

"Yes, I love that picture," Justice responds.

"Yeah, I've actually got a copy of that one too somewhere," Miguel says. "By the way, I don't know what you did to President Hogwood, but he's not your biggest fan."

"I know and I'm confused by that…I have no idea why…I'm not sure I've ever met the man."

"Well, I did a little digging," Miguel says. "He was trained as an economist at the University of Chicago, which was a very conservative economics department at the time. So he's probably not so keen on your Whole Earth Justice vision. And he was hired for his skills at fundraising from corporations and superwealthy contributors, so he may not appreciate the university being associated with such progressive activism either. Plus, when he was first hired as an economics professor, he and our grandfather were on opposite sides of a number of controversial scrapes here at the university. Anyway, he controls this probation, so you're going to have to be careful."

"Yeah, I know but I think the probation terms are fairly straightforward, aren't they?" Justice asks.

"Yes, but there are media requirements, for example…restrictions on the university being associated with certain positions, that could be open to interpretation, I suppose," Miguel responds. On the other hand, I'd say the media exposure is one of the reasons you were reinstated."

"I'll be careful, but I intend to continue my new career as Whole Earth Justice TV commentator and all around media, darling." She laughs.

"And I think you should, just recognize that man doesn't like you for some reason and he holds your contract in his hands."

"Thanks again for your help, Miguel. I look forward to seeing you and Alesha this summer up at the lake."

Chapter 2

BACK TO SCHOOL

It was a beautiful summer morning. A lone bike rider had the trail to herself just after sunrise, pedaling along the Mississippi River at the edge of downtown Minneapolis. As the trail dipped into a tunnel under the freeway, she notices the roadway above is already jammed with cars. Picking up speed down the hill, she turns onto the old rail bridge that now carries bikes and pedestrians across the river, and she glides onto campus. She's excited but apprehensive to be getting back to teaching economics after being arrested with a group of students during a protest seeking divestment of the university's endowment from socially and environmentally detrimental companies. While the students were given citations for trespassing and disorderly conduct and released, she was terminated from her job and then later put on probation and reinstated. The change of heart on the part of the administration apparently related to the spontaneous growth of her online series of classes on the evolving interdependence of the world's economy. Professor Justice Miller's summer class was moved to Northrop Auditorium at the University of Minnesota because of demand.

As a child visitor, she had attended a class at Northrop Auditorium that was being taught by her grandfather Bill, who was a popular anthropology professor at the university. As a student, and then faculty she attended many concerts, lectures, and dance performances there over the years as well, including one in which she and her teammates on the Gopher women's hockey team were honored for their NCAA Frozen Four Tournament appearance.

She rides down Pleasant Street to the bike racks on the side of Northrop. They're all full, unusual for summer session she thinks as she pedals to another set of racks several blocks away. Locking her bike, she hurries to the building where she finds a huge crowd of students in front of the building. Spotting her, several students rush up to her and tell her the police have canceled the class.

"What? Why?" she responds.

Several officers from the campus police force stand at the top of the steps blocking the entrance. Justice takes a deep breath and walks up to them. "I'm Professor Justice Miller and this is my class. Why are you not allowing us in?"

"Sorry, Professor. We're just following orders."

"Whose orders?"

"Chief of police, ma'am."

"Could you get the chief of police on the phone for me right now please?" she directs in a polite, firm tone.

"Sure." The police officer dials a mobile phone and hands it to Justice. Chief Thompson. "Ma'am."

"Chief Thompson, this is Professor Justice Miller. Why is my class being shut down?"

"Your suspension has been reinstated and your class terminated on orders of President Hogwood," he says flatly.

Justice pauses and thinks for a second, then says, "Chief Thompson, could you kindly relay a message to President Hogwood for me? Tell him I'm going to be on TV a lot in the next few months, and I intend to tell the truth...so he's deciding right now what's going to be said!" Then without waiting for an answer she hands the phone back to the officer.

She hears the officer say to the chief, "I don't know, maybe one thousand or more, I'd say."

Justice turns and looks at the throng of students, from the top of the stairs. They begin to chant, "JUSTICE IS THE ONLY WAY, THAT IS WHY WE'RE HERE TODAY! JUSTICE IS THE ONLY WAY, THAT IS WHY WE'RE HERE TODAY!"

A minute later the officer gets a call back. "What's that again?… I can't hear you… Oh…I don't know, but they keep coming… It's well over a one thousand, I'd say…" The officer places his finger over the other ear and struggles to hear. "Yes, sir, yes, I understand… Okay, will do." And he hangs up.

"It was apparently a misunderstanding of some kind, Professor. The building is all yours." And he opens and holds the door for the professor.

Justice and the students file into the auditorium, and soon every seat is taken and a couple dozen students have plopped down in the aisles and are standing in the back.

Justice steps up to the lectern. She's clearly a little rattled and says, "Wow…I guess nothing is easy in this world…but we just had a good demonstration of the power of collaborative action." The auditorium erupts in claps and shouts. Justice regains her composure and raises a hand to quiet the crowd. "I know many of you are auditing this class or have not taken the previous class in the series called Futurama. So we're going to put some review materials on the website for you to use. These classes are about us…and our future. About where we're going and how we're going to get there. Let's get started!"

Some of the students start chanting, "JUSTICE IS THE ONLY WAY, THAT IS WHY WE'RE HERE TODAY! JUSTICE IS THE ONLY WAY, THAT IS WHY WE'RE HERE TODAY!"

Justice smiles then raises her voice as the chants continue. "This is a college course, not a protest rally!" When the class quiets, she says, "I wasn't going to say anything about the activities of the past several months…but…well, I just want to say thank you! I know this is inappropriate language for a classroom setting, but it's appropriate for me to say, I love you for coming to my rescue, and I love you for coming to the rescue of the world. Thank you!" She walks out from behind the lectern and begins to clap, directing it at the crowd. The students stand and break into another round of applause.

"Thank you, Professor," several of them call out.

She turns and writes Justice Miller on the white board, and then says, "Please…everybody call me Justice."

Chapter 3

FUTURAMA 2.0, ROAD TO AN INTERDEPENDENT FUTURE

Northrop Auditorium

Despite being an introvert by nature, Justice had developed an animated style of lecture presentations. She prowls the stage moving from side to side like a cat, always maintaining eye contact with the audience. She points, uses hand gestures, allows uncomfortable pauses, and raises and lowers her voice to keep the audience engaged and elicit reactions from them. All nods, smiles, laughs, cringes, doubts, questions, and rebuttals from the class are good as far as Justice is concerned. As a little girl she would play teacher with her grandpa Bill as the student, and he would give her tips. You need to be a bit of an actor, she remembers him saying, "Hold the audience's attention with drama, suspense, humor…whatever you can…let the performer inside of you out!"

"We live in uncertain times," Justice explains. Our culture is becoming tribalized, our politics polarized, and our problems globalized. The challenges we face threaten our health and wellbeing…and possibly our survival. While I cannot dismiss the darkness and gloom that exists, I think there is another way to see our future. And that is what this class is about. Not that the threats we face aren't real…I think they are. I just don't think the outcomes are determined yet. I see opportunities hidden in the darkness. Not just opportunities to survive, but opportunities to thrive."

"What makes you optimistic, Professor, I mean Justice," a young woman calls out.

"What makes me optimistic?" she repeats the question. "Let me answer that this way…Even as we hear every day constant news of melting polar ice caps, droughts, superstorms, heatwaves, wildfires, staggering inequality between the haves and have nots, and millions of refugees seeking to flee places where climate change combined with poverty and political breakdowns are making life miserable if not impossible, I don't believe we've lost the battle. At least not yet.

"I've spent my life studying human civilization, and I've learned a couple of truths. One is that the human capacity to create and innovate and adapt is far more powerful than we give it credit for. The story of the human journey is about our capacity to create and civilizations' capacity to build upon our collective knowledge, one generation after the other.

"Also, the history of civilization reveals patterns. Patterns that we can use to navigate with. Patterns that can transform our fears into visions of opportunities. We're on the cusp of a great transformation, and we're going to be studying and analyzing the evidence for it in this class.

"Lastly, I've learned that we should expect the unexpected. This class is a perfect example, it looked doubtful just a few minutes ago. And now, here we are."

A couple of students begin to chant again but quickly grow quiet as Justice raises her arms. "What I'm saying is that history is full of examples in which the outcome is determined at the last moment, in an unexpected way. Some of you may know that I was a goalie on the women's Gopher hockey team several years ago, and I can share something from that experience as well: Goalie is the ultimate defensive position, but it's played offensively. You attack the shooter. You take away their shot options one by one until there is nothing left for them, except to miss the net or hit you. Offense is the best defense! So don't ever give up! Do in life what your gym teacher taught you in junior high…run through the tape.

"So why am I optimistic?" she repeats the question for dramatic effect. "I'm here today, we're here today, because you decided to show up. We, and millions more like us, have decided to show up. I'm a big fan of humans, and I'd bet on them, even when the odds are long. We aren't going down without a fight." A ripple of laughter streaks across the auditorium.

"Okay, now onto the work of this class. In our world, hyperbolic claims have become common. As a result, most of us have developed a skeptical approach to what we hear. If it sounds too good to be true, it probably is—that's the common wisdom. This, of course, makes it difficult to discuss important, life-changing breakthrough ideas. This poses a dilemma for me teaching this class because I'm going to offer some extraordinary predictions about the socioeconomic character of the world, we're all going to live in soon. The information is so hopeful that it will trigger your skeptical reflex. But that's a good thing because I am going to encouraged you to embrace your skepticism by trying to disprove what I say. We're going to explore the evidence together ourselves, so you can make an honest determination on your own.

"The name of this course is Futurama 2.0, the road to an interdependent future! Futurama is a reference to the General Motors Futurama Exhibit, at the 1939 World's Fair, in New York City. What was important about the Futurama exhibit was that it created a vision for the future that was so compelling, it literally changed the expectations of the American public. Futurama painted a picture of a future in which middle-class Americans were going to be able to afford a car, or two, and live in a single-family home with a yard in the suburbs. These new suburbs were going to be appointed with schools, hospitals, shopping centers, and the whole metropolitan area would be connected by a freeway system allowing people to drive between locations quickly and safely. And according to the Futurama exhibit...it was all going to happen within twenty-five years. Futurama presented a dramatic, revolutionary vision, which was going to reshape the lives of the very people lining up to see the exhibit—not some far off generation in the future.

"So Futurama 2.0 is a bold and aspirational title for this class, which focuses on social and economic changes that are beginning to sweep the US and the world *now*! And which will transform and improve the way we live our lives. These changes are going to allow us all to have more…significantly more…and pay less. These changes are going to open vast entrepreneurial opportunities for wealth creation. And they're going to set the stage for a far more sustainable and socially just world.

"Anybody's skepticism meter go off yet?" A few people chuckle and raise their hands. "Just keep listening she says, with a smile.

"To be clear, we're still going to have problems twenty-five years from now, but many of the economic, environmental and social issues that are currently plaguing our society will improve rapidly. You're going to be more prosperous and secure than you think…and so is everyone else!

"Now, I'm going to start by telling you a story. A story some of you will be familiar with from your studies. The story goes like this:

"Great transformations in the economic and social character of Western civilization happen when large communications innovations and large energy innovations coincide. She raises her voice and repeats the point for emphasis. WHEN COMMUNICATIONS AND ENERGY INNOVATIONS COINCIDE!

"We call these periods of rapid economic and cultural change, Industrial Revolutions. For example, the First Industrial Revolution happened when the development of steam power, coincided with the development of the printing press. These combined developments led to a massive reduction in the cost of media and vast increases in availability of print materials. This in turn, led to large increases in literacy and education. And that led to more social organizing and awareness. And that led to industrialization, urbanization, and wealth creation. Energy and communications combined!

"Likewise, the Second Industrial Revolution happened, when the development of electricity coincided with the discovery and development of oil. Electricity which is an energy development also provided for vast communications innovations including the radio, TV, movies, sound recording and playing devices, the telegraph and telephone to name a few. And the oil industry gave rise to the internal combustion engine and the automobile industry, air travel, and new products including plastic's and fertilizers, building materials, solvents, and lubrications. And of course, this combination of oil and electricity also led to the geographic development that is the namesake of this class…Futurama, the development of a car-dependent suburban society. We will explore these periods and developments in much greater detail during this course.

"So large energy innovations, combined with large communication innovations, lead to large socioeconomic transformations. When we look at today through that lens, do we see transformative communications and energy innovations taking place now? I think we do. On the communications side of the equation I'd point to what I call 'networked information sharing.' Networked information sharing is what allows the shared economy to happen. It's what allows you to purchase things online. It allows you to connect with a neighbor that wants to sell his bike. It's what allows you to connect with someone willing to give you a ride someplace. It's what allows you to get reviews from past customers when you're hiring a plumber, or going to a restaurant, or investing your IRA funds. And it's what allows you to find and connect with like-minded people.

"I would also argue that we're still in the early stages of its development.

"Okay, now energy. What do we see there?"

"How about renewables?" someone shouts.

"Good, yep, renewables! In 1977 to generate a watt of power through a photovoltaic solar panel cost $76.76. In 2018, that same watt of solar power cost $0.34. I'd also include advances in battery technology here as well. They've led to electric and hybrid cars.

"And there's also improvements to wind, geothermal, and a host of other new renewable energy sources in the pipeline. And we—think about this—are still much closer to the beginning of this transformation than we are to the end of it.

"Today, the largest corporations in the world are all in a race to become 100 percent renewable. With most declaring they will do so within the next ten to twenty years. So is networked information

sharing combined with renewable energy going to be as transformative as electricity and oil in the twentieth century or steam and printing in earlier centuries? Some say we are entering the Third Industrial
Revolution. We're going to study whether that is true in this class.

"The Third Industrial Revolution is a big deal in terms of its
economic and social effects for sure…but we're not quite done yet.
I have a second story to tell you. This second story is about patterns
that have an even longer time horizon and a far greater potential
impact than the Third Industrial Revolution.

"Does civilization mature through recognizable phases, like
people do—from a dependent childhood to an independent adolescence, to an interdependent adulthood? If we impose that model
over our history, we see that prior to the Renaissance, most people
lived a dependent existence. Few had property rights, educational
opportunities, or sovereignty over there life in any way. The world
was controlled by authorities including the church, monarchs, and
various other types of nobility or elites. People were dependent on
those authority figures for everything. It was a dependent child-
like existence. In this second story, transformative change happens
through a fixed development process and the imposition of catalysts
for change. Meaning, prior to the Renaissance, there was only one
direction civilization could go. It would either remain in a dependent state or it would move toward greater independence, autonomy,
and liberty. The values and characteristics we typically associate with
adolescence! And what happened? The advent of liberal democracy
and liberation movements through the Enlightenment period and
beyond, the expansion of public education, and successive waves of
development through the industrial revolutions. Individual liberty…
independence! And as a result, the world's economic output went
through the roof. Turns out, self-interest is a big motivating factor! So
in this story, the Industrial Revolutions represented successive waves
of developments owing their existence to cultural shifts that moved
civilization away from dependence and embraced independence.

"But what catalysts led to this move from dependence to independence?" Justice waits and scans the audience. Then she says,
"Science and the discovery and development of the Americas by white

European men. I say it that way because independence only applied to the people included...and at the time, only white European males were included. During this time, at the beginning of independence, a tremendous amount of genocide and slavery also happened. We will talk much more about this in coming classes because it's still relevant to our future today. Anyway, I didn't want to pass over this history without mentioning it. So science and the discovery of the Americas were the catalysts. Science: from Copernicus and Galileo's heliocentric world, to Newton's mechanical world, to Einstein's relative world, to Schrodinger, Bohr, and Heisenberg's quantum world, science created a new narrative to explain and manipulate the natural world, and the church's authority was eroded in the process.

"Second, the discovery of the new world in the Americas. These new lands represented compelling opportunities but were too far away and too large to be controlled easily by European monarchs. Independence, self-reliance, opportunity, and manifest destiny were the only way these great lands could be settled. And there was no going back, civilization embraced independence through the Enlightenment, and through the First and Second Industrial Revolutions which were both part and parcel of this transformation from a dependent to an independent civilization.

"So the process is from dependence to independence to interdependence, and we've just described how we moved from dependence to independence. So what does interdependence look like? Interdependence means cooperation. Cooperation and benefit sharing. So the road from independence to interdependence can be characterized as moving from competition toward cooperation, from scarcity toward abundance, and from injustice toward justice. Does everybody get what I mean when I say scarcity and abundance? Scarcity is the idea that if you have something, then I can't have it. The idea that we are in competition for a fixed amount of stuff. Abundance is the idea that if we cooperate, we can make more together, and both have it. So adolescence, independence, is more focused on scarcity and interdependence is more focused on abundance.

"Do we see anything today that is moving society toward greater cooperation and interdependence? How about our global environmental problems, immigration problems, economic disparity problems, food insecurity, drug resistance and adaptation, and species die-offs and biodiversity. These are just some of the problems that will require cooperation and greater interdependence to solve. In each of these cases, individual countries are helpless to solve the problems without cooperation between them. So I would assert that global environmental and social justice issues are not just scary problems threatening our existence, they're also catalyst, moving us toward the solutions. Problems and solutions are in a dance in which neither can exist without the other.

"For a second catalyst, I'd go back to the networked information sharing from the first story as being a second catalyst because it greatly enhances our ability to cooperate. All the shared economy ventures are perfect examples of this new type of interdependent development.

"So we're describing two socioeconomic narratives playing out right now that point to massive transformational change happening in our economy and world in the immediate future. And we know something about the nature and character of these changes. They're going to involve

- more interdependence, greater cooperation, and less predatory behavior and injustice;
- more networked information, less ownership, and more sharing;
- solutions to global problems, including climate change and other environmental concerns as well as other global social justice issues;
- greater use and exploitation of renewable fuels and less fossil fuels.

Justice's delivery borrows a bit from TV pitchmen or game-show hosts.

"But wait, there's more! We'll be discussing why you, personally, should care about all this? What's in it for you to build a more interdependent sustainable world? Here's a preview:

"**More from less:** Transportation is the second biggest expense for the typical American household at about 20 percent of household income. That cost is predicated upon car ownership. But as new alternatives enter the market including rideshare, bikeshare, carshare, scooters, e-bikes—better conditions for walking, biking, and transit—and autonomous vehicles, car ownership becomes optional. Projections suggest transportation costs may be as little as 5 percent for the typical household in twenty years. Transportation is going to be more convenient, cost less, and be cleaner. And this type of thing is happening in every sector of the economy.

"**Less predation equals more:** Who here has run with weights on your ankles or tried to run in the sand? It takes a lot more energy and you go a lot slower. Well, what do you think it costs us, every time a corporation uses bankruptcy or other tactics to avoid paying environmental cleanup costs of its actions while privatizing the profits? What does it cost us when they funnel profits offshore to avoid paying their fair share of taxes? What does it cost us every time the CEO of a public corporation gets tens or even hundreds of millions of dollars in compensation?

"The economy is suffering from millions of these tiny little rip-offs every day. But there are practical, fair solutions to these problems that will boost business rather than squeeze them—and we're going to study them in this class.

"It's not just new…it's different in kind! Today, we're living in a world where an individual with a smartphone can make a video and place it free on the internet, and it can be seen by more people than a Hollywood movie. A world in which retailers that only live in cyberspace, with little or no real estate, can challenge the biggest retailers in the world. A world in which crowdfunding and other technology-based financial alternatives permit entrepreneurs and consumers to cut banks out of the process. A world in which excess capacity, like a spare room in your house, or your idled car or boat, can become a productive asset, significantly changing the value proposition of the product. A world in which an individual or a neighborhood can form their own energy utility. A world in which consumers find the contractors they need online along with reviews and ratings from previous customers. A world in which publicly traded companies work to meet environment, social, and governance goals or risk having their earnings ratios diminished through market forces. Not just new… different in kind!

"Okay, that's it for today. Please read the listed materials for the next class, including President Barak Obama's speech to the UN upon passage of sustainable development goals, as well as Pope Francis's encyclical and statement on climate change. These materials document the profound changes in attitude taking place in our culture. [Materials are included in the appendix at the back of this book.]

"I will stick around for a few minutes if any of you have questions or you want to hear more about what we covered in the first Futurama course." Justice walks down the steps from the stage and is surrounded by a group of students wanting to ask questions or talk about the protest rally and aftermath. After about thirty minutes, all the students have left, and she goes back to collect her backpack. On top of the backpack is a sealed envelope. On the envelope is written "To Justice Miller, From Whistle-Blower."

Chapter 4

THE BIRTH OF JUSTICE

Middle of the 1980s Minneapolis Minnesota

The temperature begins to plummet just as the Miller family is gathering for their annual Christmas party over at Uncle Paul's house. It's always a festive occasion with as many as fifty people in attendance most years. Emma, called E by most, and Matt Miller have no children yet, although they're twenty-four weeks into their third pregnancy. The first two pregnancies ended in miscarriages. While Emma wants to go to the party, she's a little apprehensive because it can be a loud and exhausting event. She's been tired lately and worries she might need to pull Matt away from the party early.

"Just give me a sign, E," Matt reassures her. "I'll go right up and get our coats, and we'll be out of there in two seconds."

"Okay, I like the party too ya know," she says a little defensively. "I'm just afraid of overdoing it! You know lots of questions! Lots of noise! Lots of Millers!"

"Believe me," Matt says, "you give the sign and we're out of there."

"How are you feeling?" he adds.

"I'm just tired. I'll perk up at the party."

By the time they arrive at Uncle Paul's house, the temperature has plunged to minus five. The packed snow and ice on the street makes a crunching sound as Matt and E shuffle their way up to the door of the house. They open the door and are immediately enveloped with the sounds, sights, and smells of an unrestrained party. As they stand in the foyer removing their coats and the rest of their winter gear, they're greeted with hugs and welcomes and inquiries.

"How are you feeling?"

"When are you due again?"

"Do you know what gender?"

"Do you have names picked out?"

Matt leans back, takes E's coat, and looks her right in the face and says, "Anytime!"

She smiles and mouths "Thank you" and they wade into the party.

The extended Miller family is bigger and closer than most, owing their success to among other things, a pair of modest cabins on the shores of Sugar Lake, a spring-fed beauty about an hour-and-a-half drive west of the Twin Cities. Purchasing cabins together as they did in the midsixties might have been considered unwise by some, but to Bill Miller and his younger brother, Paul, it just seemed right. Dr. Bill Miller is a professor of anthropology at the University of Minnesota, and Paul a plaintiff's attorney with a penchant for disadvantaged clients, in fights with big and powerful adversaries. On summer weekends, Bill and his wife, Marilyn, and Paul and his wife, JoAnne, raised their combined ten children, together, on the shores of Sugar Lake. Bill the patriarch of the family spent many hours on weekends talking to his grandchildren and nieces and nephews as he baited hooks and removed small perch and sunnies from their lines, while they fished the waters around the end of dock. The extended Miller family shared meals, campfires, laughter, tools, chores, board games, births, career failures, and many successes.

While the decades of the sixties and seventies were defined by suburban migration, both Bill and Paul stayed in the city. Bill works at the University of Minnesota campus just outside downtown Minneapolis, and Paul's practice is right downtown. The kids all go to public schools and earn undergraduate degrees from Minnesota colleges. For the most part, Bill's and Paul's children marry and have children of their own and many remain in the Twin Cities, although they're geographically distributed from edge to edge. The Millers see each other a lot less during the winter season when the cabins are closed, so the annual Christmas party has become the one big family gathering of winter. For many years the Christmas party took place at Uncle Paul's house, a large beautiful turn-of-the-century home in a well-preserved neighborhood, near downtown Minneapolis.

After a traditional dinner that includes Irish stew, Swedish meat-balls, and German fry sausage, everybody gathers in the living room to sing Christmas songs accompanied by various nieces and nephews playing guitars, violins, and whatever other instrument someone has taken up. E loves music and has an extensive choral background from her school days. With a beautiful soprano voice, her training and exuberance, she's always one of the most recognizable voices in the group.

Matt notices that Emma isn't singing with her usual enthusiasm.

"You okay?" Matt asks, looking into her eyes.

She pauses and then finally says, "I've developed a headache."

"I'll get our coats and warm up the car," Matt says.

"Okay, maybe that's a good idea," Emma whispers.

A minute later Matt comes down the stairs with their coats, fighting off protests from family members wondering why they're leaving so early.

Matt hands E her coat and goes out to start and warm up the car.

As he opens the door and walks back into the house, the sounds in the house have changed dramatically from a party to something else.

"E fell," Matt's cousin Jim tells him.

"What do you mean?" Matt says in an urgent voice.

"She got up to put her coat on and collapsed," Jim answers. "An ambulance is on its way."

As Matt enters the living room, E is lying on the floor. His cousin Nicolette, known as Nicky, is an internal medicine MD, is kneeling on the floor next to her. Emma's face is pale, but she's conscious.

"She's okay," Nicky says. "We should get her into the hospital though and see what's going on."

Nicky's presence is very reassuring to Matt, and she rides with them to the hospital.

At the hospital, the emergency room doctor tells Matt that, with the headache and Emma's high blood pressure, they need to do a CT scan of her head right away.

E is wheeled to a prep area for the CT scan. Matt sits quietly next to her, tightly grasping her hand.

A nurse enters the room, looks into Emma's eyes with a scope of some kind, and asks, "Do you know where you are, sweetheart?" E nods but doesn't say anything. "Can you tell me what happened?"

Matt starts to say, "She collapsed when I was getting the car started."

The nurse looks at him and says, "Let's let her talk."

Emma says in a slightly slurred tone, "I have a headache."

"When is your baby due?"

E mouths, "May."

"Is this your first child?"

She nods yes.

"Do you know the gender of the baby?"

She nods yes.

"It's a girl," Matt interjects, then apologizes.

"Okay, they're getting you ready for the CT scan," the nurse says. "Do you have some names picked out at this point?"

E mouths, "Brenda."

"Brenda...I like it," the nurse replies as she stands up.

As they move her down the hall, Matt walks alongside holding her hand.

Then the nurse directs Matt to the waiting room. He kisses Emma and tells her everything is going to be fine.

As he watches her disappear around the corner, however, he feels helpless and fearful for what is about to happen.

After what feels like a long time later, a nurse comes to tell Matt the procedure is done, and Emma is back in her room and he can go in.

As Matt enters the room, E looks like she's asleep. He sits in the chair next to her and takes her hand in his. She opens her eyes slightly, squeezes his hand, says nothing, and then closes her eyes again.

Later that evening, the attending doctor enters the room and pulls the CT scan images up onto the monitor. "What we've discovered is an aneurysm on the left side of your brain," he tells Emma and Matt. "The good news is that it has not ruptured and we think we can repair it with an operation. If the aneurysm were to rupture, it could cause lots of damage to you and the baby. Surgery to repair the aneurysm is the best option, however, in most circumstances, we should deliver the baby by cesarean section first. Your obstetrician, Dr. Stewart, will be coming in this morning to discuss her concerns regarding delivery. Babies are often viable at this point, but it is very early."

"When would the cesarean section happen?" Matt asks.

"For the baby's sake, we would like to hold off as long as possible, maybe a few days to a week, as long as her blood pressure remains stable."

Early, the next morning, Dr. Stewart and Dr. Adams, the neonatologist, the doctor who will take care of the baby once she's born, come to see Emma and Matt. They agreed with the other physicians about the plan of care. Emphasizing the fact that since she was just twenty-four weeks into the pregnancy at this point, it would be best to wait since the baby is just on the edge of viability.

Suddenly, in a voice with strength and power that Matt hadn't heard in a while, Emma looks Dr. Stewart right in the face and says, "Nobody touches this baby until she's viable. She gets a chance too!"

An awkward pause hangs in the room, as the doctor examines Emma's face for doubt. Seeing none, she purses her lips and nods, saying, "Okay, I understand."

Dr. Stewart pulls up a stool and sits down. "Every day we can delay the birth helps at this point. One of the problems with babies delivering this early is that their lungs have not fully developed yet. However, once the baby is born, we can administer a medicine directly into her lungs called Surfactant. Surfactant is a new drug, but it has proven to be very effective in improving the lung function of premature babies. In the meantime, we will do everything we can to keep your blood pressure stable and the aneurysm from rupturing. They will put you on bedrest and administer medications to try and keep your blood pressure down."

Then Matt speaks up. "What are the prospects, Doctor?"

"It's a narrow window, but I think we have a good chance of success for both the mother and baby," Dr. Stewart replies.

"Thank you," Matt says. Matt looks at E, somewhat relieved.

E turns to Matt and says, "I mean it, Matt, no matter what, this baby gets a chance."

Matt nods his agreement.

Time inched by for the next few days, with Matt hardly ever leaving his wife's side. He feels helpless and frustrated about being unable to do anything about the situation. He thinks about whether he coerced her into attending the party or missed or ignored early signs of trouble.

Knock, knock. Matt's father, Bill, enters the room. He's carrying a large bouquet of cut flowers in a vase and places them on the windowsill.

"How are you feeling, sweetheart?" Bill asks Emma.

"Pretty flowers," E says as she tries to straighten herself a little for her father-in-law.

"Have you been able to sleep?" Bill asks.

"Yes," E says softly.

"And how about you, Matt, are you getting any sleep?"

"No not much," Matt says. "I just feel so useless and helpless."

"Yeah," Bill says and nods his agreement at the difficult situation. "Have they given you any new information on the plans or schedule?" Bill asks.

"No, we're still waiting to let the baby get as strong as possible before the cesarean section is done, and then the repair operation on E's aneurysm will follow," Matt replies.

"Have they said any more about when?"

"No, although we're now in the window they originally set out…anywhere from a few days to ten days or so," Matt says.

"Well, how about if you start your daughter's education?" Bill asks.

"What do you mean?"

"Well, start reading to her."

"The baby?" Matt asks.

"Yes, she can hear you. It might be reassuring to her."

"That's a great idea," E says.

"I think there's a bookstore just down the block. I'll keep Emma company while you go find something," Bill says.

Matt returns an hour later with a book under his arm.

"What did you get?" E asks.

Bill reaches out and Matt hands him the book.

"It's a novel called *The Dandelion Insurrection*," Matt says.

"What's it about?" E asks.

Bill flips it over and reads the jacket cover.

Close your eyes and imagine the force of the people and the power of love overcoming the force of greed and the love of power. Then read *The Dandelion Insurrection*. In a world where despair has deep roots, *The Dandelion Insurrection* bursts forth with joyful abandon.

"I love this book! It beautifully captures the revolution of love that is sweeping the globe, told as an epic novel that will set your heart on fire. A rare gem of a book, a must-read, it charts the way forward in this time of turmoil and transformation."

—Velcrow Ripper, Canadian Academy Award (Genie) winner, director of *Occupy Love*

E smiles at Matt. "You're a revolutionary at heart, just like your dad."

Bill says, "Hey!" But he is really flattered at her suggestion.

Bill excuses himself, gives Emma a kiss on the head and a hug to Matt, and leaves the room.

E looks at Matt and says, "Your dad always knows what to do, doesn't he?"

"Yeah, he does," Matt says with pride.

Matt begins to read and E drifts off to sleep.

As Matt reads to E and the baby, a funny thing happens. The baby becomes more active, kicking and moving around. The nurses notice too. "I don't know what you're doing, but keep doing it," one says, "she seems to like it." Matt reads and reads and reads.

After about ten days in the hospital, E's blood pressure becomes unstable.

Dr. Stewart enters the room and says, "It's time to deliver the baby. E's blood pressure has become unstable and that can have implications for the baby as well as the mother. You've done a great job, Emma, but we need to deliver the baby now and repair the aneurysm before it ruptures. It needs to happen now!"

With great trepidation, Emma and Matt agree to proceed.

As they wheeled Emma into the bright, sterile operating room, Matt is invited to accompany Emma and sit beside her at the head of the bed to give her support. Sitting behind a blue cloth, not knowing what was happening on the other side, they huddled together hoping for the best. Moments later, they hear a weak little cry and the new baby is handed off to the neonatal team. Matt was able to get a short peek at his beautiful baby girl before she was taken to the NICU (neonatal intensive care unit).

As they were finishing with Emma, her vital signs changed dramatically requiring immediate attention from the neurosurgeon, who was standing by in case anything went wrong during the delivery. Unfortunately, the aneurysm began to leak, and Emma required another immediate surgery. As the neurosurgeon takes over, Dr. Stewart places his hand on Matt's shoulder and says, "Emma, hung in there until the very last minute." There is no question she gave your daughter a chance.

"Is E going to be okay?" Matt says.

"We will know more in a few hours," the doctor says. "Do you want to go to the NICU and see the baby?"

"No, I'm going to wait here for E," Matt says.

Finally, after what felt like an eternity, the neurosurgeon shows up in his scrubs to speak to Matt. "Emma came through the surgery fine, she's very tough. Your wife has been through a lot and will require intensive care for quite a few days. We can certainly hope for a full recovery, and we will know more in a few days. The nurse will come and get you soon so you can go see her."

When Matt walks into E's room, her head is bandaged like a mummy. She's attached to tubes of various sizes coming out of multiple places. Matt whispers into her sleeping face. Suddenly her eyes open wide, and she whispers, "Is Brenda okay?"

"She's alive and they tell me she has a good chance thanks to you," he says. "I haven't seen her yet. We'll go together when you can go. She's in good hands."

E drifts back to sleep and Matt decides to go see his daughter for the first time by himself.

Over the next few days, while Emma is recovering, Matt spends his days going from one intensive care unit to the other. He brings updates to Emma, in the form of polaroid photos taken by the NICU nurses of their sweet little Brenda. Soon E is able to make the journey herself to see her baby for the first time. As they push Emma in the wheelchair to the NICU, her energy rises and she has many questions. "How big is she? Have they found any problems? How do they feed her?"

"Just wait and see," Matt says, "it's pretty amazing."

In the NICU, baby Brenda lies in an Isolette, motionless with her eyes closed. She has a breathing tube attached to a ventilator to help her breathe. She weighs about one pound and is not much bigger than the nurse's hand. Emma leans forward and puts her hands on the Isolette. A growling involuntary sigh of emotional pain comes out of E at the separation between she and Brenda. Look at her Matt, she's beautiful. The nurse opens the little door to the Isolette and encourages Emma to put her hand in and touch the baby. Emma reaches in and strokes her baby's tender skin with tears in her eyes.

"How long will she be here?" E asks.

The nurse replies, "Babies typically go home around their due date."

Emma and Matt both silently do the math—four months.

"When can I see her again?" E says.

"We can come down again tomorrow," the nurse responds.

The next day Dr. Stewart comes in the morning to check on Emma.

He tells Emma and Matt about the complications that could occur with a baby as premature as Brenda as well as the milestones that happen along the way.

"Okay, thank you, Doctor," E says. "By the way, we decided to change her name to Justice."

"Justice, I like it," Dr. Stewart says. "Strong! That's an unusual name. How did you come up with it?"

"Well, Matt started reading to her while we were waiting for the birth. Anyway, the book Matt was reading is a novel about people seeking social justice, and the baby seemed to respond to it," Emma says.

"Well, Matt if you'd like to, the nurse interjected, you can continue to read to her here. You can also record your voice on a tape, and we can play it for her in the Isolette."

Over the next few weeks, it became clear that Emma was recovering without any further complications. However, that was not the case with baby Justice. She seemed to be in a suspended state. She continued to have breathing issues requiring the ventilator. She made very little sound. She just laid there, hooked to the ventilator. Matt had finished *The Dandelion Insurrection* and went on to other books, but he kept with the social justice theme given that baby Justice seemed to respond to them. As he was reading to her, he would place his finger in Justice's hand, and she would respond by squeezing his finger.

One day several weeks after the birth, while Matt was reading to Justice, an alarm goes off. The nurses rush to her bedside. Justice had stopped breathing again; the nurses called it apnea. Apnea was a common problem with premature babies, but this was happening more frequently, not less.

There was concern that baby Justice might have developed an infection. The neonatologist Dr. Adams comes in and examines Justice and orders lab tests and an x-ray of her abdomen.

A short time later and Dr. Adams enters E's room and begins to explain the findings of the tests to her and Matt.

"I'm sorry but Justice is quite sick," she says. "The x-rays have revealed perforations in her intestine, causing toxins to spill into her system. The pediatric surgeon is reviewing all the data now and will be in to speak with you soon."

Just then the pediatric surgeon Dr. Davis enters the room. He walks over to Justice and examines her. He turns to Matt and Emma, who are visibly shaken, and says, "I'm terribly sorry but your baby is very sick. I'm afraid she is too fragile to survive a surgery to fix her intestine. However, we can put a temporary drain into her abdomen to get rid of the toxins. If we don't do something, she will not survive."

"What are the chances she will survive without the surgery?" E asks.

"Not good either way, I'm afraid," Dr. Davis says.

"Please, Doctor," Emma begins to cry. "We must try! Please!"

"I'm sorry, it's a terrible spot to be in," he says.

Then a strange thing happens.

As Emma pleas for help, baby Justice squeezes Matt's finger. It was harder than she had squeezed before. It was as if she was listening. Her grip on his finger seemed to declare, *I'm here, I'm not afraid, don't give up on me.*

Matt demonstrates her grip to the doctor and says, "Please, Doctor, we have to try."

Dr. Davis bends down and looks at the child's grip on her father. Dr. Davis pauses as if thinking and then says, "She is very fragile...I'm not sure she can survive the surgery, but I'm willing to try, and if we can't repair the intestine, we will at least put the drain in."

Emma and Matt waited and prayed together as the surgeons worked on Justice.

When they were done, Dr. Davis the pediatric surgeon comes into the room and says, "Well, so far so good, she survived the procedure. She's a courageous but very fragile child. Only time will tell."

"Were you able to fix the perforations in the intestines okay, Doctor?" Matt asks.

"I don't honestly know," Dr. Davis says. "We did the best we could, but her intestinal wall is so fragile that we just don't know for sure if we were able to close everything. But we did place the drain in so we can eliminate the toxins from her body."

"Thank you, Doctor," Matt says.

Back in the NICU, Emma and Matt notice how small and vulnerable she looks.

"Her life has been six weeks of misery and pain," Emma cries.

"Yeah," Matt acknowledges, "but she's still alive and still fighting." Matt pulls out the book and begins reading where he left off. He reads all that night until he falls asleep in the chair next to the Isolette, the book still open on his chest. Waking up, he immediately checks on Justice. She is still alive, and the monitors are humming away. Matt begins to read again. He reads all day and baby Justice hangs in there. Every day she continues to live seems like a miracle at that point. At times it feels to Matt like they are waiting for Justice to get better, and at other times it feels hopeless, like they are waiting for her to die. He just keeps reading. It is the only thing he can do. He imagines that baby Justice is somehow being strengthened by the characters in the books, as they fight for social justice themselves. Finally, nine days after the surgery, baby Justice's begins to breathe on her own, and it appears she has started to add a little weight. Then one day, out of the blue, Justice begins to cry. It is the most beautiful sound Matt and E have ever heard. It seems like a declaration. Justice is no longer suspended in between worlds. She is here, with them, and making her presence known.

It takes several more months of hospital care. But Justice continues to gain weight and strength. She learns how to nurse. Justice becomes increasingly more animated and interacted with everyone.

By the time Matt and E are ready to take Justice home to meet the whole extended family, she has transformed into a wiggly and demanding infant.

As Emma packs up to be discharged, Katy, one of the NICU nurses who was involved in her care, comes into the room to say goodbye to Emma and baby Justice.

"Thank you so much," Emma says as she gives Katy a hug.

"That little girl of yours," Katy says, "she has quite the fighting spirit. Only a pound when she starts but a heart, and will to live, as big as a mountain. I feel like she's already taught me things about life."

"How so?" E says.

"Life is worth fighting for! Don't ever give up!" Katy says. "I suspect this world will be hearing more from Justice Miller!"

Chapter 5

CRETE, 2005

The Plati-Summit Trail is a wilderness hiking trail in central Crete that rises and falls 2,500 feet in elevation, passing two summits along the way. Rated as difficult in the guidebooks, its estimated to take seven to nine hours to walk in good walking conditions. The largest of the Greek islands, Crete has a beautiful coastline that is dotted with small villages. The interior is mostly wild with small mountain ranges, spectacular river gorges, and ruins, some of which go back to the Minoan civilization, which predates Ancient Greece.

Holly, Kat (Kathy), and Justice are friends from high school. They're between there freshman and sophomore years at different colleges and they've come to Greece during summer break to do a little budget-conscious touring. They all played on the same high school hockey team and were veterans of long hikes in Minnesota's rugged North Woods, so they decide to try a challenging trail that winds into the interior of the island to some spectacular ruins. In some places, the trail is no more than a worn spot on the grass. The only water is a spring-fed well several hours in. They each pack a lunch in their backpack and carry a jacket they can put on, if it gets cold or starts to rain. They leave the hostel early so they can get back before the sun sets.

About two hours into the hike, they decide to stop for a rest.

"You know, we haven't seen another person since we entered the trail," Holly says.

"How much farther do you think it is to those Byzantine-era ruins?" Kat asks.

"The guy at the hostel said they are at the top of the second summit," Justice answers. "I think we should be coming up on the first within an hour and the second an hour after that. Let's plan on eating our lunch at the second summit," Justice says.

Kat pulls her sandwich out of her bag and begins eating it.

Justice doesn't say anything; she just looks at her.

"What? I'm hungry, I need fuel," Kat says defensively.

Ten minutes later and Justice is back on her feet. "Come on, let's go!"

"Don't be so controlling," Kat says.

Justice doesn't respond but looks at Holly and rolls her eyes.

"You could loosen up a little," Holly says as she stands up to put on her backpack.

Justice says nothing and heads out walking faster than before. Soon the other two are out of sight. She waits for them at the first summit, but they say little upon reuniting. This time Holly takes out her sandwich and eats it. Fifteen minutes later, Justice is once again saying, "Come on, let's go!"

Kat and Holly just keep talking and remain seated.

"Fine, I'll see you back at the hostel." Justice heads out by herself.

When she gets to the second summit, she eats her lunch and explores the ruins. They're stone ruins of a small fort or encampment of some type. She walks inside what looks like it might have been a lookout. From that vantage point, she could see many miles in every direction. Far off in the distance she can see the ocean, with many miles of wilderness in between. Justice looks out and tries to imagine the life of the person who would have been assigned to that post many centuries ago and looked out over the same landscape from the same vantage point.

By the time Justice is done and ready to go, she looks back down the trail and still sees no sign of the Kat and Holly yet so heads back out onto the trail by herself. About an hour later and she stops and looks around. The trail seems to have ended. She decides she must have missed a turn, and she begins to trace her steps back the way she came, but she isn't able to find the trail or even familiar territory. She calls out but hears nothing back. "KAT, HOLLY! ANYBODY!" *It must be this way*, she thinks and heads out across a field. In about half an hour, she comes across a partially eaten carcass of a mountain sheep. "KAT, HOLLY! ANYBODY! "Nothing. She walks for another hour and then she comes across the same sheep carcass again. The sun is now getting lower, and she realizes that here, closer to the equator, the summer sun sets much earlier than in Minnesota. She picks up the pace of her walking. Off in the distance she sees a high peak. *I wonder if that's the peak where the second summit is?* She drinks the last of her water and scales the hill. At the summit, nothing looks familiar. It's wilderness as far as she can see, and the sun is now an orange disk threatening to disappear over the horizon. Panic and despair set in and she sits on a log and begins to cry. She's exhausted, lost, hungry, and out of food and water, and it looks like she's going to have to spend the night alone in the wilderness with who knows what predators lurking in the shadows. After a few minutes, she pulls herself together. *You can't afford to panic now*, she thinks. *Work the problem.* She looks through the backpack for anything useful. A small lighter. *Thank God, it works. Fantastic! Now, first things first…I'm probably going to have to spend the night, so find a rock wall or something I can have my back to. This will cut down the directions I could be attacked from. Build a campfire in front of me so I can be between the rock wall and the fire. Find a stick I can use to defend myself if I need to fight something off.* Within thirty or forty minutes she's built a fire and stockpiled a small amount of wood for the night and is ready to climb into her protective space for the evening. Just before the sun disappears over the horizon, she marks an arrow in the dirt pointing at the place where the sun goes down and marks a *W* for *West* into the dirt. As darkness settles in, she goes through a mental checklist looking for something else she can do before its dark. Thinking of nothing her mind wanders back to a time when she was a little girl fishing on the end of the dock, with her grandfather.

With a small sunfish on her line, she walks over to her grandpa Bill to have him remove the small fish from her line.

"Grandpa, does God live in the fish too?"

"What do you mean?" he says as he takes the sunny off the line and releases it back into the lake.

"Well, in Sunday school, the teacher said God lives in us all. Does that mean he lives in the fish too?"

"Oh, I see," Grandpa says. "Well, let me answer that this way. First, God is a *she* too, you know!"

"God's a girl?" Justice says.

"Yes, and a boy, God's both," her grandfather says. "Also, I don't think God lives in us or the fish."

"You don't?" Justice says with surprise.

"No, I think both us and the fish live in God," Bill says. "God is like the lake water—all the fish live in it," he instructs. "When we catch the fish and take them out of the water, what happens?" her grandpa asks her.

"We have to put them back in the water or they'll die," Justice answers.

"Right," Bill confirms. "We all live in God and we can't really be removed from God. We couldn't live outside of God. So if you're ever really scarred, ask yourself, if you're still alive, if you are…you'll know you're still with God. And then you can say thank you for still being with you and ask her what you should do!"

A smile creeps over Justice's face as she pokes the fire with her stick. "Thank you, God, for being with me tonight. Thank you for this fire. Thank you for this rock and stick. And my health, and mind, and memory and strength. Thank you, God, and please help me to know what to do and give me the strength to do it. Amen."

Throughout the night, she hears noises in the brush and animal sounds in the distance. She also thinks she sees eyes looking at her from beyond the tree line. She sleeps in short stints. By dawn, the fire is cold and so is she, but she's made it through. She gets up and collects more wood and restarts the fire. She marks another arrow in the sand pointing to where the sun came up on the horizon and writes E by the arrow for east in the sand. She marks *N* and *S* with her stick. How long had she walked past her last known trail point at the second summit? *Maybe six hours*, she thinks. Fifteen miles maximum distance if she walked in a straight line. Since she was probably walking in circles, she cuts it in half. *I'm probably no more than seven miles from the second summit*, she thinks. The trail loops and ends where it began, and in the morning when they started the sun was at their backs, so they were probably moving west. In the afternoon, even though it was cloudy, she was probably going east, she thinks. She looks out from the top of the hill she's on and sees a group of peaks that look like they might be five to ten miles in a southwesterly direction. One of those must be the second trail summit. *So if the trail was headed east from those peaks…I should walk straight south to intersect the trail. That means I need to keep the sun on the left side of my face in the morning and on the right side of my face in the afternoon.* Justice walks due south for four hours, ever vigilant to keep the sun to her left side as it rose above her head.

Finally, about midday, she sees a little car moving down the hillside in the distance, trailed by a cloud of dust. She runs south hoping the roadway crosses her path and she can get there first.

Oh, please, please, please!

She's confronted by a thick grove of tall, prickly bushes. Seeing no way around, and fearful of missing the car, she puts her arms up over her face and plows straight through. She sustains widespread laceration and her clothes torn. But there it is, the road, down a steep sand and gravel hill! She rushes down the bank. She falls and her shoe goes flying off. She picks it up with her hand and gets onto the roadway just in a nick of time. She steps onto the roadway hands up and waving just as the small car reaches her location. The car swerves and stops. Justice limps over to the car. Inside are an old man and woman.

"I'm lost. Do you speak English?"

The old man points at her and says, "American? Justice?"

"Yes, yes, Justice," she says. "Oh, thank you!"

The driver opens the door and she climbs in. As the car pulls away, Justice begins to cry in the back seat.

The old woman reaches back and touches her leg as if to say, *It's okay.*

As the car enters the village, the old man starts honking his horn at a large group of people gathered in the village square. He rolls down his window and starts yelling, "American Justice! American Justice!" Kat and Holly run up and greet her with hugs shrieks of joy as she climbs out of the car. The crowd cheers as the three American college students jump up and down while embracing each other.

"I am so sorry I was so bossy," Justice blurts out.

They hug her again, explaining that when they got back at the hostel, they were surprised she wasn't there to greet them in the garden with a glass of wine. By nightfall they panicked. By noon on the following day, with help from the hostel manager, they had organized the entire village into a search party. Finding the lost American Justice became every one's mission.

Several days later at the airport in the Crete capital of Heraklion, waiting for the flight home to Minneapolis, Justice pulls out her diary and makes an entry: "I was wrong to be so insistent that my hiking partners go at the pace I wanted to go at. I'm grateful for Holly and Kat's friendship. I've repeatedly apologized to them both. I've learned a couple of other things from the experience as well. I allowed myself to have emotional moments in which I cried, but I could also pull myself out of them and do what needed to be done. I discovered that panic and despair are controllable choices. I could close my eyes and focus my attention on my breathing and the panic moment would pass. I realized I could remain calm and engaged. Don't let fear or depression or denial stop you from doing what needs to be done. Search for fixed points and patterns that can be used to navigate with. Work the problems deliberately and judiciously and don't give up. Never give up! And check in with God."

Chapter 6

AMERICAN DREAMLESSNESS

Justice, a recent graduate of the University of Minnesota, pulls her parents' Honda to the front entrance of her grandfather Bill's assisted living facility. Bill, eighty-five, a retired cultural anthropology professor at the university waves, opens the passenger door and exclaims, "Quick, let's break out of here before they're on to us!"

Justice plays along. "Trouble with Nurse Ratchet?" She alludes to the infamous character from *One Flew Over the Cuckoo's Nest*.

"No, it's just that I've got a lot of girlfriends in there, and it's about dinnertime." He grins. "Apparently, I was overbooked for this evening, so your graduation party is a very well-timed event."

"Well, I'm glad to help out," Justice says.

As Bill buckles up, Justice puts her new iPhone into the cup holder and turns into the busy street.

"What's that?" he asks.

"It's a new Apple iPhone 3G. Mom and Dad got it for me as a graduation present. You won't believe what it can do, Grandpa."

Bill picks up the small black device and looks it over. "Is this the thing that's been on the news because people are lining up in front of the store for hours to get one?"

"Yep, that's it!"

"It's really thin, isn't it?" Bill observes. "What's the big deal about it?"

"Well, it has a camera in it, and a calculator. You can get your e-mail and text messages and has tons of different apps that do amazing things," Justice responds.

"Can you still call someone with it?"

She laughs. "Yeah, Grandpa, it's still a phone too."

"Amazing," Bill says.

"I just downloaded a new app called Uber. It's a new company that allows you to get a ride from someone nearby. A driver who is in the Uber system lets the app know when he or she is willing to take a passenger, and then people who are looking for a ride somewhere can contact them. When the ride is over, one person's account gets credited and the other person's is debited. No cash anywhere!" Justice says.

"And how do you see yourself using Uber?" Bill wonders.

"To me, it means flexibility. I don't have to own a car if I don't want to. And right now, I don't want the expense of a car. So I can use Uber to get rides if it's too cold to bike or I am going somewhere not close to a bus or light rail line. That's worth a lot to me. Freedom, I'd call it."

"Smart kid," Bill says. It's funny but I remember describing my graduation gift in the very same terms—freedom."

"What was your graduation gift, Grandpa?"

"It was an old car. My first. Just like you, it meant I could get where I needed to go when I needed to go there."

"Yeah, but cars are expensive! According to AAA it's almost 8,500 bucks a year to have a car. But it's not just about money, Grandpa. Not having my own car is good for the environment, and for my personal health since I'll walk and bike more."

"You make me optimistic about our future, Justice! Are you thinking about grad school yet?"

"Come on, Grandpa, we're just on our way to my graduation party," Justice protests.

"All right, I'll give it a rest. For the rest of the day anyway. I understand you're playing goalie again, this time on a men's team?"

"Ha, who told you that?"

"Your dad," Bill acknowledges. "And I understand it's for your cousin Miguel's team."

"Well, yes, that's true, but it's not a big deal, it's just an old man's league," Justice responds.

"As I recall, Miguel is a pretty good defenseman, and he's a year younger than you...I'm not sure I'd refer to that as an old man's league," Bill says.

"I know, I just mean it's a league of former high school and college players, playing for fun. They didn't have a goalie, so his teammates asked him if he'd ask me to play."

"That must have made you feel pretty good," Bill says.

"Yeah, I guess so, it was nice of them to ask, and after a couple of games, I feel like I can do the job okay."

"And how does Miguel feel about having his cousin playing on his team?"

"Well, he hasn't said specifically, but I get the impression he's okay with it," Justice says. At least as long as we keep winning!"

"Well, I actually saw Miguel the other day and I asked him about it."

"And what did he say?" Justice asks.

"He said he didn't think there was another woman on the planet that could do it as well as you," Bill tells her.

After Justice's traumatic birth, and Emma having had multiple miscarriages, Matt and E Miller decided against trying to have additional kids of their own. They always thought they would like to adopt a second child, but money and careers and life conspired against them and it just never happened. So Justice grew up as an only child; however, with the extended Miller clan and Sugar Lake, she had plenty of close-related kid relationships. Among the closest to her age was a cousin named Miguel Miller. Miguel's mother, Maria, was born in Mexico and is married to one of Paul's sons, John. John and Maria live in the Twin Cities suburbs and would typically go to Sugar Lake on summer weekends. So Miguel and Justice became as close and as rivalrous as siblings.

Since hockey was the Miller family sport, Miguel also played in high school but for a different school and a year behind Justice.

Miguel was an accomplished defenseman, on a great high school team that made it to the state high school hockey tournament during his tenure. He tried out for the men's gopher hockey team but didn't make the cut. He could have gone to a division III school and played or gone to the junior leagues for a couple of years, but he decided it was time to just go to school and play for fun.

Miguel and Justice grow up with separate groups of friends, but they're as close as most brothers and sisters growing up a couple of years apart. He's got a big personality and charismatic smile, and Justice would become annoyed at her girlfriends when they pleaded with her to fix them up with Miguel. While they were only a year apart in age, they were a couple of years apart in class because after not making the gopher hockey team, Miguel spent a year traveling, particularly in South and Central America. Justice was really the hockey star, but Miguel was really the bigger personality on campus. They were frequently seen together on campus and Miguel provided an entrée into social groups that Justice, who was often tentative outside the hockey rink, would have had trouble accessing on her own. During those undergraduate years while Justice was the goalie on the university's women's varsity hockey team, and competing for the NCAA Championship, Miguel was a journalism major and writing for the *Minnesota Daily* campus newspaper.

A few hours later, after Holly and Kat and the last guests have left the graduation party, Justice finds herself in the den at her parents' house, sitting with her grandfather Bill. The TV is on in the background and the new American president, Barack Obama, steps to the microphone. Bill turns the sound up. The president is announcing the bankruptcy of General Motors. "*Its stakeholders have produced a viable, achievable plan that will give this iconic American company a chance to rise again. It's a plan tailored to the realities of today's auto market.*"

"Wow, that's sure interesting given our discussion earlier today," Bill remarks.

"How so?" Justice responds.

"Well, General Motors was one of the companies that really convinced people that the American dream meant individual car ownership. When I was about fifteen years old my father took me to the Futurama exhibit that General Motors put on at the 1939 World Fair in New York. That gave us a real feel for what the world would look like in the 1960s, with tall skyscrapers and vast freeways where people could drive to their own homes in the suburbs. It was powerful stuff that really excited people, and most of it came true. That's why I loved my first car so much. It represented the future to me. And freedom, like you said. Now, you're graduating from college and were given a gift that you described as representing freedom and the future to you. But it wasn't a car—it's that fancy phone. Maybe it's the anthropologist in me," Bill adds, "but the bankruptcy filing of General Motors combined with the popularity of the smartphone around the same time feels like the ending of one era and the beginning of another."

Justice thinks this over. "I remember learning in my environmental studies class about the consequences of our auto-centric lifestyle and our fossil fuel–dependent economy that grew up after World War II."

"It's definitely true," Bill acknowledges, "there have been a great many unforeseen consequences to our development patterns. As a kid, I remember city streets filled with people going in and out of all the shops and stopping to talk with each other on the street. The city was much denser then, with the primary commercial area concentrated downtown. Then after the war cars came along in a big way and we built the suburbs, and then suburban shopping areas followed, and acres and acres of parking lots to support all the cars. We thought we were building communities, but in many ways, we were destroying and stratifying them. We didn't really understand how we were affecting the natural systems of the environment either. Look at global warming. Eventually a consciousness-raising about the environment started to take place, but it was a slow process that went through a number of steps. Take your environmental studies class," Bill continues, "you wouldn't find anything like it on campus fifty years ago."

"And it's one of the most popular classes on campus," Justice explains. "Grandpa, when did you start to become aware of the environmental movement?"

"Well, that's a good question. You know my first real memory of it was in the fifties and the issue was an avalanche of garbage going into the landfills. Then came along the idea of recycling. That was in the sixties, I believe. There was also a lot of talk about pesticides, smog, and industrial pollution in the lakes and rivers. After that concerns about nuclear waste from power plants, acid rain, ozone depletion, and climate change."

"And that's not the end of it either," Justice chimes in. "There's also been a reduction in biodiversity and the extinction of species."

"Yes, I know," Bill says with a nod and a frown. "We fixed some of those issues, but it seems like new ones keep popping up. For a long time, we saw these problems, as individual problems needing individual solutions, but recently it seems they are now being looked at it in a more wholistic way under the term sustainability."

"Yes," Justice says, her voice rising. "And sustainability just doesn't mean nature. It's also the social consequences of environmental problems—economic deprivation and exploitation, food insecurity and refugees, and the resulting break down of the social order and governance."

"Can I get in that environmental studies class?" Bill asks with a smile. More serious again, he says, "You're absolutely right, and it's made more difficult by the fact that we're not living in an equitable world. The 'haves' are the developed countries, and they, including the United States, are responsible for the largest share of greenhouse emissions to this point. And the developing nations, like China and India, have an absolute need to develop as fast as possible to maintain some social order and prevent catastrophic humanitarian disasters. The solutions require cooperation, and cooperation requires justice. And justice in an unequitable world is a huge challenge," Bill says.

"Why is that? I mean, everybody seems to benefit."

"Well, how about if we continue this conversation in the car on the way back to my place?" Bill says. "And I sure would like to take home another piece of cake."

"You got it, Grandpa," Justice says.

Once in the car, Bill says, "Now back to our question on why cooperation is difficult in an unjust world. I mean the first thing I'd say is, why would we expect people to cooperate with us, if they think we're treating them unfairly? The truth is, they won't. Cooperation requires a sense of justice to work. Suppose you and Miguel were sharing a car for example. Let's further suppose that even though you go to great effort to keep the car full of gas, every time you get the car after him, the gas tank is on empty," Bill says.

"Closer than you know, Grandpa," Justice says.

"Okay, now let's further suppose he gets a flat tire and it needs to be replaced before the car is usable again. What happens?" Bill asks.

"Well, I think he should buy the tire because I buy most of the gas!"

"Exactly," Bill says. "On the other hand, if both you and Miguel shared the gas fairly, the tire probably wouldn't be an issue! And the problem is further exacerbated as we become less familiar with the people we're dealing with. People are pretty good at cooperating with people they know and identify with—like their family and their neighbors. But not so good with people who seem different or live far away. But advancements in communications like the internet, and your new phone should make it easier for us to connect and identify with more people around the world. That could make a big difference. Do unto others as you would have them do unto you!" Bill says.

"The golden rule," Justice exclaims.

"Yes, the golden rule," Bill responds. "Do you know that the sentiment expressed in the golden rule has made it into every major religion on earth?" Bill proclaims.

"Wow that's interesting," Justice responds.

"To me, it says exactly what we're talking about, that without a sense of justice, there can be no lasting peace in the world, no cooperation, nor can humanity reach its potential," Bill says. "I wish I was going to be around for a little more time to be part of this new movement to connect people everywhere. But I'll have to leave it up to you and your generation to keep up the good fight."

"We'll get there, Grandpa, we'll get there."

"Y'know, this conversation reminds me of something."

"What's that, Grandpa?" She keeps her eyes on the traffic ahead since this stretch of road was notorious for crashes.

"Well, a long time ago now, I think it might have been thirty-five or forty years ago, I was asked if I could lead a weekly discussion group at our church on the relationship between science and religion. It was really a forward-thinking group, and as part of that effort, I started scribbling thoughts about the interdependent nature of the world in a notebook. After the discussion group ended, I kept adding to the notebook from time to time as questions surfaced in my mind. Anyway, it's been quite a while now since I've added anything to it, but I think I might still have it if you'd be interested in it?"

"Yes!"

"Okay, I'll see if I can find it."

When they get to Bill's apartment at the assisted living center, Justice tucks the piece of cake into the fridge and Bill goes to the bedroom closet, scanning the upper shelf. "Here it is," Bill sings, bringing out a three-ring notebook with accompanying sheets of typed pages. It's maybe an inch thick with the loose pages stuffed into it. The cover of the notebook reads, "My Big TOE."

"What does *TOE* stand for?" Justice asks.

"*TOE* is shorthand for *theory of everything*. At one time physicists were confident that they were going make a breakthrough that would unify all we know about the nature of the universe into a single theory—the theory of relativity, quantum mechanics, everything. They started referring to it as the theory of everything, or TOE. Our church group wasn't studying physics obviously, but we were dealing with what I would describe as fundamental questions about the nature of the universe and the implications for us as Christians and for people of all beliefs. Anyway, as time went on this notebook became the record of my own search for understanding. Maybe something in it will stir your own thoughts and we can continue this discussion?"

"For sure, Grandpa. Thanks for sharing it with me," Justice says, slipping the dusty notebook into her backpack.

Chapter 7

MY BIG TOE

Nobody close to Justice had ever died before. Her grandparents, other than Bill, had all died before Justice was old enough to have much of a relationship with them. Bill came over to the house for dinner frequently while she was growing up. He went to all of Justice's ice hockey games and dance recitals. And he always made a point of sitting down to talk with her, just the two of them, asking questions as well as telling her his own intriguing stories. And Justice was a member of the Minnows, a name Bill had given to the generations of kids including Justice and Miguel, he spent years baiting hooks for at the end of the dock on weekends. A retired professor, Bill was always nudging Justice to go back to graduate school.

"It's an amazing world out there," he urged, and you are a bright, passionate young woman. Give yourself the best chance you can to make a difference in the world."

Justice would dodge the question, talking vaguely about plans to travel or volunteer for a global justice organization. But the truth is, nearly a year after graduation from college, Justice was living in her parents' house, working at a coffee shop, and hanging out with friends.

At Bill's funeral, Justice is seated next to Miguel. It was a large event because Bill had been such a big influence on so many people— faculty and students from the university, people from his church, and people he had met along the way with no obvious connection.

After a short eulogy delivered by Justice's and Miguel's uncle Mark, the podium is open to anyone who would like to tell a short story. Without hesitation, Miguel jumps up and walks to the podium. He asks that all the Minnows come up to the podium. Justice and many of her cousins from several generations walk to the podium and stand behind Miguel. He tells the story of how Bill would sit on the end of the dock helping us bait hooks and removing small fish from our lines.

"He would teach us stuff while we were fishing, particularly about nature," Miguel says. "He loved us and he loved the wonder of this world we live in, so he couldn't help but show us what he was learning." Then with his hands Miguel demonstrated the proper way to remove a sunny from your line so you don't harm them in the process.

"You are one smooth dude," Justice says to Miguel as they sit back in their seats. Miguel smiles broadly.

Home from the funeral, Justice thinks about some of the last conversations she had with Bill. Justice goes into her bedroom to change clothes. Hanging up her dress in the closet, she spots the notebook Bill had given her months earlier. She pulls it off the shelf and sits on the edge of the bed. Justice hadn't looked at it since Bill gave it to her. As she opens the cover a small handwritten note falls out. It's a note written in Bill's hand.

> To whoever is reading this notebook:
> Curiosity is the doorway to meaning!
> Love, Bill

How many times had he said that exact same thing to her? Justice wonders. A wave of remorse washes over her as she remembers her promise to read the notebook and discuss it with him. Now, there will never be the chance.

"My Big TOE" is organized into sections, and each includes background study materials written by Bill, a list of thought-provok-ing questions for discussion, and a summary and analysis. Even the loose pages of thoughts are carefully filed into the section where they fit the best waiting to be punched and added.

Ever the academic, Bill meticulously added footnotes and citations for the materials referenced. Notes in the margins expanded on the original text. He intended for someone to read this book, Justice realizes. Justice felt curious—and excited—for the first time in months. She starts reading it right away, even before changing into her jeans and sweatshirt.

Chapter 1

Dominion?

Background Materials

Dominion refers to the power to control something. To act as a sovereign or authority over it. In the book of Genesis, it says the following about our dominion over the living creatures of the world we inhabit:

Genesis 1:26–29: "And God said, let us make man in our image, after our likeness: and let them have dominion over the fish of the sea, and the fowl of the air, and over the cattle, and over all the earth, and over every creeping thing that creepeth upon the earth. So God created man in his own image, in the image of God created he him; male and female created he them. And God blessed them, and God said unto them, be fruitful and multiply, and replenish the earth, and subdue it; and have dominion over the fish of the sea, and over the fowl of the air, and over every living thing that moveth upon the earth. And behold I have given you every herb bearing seed, which is upon the face of all the earth, and every tree, in which is a fruit of a seed yielding tree; to you it shall be for meat."

---

1. Some have interpreted these passages as meaning we have no responsibility toward the rest of the natural world. Dominion grants us the power to do as we want with respect to the natural resources of the world free from any notion of responsibility for its well-being. Some have even interpreted dominion as being a religious command to conquer the whole world. Some Christians as well as Islamic sects have sought world domination under such an interpretation.

2. Others have interpreted dominion as meaning stewardship, arguing that we humans have an obligation to act with knowl-

*edge and wisdom and with sincere intentions for the well-be-
ing of ourselves as well as the balance of the natural world.*

Study Questions

1. *Do we humans have an obligation to understand the natural
   world we are a part of?*
2. *Do we have an obligation to act in the best interest of the natural world, including ourselves?*
3. *Do we have an obligation to act in the best interest of humans
   we may see as different from ourselves?*
4. *Do we have an obligation to act in the best interest of all other
   life upon this planet we call home?*

Summary of Discussion and Findings by the Group

*The group firmly concluded that we have an affirmative obligation
to learn about the natural world we are a part of. The group was less
clear as to the order of responsibility we owed to ourselves, other humans,
and the rest of the natural world in general. The command to "love your
neighbor as yourself" was discussed extensively, as well as how human
activity has affected the rest of the natural world. In the end, a consensus
was reached around using words like "respect for" and "appreciation of"
the wholeness of the natural world. The group stopped short of asserting
a right to exist for the nonhuman natural world. The group did say,
however, that our research and study about the natural world was of par-
amount importance to our survival, and if we do not use the power we
gain for the benefit of the whole, we will not survive ourselves.*

*There was also lots of discussion about the inevitability of the
human effect upon Mother Nature and when it was necessary and when
it was not? How do we draw the lines between reasonable and unreasonable in terms of the externalities associated with human civilization?
Are economic considerations the only language we have for describing the
lines between reasonable and not reasonable?*

In the margin Bill wrote, "Good discussion. I recommend we
move on to exploring the nature of our reality."

Underneath that, Justice writes, "I agree! Curiosity is the doorway to meaning!"

The next section includes a note from Bill to the group.

"Fellow searchers," the note starts. Justice smiles, that was so Bill. He always made everybody feel like they were an important part of everything. Even though he was usually leading the way. A wave of sadness sweeps over Justice. Her throat tightens, her eyes fill up, and she wipes her running nose. She can hear grandpa's voice in every word.

> *Fellow searchers,*
>
> *The next section is on knowing Mother Nature better. To do this I have put together a small easy piece on some of the important science about our mother. There is a piece on general relativity. One on quantum mechanics. One on emergence. And one on our perception of boundaries. Trust me, you're all highly capable of this discussion. There is no test on this. In the end, I think we will discover the world is more interdependent and connected than we perceive.*
>
> *—Bill*

The note reminds Justice of a conversation she had with Bill after one of her hockey games long ago. At the time, she remembered thinking it was a strange conversation. She didn't quite get what Bill was telling her. During the game, Bill noticed that sometimes Justice's team passed the puck to one another without even looking. The team had reached a level of coordination where they just knew where each other were. Then as she remembers it, Bill dropped a pencil on the floor and bent down to picked it up. He looked at Justice and said, "Do you know how many millions of bits of information had to be perfectly coordinated for me to be able to do that? Several hundred individual muscles must contract or loosen in just the right sequence, so I can make the necessary moves. The eyes need to focus and adjust. I need to maintain my balance while all this is going on, and I need to maintain my temperature, and heart rate, and blood pressure and everything else at the same time. These millions of bits of information are instantaneously sent to remote locations in my body, in a precisely timed sequence. That process and coordination happens," Bill explained, "partly because each part of the body does its job in sync with all the others. It's harder with a group of people because we all work so independently. But with a lot of practice, a group of people, like your team, can achieve some of the benefits of this type of connection. And when that happens, when people work together in a coordinated way, amazing things happen. The potential impact of every action goes through the roof."

Remembering that conversation reminds Justice how much she misses her grandfather Bill.

She turns to the next chapter.

Chapter 2

The Nature of Reality

Background Materials

Relativity

Light travels at 186,000 miles per second. What's perplexing is that light intercepts objects at that speed whether the object is moving toward the light source or away from it. Another way to express this is to say that the speed of light is a constant that is unaffected by the speed or direction of the source. *This just doesn't make any sense to us. How could the speed of two objects flying through space not be affected by each other's speed or direction? Scientists and philosophers wrestled with this for a long time. It was a great mystery.* It couldn't be, and yet it was. *In 1905 a new view began to take shape. Instead of saying "It couldn't be, and yet it was," Albert Einstein concluded, "It couldn't be, unless time and space aren't what they appear to be." With that little alteration in the orientation of the problem, man's view of the entire universe was transformed. Einstein's theory of relativity describes a universe vastly different from the one we perceive with our senses. Relativity suggests a universe in which space itself has distinguishing features. A universe in which time is not a constant. A universe in which everything objective exists in relationship with, or relative to, everything else. A universe in which space is neither empty nor a void, but rather, a textured element, like a fabric or a sponge. A universe in which space isn't something objects pass through, but rather, something they're attached to.*

Relativity was a huge breakthrough. It explained the actions of everything bigger than the size an atom. Whether it was the mass, location, or velocity of an object or phenomena such as gravitation, energy, or electromagnetism. All were explained through a new frame of reference known as space-time. Relativity describes an interdependent reality in which everything is connected to everything else through the fabric of space-time.

Waves of Nonthings

Quantum mechanics describes a vastly different world than that of relativity. Relativity describes the workings of things that are as big or bigger than an atom. The world smaller than an atom—made up of electrons, positrons, quarks, gluons, and the rest of the exotic subatomic particles—doesn't conform to relativity like the big stuff does.

Quantum mechanics developed at about the same time as Einstein was developing relativity. The results were startling to say the least. Niels Bohr, one of the preeminent physicists of the twentieth century, put it this way: "If a person does not feel shocked when he first encounters quantum theory, he has not understood a word of it." And that's from one of its leading proponents. The big problem with electrons is that they demand attention. Literally! One of the main tenets of quantum mechanics is something called the uncertainty principle. The uncertainty principle says that before the location of an electron can be known, it must be observed. That's right observed! Before it's observed, it can only be accounted for as a wave of possibilities. A wave function, or wave of possibilities as they're referred to, means that all the possibilities exist simultaneously, but none of them is present until observed. When the electron is given the attention it needs, it manifests with singular characteristics. WOW! Okay, so if you're thinking I don't get it! I must have missed it. You are right where you are supposed to be. Suspend your disbelief. It just can't be, and yet it is!

One of the implications of quantum mechanics I find most interesting is the connection between the objective, relative world of things and the subjective world of conscious thought. As I see it, observation is a function of consciousness. Without consciousness there can be no observation. So it boils down to a chicken-and-egg story fairly quickly. The story we're familiar with goes like this: There is a big bang thirteen billion years ago, followed by the development of the cosmos, followed by the advent of a solar system and at least one planet with a natural environment conducive to life. Next there was a spark of life, then evolution produced ever more complex life until it had subjective thoughts. In other words, the subjective thought flowed out of objective life. Objects beget subjects. What quantum mechanics is saying is the opposite. That objects can't manifest until they're observed. Subject begets objects. Quantum mechanics describes an interdependent world in which the observed and the observer are cocreators together. *Without a subjective observer, objective reality can only exist as a wave of possibilities.*

Quantum Connectedness

The idea that things, including people could be connected at a distance without any known connection is part of quantum mechanics as well. It's called phase entanglement, and as I understand, it is a suggestion in quantum math that says: Once two quantum entities have been in a relationship, their possibility waves get tangled up together. This wave tangle then provides a connection, which is outside of normal, objective parameters. Maybe phenomena like a mother knowing when her child is in trouble or thinking about a loved one just as they call you are a result of such a "wave tangle" phenomenon. The world does seem to be more connected and coincidental than we can explain easily. It has also always seemed curious to me that inventions or other milestone ideas often seem to come from more than one source at a time.

In fact, simultaneous invention as it's called is so common, a body of legal presidents has been built up to deal with it. Take the telephone for example. We all know that Alexander Graham Bell invented the telephone in 1876. But what you may not know is that another American inventor named Elisha Gray filed for a patent on the telephone on the exact same day as Bell. Many other examples exist as well. Newton and a guy named Leibniz both invented calculus independently and at the same time. The discovery of oxygen, the invention of flight, sunspots, the discovery of the law of the conservation of energy, the invention of the thermometer, the telescope, the steamboat, the typewriter, color photography, and many more. Doesn't it seem odd that after thousands of years of dreaming about manned flight, several unrelated and unconnected groups that didn't know of each other were building airplanes in roughly the same way, at precisely the same time? How do we account for things like that? Maybe phase entanglement is one of the ways that we're connected outside our traditional sensory perception. Phase entanglement certainly speaks to an interdependent and interconnected world.

Emergence: The Knowledge between Us

The classic way of seeing the world is to see objective things, distributed within empty voids. According to new scholarship, however, this view is wrong. Information may be the very fabric from which our universe is constructed. It's not the objects themselves that are singularly important but rather the relationships between them. As a result, our reality cannot be separated from community.

Atoms, the fundamental building blocks of all matter, are inanimate. In fact, no portion of the atomic world is alive. It's only when a group of atoms combine into a cell that life appears. That means that, life is an emergent property of interdependent community! A community of subatomic particles makes up an atom, a community of atoms makes up cells, a community of cells makes our organs, and a community of organs makes up what we think of as us. And we, along with all the other living creatures who share this Earth with us, make up the community of life upon this planet. Our reality cannot be separated from community.

We observe emergent qualities in many types of communities, from single-celled creatures like slime molds, which can think and learn collectively but individually possess no nervous system, no brain, no means to harvest information about their environment. How could it be that a group of creatures that possess no individual means of thought can reason and solve problems together? This just doesn't make sense to us. We observe these properties emerging from interdependent communities but can't explain how it happens. We see qualities emerge in communities of higher life-forms as well, in ant colonies, in migrating or flocking birds, and in communities of people as well. In people we see emergent qualities in the performance of markets, in organizational creativity and innovation, and we see them emerge from communities across time. Our unique characteristics and capabilities all carried to us from our ancestors in our DNA. Our reality cannot be separated from community.

One of the implications of this idea of properties emerging from within communities is that it makes it harder to define things. The boundaries between things become fuzzy. Let's look at ourselves for example: we breathe in oxygen, we use it as fuel, and then we exhale it as carbon dioxide. Plants take in the carbon dioxide, use it as fuel, and then send oxygen back into the world. It's an interdependent system in which *one side cannot survive without the other. And yet we think of our lungs and heart and bloodstream as being part of us, but we don't think of plants in the same way. Our reality cannot be separated from community.*

Carl Jung's collective unconscious, Rupert Sheldrake's morphic resonance, Pierre Teilhard de Chardin's noosphere, Buddhism's akashic records, quantum mechanics' phase entanglement, and uncertainty principle all descriptions of knowledge and value, and meaning, and information existing outside the confines of a thinker, as we understand them. Properties we observe emerging from communities but cannot explain. Our reality cannot be separated from community.

Mathew 18:20: "When two or three are gathered in my name, there shall I be in the midst of them."

Maybe Mathew 18:20 is a reference to God existing as the meaning or value that emerges between objects, like us? Our cocreator? Bill.

Study Question

1. *What are the appropriate definitions, distinctions, and perceptions of "me" and "we"?*

Over the course of a couple of days, Justice holes up in her room reading grandpa Bill's notebook cover to cover, including all the typed additions and handwritten notes. She finds herself penciling comments in the margin just as he had. About a week after Bill's funeral, Justice comes bounding down the steps and into the kitchen where she pours herself a large glass of orange juice and quickly gulps it down.

"You're looking good this morning," her mom, Emma, says to her. "Where are you going?"

I've got an appointment with an admissions counselor at the university," Justice replies.

"Wait, you're going back to school?"

"Curiosity is the doorway to meaning, Mom," Justice declares as she heads out to the garage and rides off on her bike.

Pleased but confused, Emma goes up to Justice's room and looks around. On the bed is a large notebook:

My Big TOE
By Bill Miller

Below her grandfather's name in smaller letters appear the words "and Justice."

What becomes clear to Justice in reading Bill's notebook is, if the true nature of our reality is an interdependent system, then it doesn't make sense that we should exert "dominion" over things that we are, in fact, dependent upon—unless the "dominion" also involves a responsibility to care for it.

Over the next couple of years after her grandfather Bill's death, Justice works on a master's degree in economics while taking additional coursework in philosophy and environmental studies. And in her spare time, she plays on Miguel's hockey team. She also continues to reread "My Big TOE," recording her evolving thoughts in a new notebook she started titled "TOE Two." She continues her grandfather's format of writing a question, and then a brief summary of contextual information. That way anyone who reads it can pick up the thread.

In the notebook, "TOE Two," Justice writes the following:

Do Our Environmental Problems Present an Opportunity?

"A crisis is a terrible thing to waste," the economist Paul Romer famously said. The obvious point being that people are motivated by fear. That fear can motivate people to do things they would not normally do. Perhaps more importantly, though, fear can motivate us to do things with people or groups with whom we would not normally cooperate. To the extent we have common enemies, we can have cooperative alliances. World War II being a clear example of this. The Soviet Union under Stalin on one side and the United Kingdom and United States on the other were natural enemies. The Soviet Union was a totalitarian state with a command-and-control economy and plans for worldwide communism. The United Kingdom and United States were democracies with free-market economies that adamantly opposed communism. And yet with Hitler's Germany threatening the world, these adversaries worked together in their efforts to counter Hitler's aggressions.

Do today's environmental and social problems present humanity with another common enemy? It's certainly true that we have reached the point where ecological devastation is global. In essence our future security no longer depends on just what we do as individuals or as a nation—we are dependent on what others do as well. We are in an interdependent relationship with them, whether we like it or not. The common enemy is universal or global.

A common enemy can make for uncommon alliances. And uncommon alliances to combat specific enemies can lead to greater trust, and greater trust, leads to opportunity. Not just opportunity to defeat the common enemy but gain all the many other benefits of greater interdependence.

Would you accept more wealth, opportunity, and security, significantly more if it meant that everybody else got more too? The difference between an independent adolescent view of the world and an interdependent adult worldview, is that independence sets up a binary choice between opportunity and scarcity. The independent mindset divides the world into "we" and "them" and thinks that only "we" or "them" can have something. If "they" have it, "we" cannot. It sets up competition for everything. The interdependent worldview is much more capable of seeing cooperative alternatives. If we work together and cooperate, we can all have more! Abundance instead of scarcity. The difference between the two views is far greater than we can imagine. It's the difference between the value of a single note, and that of a symphony, as Bill Miller said. Only when the note is played in the proper context of the piece of music can its real meaning and value be appreciated.

So for the first time in history, the biggest enemies are the ideas and prejudices that separate us and the institutions of ignorance that hold onto their exclusive ideologies at the expense of humanity. We need a new inclusive approach to life that disarms the biases and prejudices of isolation and demands more. More for ourselves and more for everyone else too. "Love your neighbor as yourself." Somebody famous said that, and it seems to fit.

Chapter 8

PERPETUITY VS. ENTROPY
DR. BILL MILLER

On the wall of Justice's on campus studio apartment, is a poster of Serena Williams stretched out and making an incredible shot with a caption that reads "Passion Rules!" The only other wall art is a signed poster of Manny Fernandez, who was the goalie for the Minnesota Wild in their first few seasons, including their second year in existence when he led the team to the second round of the Stanley Cup playoffs. Now several years after her grandfather Bill's death, Justice is finishing up her master's in economics and thinking about getting in a PhD program. Justice has many friends, but she doesn't date or even socialize very much. She works incredibly hard at school, and she continues to play goalie on the hockey team with Miguel. Ironically, Miguel is no longer a regular on the team himself because after his graduation from the university he was accepted into law school (international law program) at NYU. Miguel's career trajectory seemed to change from journalism to law in his senior year when he wrote a story for the *Minnesota Daily* newspaper that had dug up some possible corruption on a local politician. Instead of being rewarded for his investigative work, Miguel and a student editor were both sacked from the paper and received lectures from the dean. Shortly after the incident, Miguel told Justice he was looking for law schools because he thought we were living in a time when a good legal brief represented a bigger hammer than a good story.

One day Justice gets a phone call from her father, Matt.

"Justice, I'm so sorry about this…but, well…"

"What is it, Dad?"

"Well, your grandpa Bill left you something."

"What, what is it?"

"I don't know. It's a blue cardboard box sealed tight with your name on it. Apparently, when we were clearing out Grandpa's things, it wound up here in the garage. Anyway, I was just cleaning out the garage and came across it. I'm sorry it's taken so long to get it to you."

"*Wow*," Justice exclaims on the phone, "tell Mom I'm coming for dinner. I'll be there in an hour and we can open it."

Justice pedals right into the garage on her bike where her dad is piling up boxes.

"Hi, sweetheart, here it is."

Justice picks it up. "Wow, it's heavy, isn't it?"

She lugs the box into the family room and sets it on an otto-man. Her mother walks in from the kitchen with a small knife, and Justice carefully slits the packing tape and lifts the cardboard flaps.

Inside there are three smaller blue boxes and an envelope addressed in cursive script to *Justice Miller*. On the first is written "Perpetuity or Entropy," on the second is written "Code of Conduct," and on the third, it says, "Futurama."

Justice opens the envelope, unfolds the typed note, and looks at it as her Mom and Dad watch.

She begins to read silently.

Justice suddenly places her hand over her mouth and begins to cry before handing the letter to her mom.

> Justice,
>
> I have so enjoyed our time together. You arrived in this world under the most difficult of circumstances. You had to fight to be here from the very first moments of your life. It has been my pleasure to watch you grow up, tackling life with energy and grit and determination through-out school and many hockey seasons. As you read

this, I want you to know how much I regret not being there to see where you are headed now.

As you're aware, I spent my years searching and teaching. This provided me a wonderful and very meaningful life. I leave with as many questions as I had when I started and am just as excited about asking them and pursuing their answers. My hope has always been that your curiosity will spur you to start your own search. In thinking about what to pass on to you to help in that search, here's what I came up with. It's my modest contribution to your future.

This material was an early experiment done by the university in what people now call distance learning. In each box are papers and study materials from classes I used to teach. Each also contains a DVD. The DVDs were originally videotapes, but I had them transferred several years ago to protect them. They contain a combination of my lectures and some photos with voice-over commentary designed to make the materials easier to absorb. When the university decided it wanted to try distance learning for the first time, they asked me to design three classes that they could produce. It was quite an effort. I hope you find them interesting. Along with my "Big TOE" notebook, they represent my own search for the truth. I was so blessed to be able to spend my life on a journey of questions and discovery, and I so hope that you will find your own search as stimulating and exciting as I found mine.

Now, sweet Justice, I am off to get some answers. Curiosity is the gateway to meaning.

Love, Bill

With a deep breath, Justice opens the first of grandpa Bill's smaller boxes.

On top is another of Bill's tidily typed notes:

> Entropy is the second law of thermody-namics. What it says is that everything over time evolves in one direction, from more organized and usable to less organized and usable. This quality is universal and applies to natural systems as well as social systems. Entropy means decay and obsolescence and destruction and death. And the only thing that can hold it off is the perpetual application of new and more efficient energy.
>
> This class is called perpetuity vs. entropy. It explores the question, why do some civilizations survive or even thrive when others fail? What are the underlying characteristics of a healthy soci-ety? And what are the characteristics that doom a society?

Justice puts the DVD into her computer. A voice she recognizes as her grandfather Bill begins to tell a story, but the screen is filled with pictures of island life on a tropical island.

> The proposal on the table was to clear an area of forest on the far southern edge of tribal lands to provide the space and wood to build a new village. The arguments were familiar. On one side were people arguing for more develop-ment. There was a shortage of housing. Housing was unavailable or too expensive within the pre-viously developed areas. The population had simply outgrown the available resources.
>
> On the other side were the voices of con-servation. We can't continue to reduce the stock of forest lands. We depend on the resources pro-

vided by the forests. If we destroy all the forests, how will our descendants live?

The heated debate had an undercurrent of intergenerational conflict as well, with older people who were already established with housing and resources generally opposing the plans. It was younger people who needed to find opportunities to establish a life who strongly supported it. "How can you claim to be preserving resources for future generations and at the same time be denying them to us, your closest descendants? Besides, Mother Nature is powerful, how arrogant of you to think we can affect her!"

"But we have affected her," the voices of conservation countered. "Areas of previous timber harvest are eroding and become unfertile grasslands, unable to grow anything useful. We can't even get the big palms or the forest to regenerate in the harvested areas."

"Well, what would you have us do?" the younger generation would protest. "What is your solution to the problem, what is the alternative? Checkmate!" The voices of conservation recognized the problems, but they didn't have an alternative solution.

The same arguments have been made in many societies throughout history. It's the problem of success. When a community succeeds, its population grows. To put it in modern financial terms, it means the community has outstripped the renewable resources available (returns from past investments), and they're consuming their principal. In this case it was the forests and trees and plants that were being depleted and not being replaced. This can work if investments are being made in productive things that will yield future returns, but if they're using the resources to live on, their standard of living will decline over time.

In this particular case, the situation was being played out at a time of great expansion in much of the rest of the world. The sixteenth century had just begun. The Renaissance was underway in Europe, it was the middle of the Ming dynasty in China, and the age of colonialism was commencing in the Americas. But in the middle of the Pacific Ocean, on the isolated island nation of Rapa Nui, an existential crisis had begun.

It had been five hundred years, since Rapa Nui's settlement as the exiled home of Chief Hotu of the tribal Kingdom of Marae Renga. As the story goes, Chief Hotu was facing the kind of situation heads of state fear most. A hostile rival with a superior military, determined to take his tribal lands by force. After losing three military battles with his rival, his army was decimated, and Chief Hotu's choices were limited—fight to the death or surrender. Surrender of course meant that the chief and his immediate family would be killed, but some members of his tribe would be allowed to live, perhaps as slaves at first, but eventually they would be allowed to assimilate into the tribe of the victors. In the aftermath of the third battle, the chief walked among the wounded warriors being attended to by the women and considered the fate of his people. If it was just himself that was of concern to him, it would have been an easy decision. Chief Hotu was a warrior at heart. Every inclination he had was to continue fighting. Nothing could be more honorable than giving the ultimate sacrifice on the battlefield, defending his people and his homeland. But personal glory was not the only concern on the chief's mind. If he doesn't surrender, his people, including his children, will surely pay the price.

Suddenly the groans of the wounded are drowned out by the shouts from an out-of-breath sentry. A boat has been spotted on the horizon. Was it more enemy warriors coming to finish them off? The chief runs to the beach to find out, after giving orders to the rest of his forces to get ready for another battle. As the single vessel approaches, cheers of excitement ring out along the beach as tribe members realize it's one of their own boats. After the first military defeat at the hands of his rival, Chief Hotu secretly sent out a scouting party to look for possible new lands to settle in case of defeat.

A small catamaran manned by three of the tribe's best sailors left the island 180 days earlier. The chief had long ago given up hope they would return. Two of the men from the scouting party are barely clinging to life as they guide the battered boat onto the beach. As the men are given water and food, with their wounds being tended, they tell the chief of their discovery—an uninhabited tropical island approximately 1,600 miles to the east. A third option, the chief exalts.

Chief Hotu, his family, and approximately fifty of the tribe's healthiest young people set out for the newly discovered island. The chances of surviving the trip were slim, but a better option than fighting or surrendering, the chief believes. After the party left in a flotilla of small boats, a message was sent to the rival chief saying that Chief Hotu and his family had fled into the sea and the remaining tribal members would put down their arms and pledge loyalty to the new chief if he spared their lives.

After twenty days' journey, the expedition safely lands on the island they named Rapa Nui. The island is beautiful, covered by a lush tropical jungle including tall palm trees and many types of native fruits. Rapa Nui is triangular, with three ancient volcanoes in the corners—approximately fifteen miles long and about seven miles at its widest point. The expedition party and their descendants settle into the island, maintaining a small amount of contact with the outside world through voyages by small catamarans like the ones they had escaped in. About two centuries later (circa 1250 CE), Rapa Nui is a successful thriving community of several thousand people, still led by the heirs of Chief Hotu. It was about this time that islanders begin to create moai.

Moai are massive sculptures of human figures with oversized heads carved out of soft volcanic rocks and transported with the help of palm tree skids to coastal locations where they're placed upright facing inland away from the sea. The Rapa Nui people believe these statues contain the embodied spirits of their deceased ancestors and will ward off evil spirits and protect them. The bigger the statue, the thinking goes, the bigger the spirits that they contain. So bigger and bigger moai were carved in the quarry.

As the island's population continues to grow, the more remote sections of the island are settled. Each time a new village is established, more trees are cleared to make room for housing, food production, building materials, and to use in the construction and transportation of moai. By approximately 1500 CE, Rapa Nui has a population of more than ten thousand people living with a moai population of about nine hundred statues watching over them. While things might have seemed good at the time, the large palms native to the island are slowly disappearing.

The large palms were not coming back for several reasons. The first is the fact that the species of palm native to the island takes over a hundred years to reach full maturity. Second, Chief Hotu and his expedition brought to Rapa Nui a type of island rat native to Marae Renga that they could use as a source of protein. The rat flourished on the new island and soon their population was in the millions. This wasn't a problem except that the rats loved the seed nuts produced by the big palms, which of course reduced the reproduction of the big palms. In addition, when the palms were cut down, it changed the environment for the small brush plants that lived and nourished the soils under the protective canopy provided by the big palms. So as the big palms were reduced a whole interdependent ecosystem was replaced by different grasses and plants. This in turn changed the soil, making it unproductive for big palms as well as many other native plant species.

The ecological problems on Rapa Nui were exacerbated by social conflicts as the islanders separated into isolated local villages and began competing with other villages for shrinking resources. This conflict meant that moai statues became even more important as symbols of prestige among the local communities. Each village wanted the most and the biggest moai watching over them, and the fewest and smallest moai watching over their rivals. So as bigger moai were being carved at a more rapid pace, other moai were knocked over and destroyed.

As the people of Rapa Nui begin fighting among themselves, the island's production of food and resources declines. With the shrinking availability of palm trees, a reduction in boat building followed, which in turn reduced the amount of fish that could be harvested as well as further isolating the islanders from other people. Other native food crops were also declining as the ecosystem of the island drastically changed. Villages began plundering one another for resources and materials. Evidence of cannibalism was discovered in this era as well, and islanders moved underground into caves, seeking protection from each other. By the middle of the seventeenth century the last natural forest on Rapa Nui was gone.

The islands' natural flora was almost completely destroyed. Land was eroding rapidly. Lakes dried up, leaving only a swamp and a single spring as the only sources of fresh water on the island. The population declined, and the remaining population lived desperate lives due to food shortages and warfare. But this is not the end of the story.

By the middle of the eighteenth century the population was down to just two thousand people when Europeans first arrived on the island. Amazed by the moai statues, the Western conquerors nonetheless imprisoned the islanders, taking them to Peru to be slaves. The population of Rapa Nui declined to just one hundred people, about the same number who had survived the journey to the island with their founder, Chief Hotu, over seven hundred years earlier.

So what lessons can be drawn from the decline of Rapa Nui? Like most societal failures, Rapa Nui did not fail because of a single cause but rather a cascade of problems. A downward spiral, if you will. In his landmark book *Collapse*, UCLA historian and geographer Jared Diamond lists eight environmental problems that have historically contributed to the ruin of past societies.

They are the following:

1. Deforestation and habitat destruction
2. Soil problems, including erosion, salinization, and diminished fertility
3. Water management problems
4. Overhunting
5. Overfishing
6. Native species being crowded out by newly introduced ones
7. Overpopulation
8. Increased per-capita impact of humans

As these environmental woes progress, they impose increasingly higher consequences on the society in question. Eventually, tribalism and civil war bubbles to the surface as groups fight among themselves for scarce resources. Finally, in their weakened state, these declining societies become vulnerable to predatory outsiders. It's a scenario that has played itself out many times throughout human history.

One aspect of Rapa Nui's fall that is particularly relevant to our own global society today is the effects of universality. When most societies decline and fail, people simply move away and are absorbed into another society in a more hospitable area. This wasn't a possibility for the people of Rapa Nui. Their isolation on an island meant the ecological damage they were experiencing was inescapable. There were too many people and too few resources to build boats to flee as their ancestors had. The ecological conditions were universal for the people of Rapa Nui.

This is analogous to our own situation today because many of our own ecological problems are global in nature, and there is no other planet to which we can escape. For example, it doesn't really matter how much one country switches to renewable energy, if others continue to burn carbon, which fuels global climate change.

What universal or global means is that we are all in this together, whether we like it or not. There's no boat that can take us away from the whole mess.

In addition to the eight environmental impacts responsible for societal declines and collapses in the past, Jared Diamond has updated his list to include four new environmental threats for our time:

1. Climate change caused by humans
2. The proliferation of toxins in our environment
3. Looming energy shortages
4. Full human use of the Earth's photosynthetic capacity

Photosynthetic capacity is the measure of the amount of carbon that leaves can fix during photosynthesis. By some estimates, humans currently use 50 percent of this capacity and that amount is increasing with both population growth and development. The fear is that

humanity could soon reach a level that could prevent other life from living.

Understanding the pathology of how societies fail is obviously important. But perhaps
more important is understanding why societies
sometimes fail to respond to dire threats. While
human history is filled with stories of societies
that successfully responded to threats and survived. There are just as many examples of societies that have not responded, suffered the consequences, and failed. The Maya in the Americas,
the Romans, the Viking Norse of Greenland,
and many others. What explains the difference
in how various societies react to an acute crisis?
Why have some responded successfully while
others failed?

So rather than asking how Rapa Nui failed,
we should be asking why did they miss the chance
to save themselves when they had a chance? A big
part of the answer is their isolation—not only
isolated geographically or historically from their
own past because they had no written language
but also isolated culturally by their beliefs and a
worldview that went unchallenged for centuries.

Isolation: One of the reason societies do
not act until it's too late, is because they fail to
see the gravity of a situation they're facing. It's
the frog in the boiling pot story. As the temperature of the water slowly rises the frog is never
shocked enough to jump out. Without a written
language, without a tradition of experimentation
and change, without challenges to their worldview or an evolution of subjective analysis the
Rapa Nui people were isolated from a capacity
to respond.

Subjective Isolation and Alienation

We are bound together through social institutions. When those institutions begin to break down and they're not replaced by new social institutions, people become isolated and alienated. Families, churches, schools, the library, local kids' sports teams, businesses, social clubs, political parties—these are the types of social institutions that people connect through. If these institutions don't remain relevant and renewed, they begin to diminish. As they diminish, if they're not replaced by something new, the people become more isolated and alienated from each other. As was the case on the island kingdom of Rapa Nui, over time tribal brothers and sisters became the other. First alienated and isolated, then enemies and competitors.

Do we see signs of growing isolation and alienation in our own time and in our own society?

In the past few decades we've seen a significant reduction in the number of people per household. We've seen significant increases in the incidence of divorce, we've seen the rise of the single-person household as the most prevalent. We've seen the decline of churches and the rise of the nonpracticing, nondenominational, spiritual, or nonbelieving as the predominant categories. We've seen the diminishment of neighborhood schools. The diminishment of local kids' sports teams. The closing of neighborhood libraries. The aging and disintegration of social clubs like the Elk's or the VFW. The shrinking of political parties as a percentage of the voting age population. The lowering of the percentage of people actually voting. The closing of factories and businesses as they move within a global market.

The increasing stratification of wealth. Increased incidents of domestic terror and mass shootings. The diminishment of science and knowledge and the elevation of ignorance, particularly through voyeuristic entertainment and personality cultishness. And we see increases in gang violence and drug addiction problems.

As the isolated and alienated suffer and become more cynical, they lash out at the perceived other. The refugees and minorities are further isolated, and the elites who study and teach are rejected. Science and education themselves lose their influence. Religion loses its moral authority, and government loses its ability to govern as "we the people" descend into we the tribes.

Cynicism increases every time a clergy member is found to have engaged in sexual activity with minors, when politicians cheat or don't pay their own fair share of taxes. Every time a company acts to socialize or leave behind pollution and environmental problems and privatize the profits. Why should we pay our taxes when the people at the top don't pay theirs? The system is rigged in plain sight. And then, just as the people are becoming more and more isolated from each other, a new set of inescapable universal problems appears. Problems whose solutions require cooperation among the alienated and isolated and cynical people.

As conditions deteriorate simplistic solutions like, going back to the old ways gains resonance as the definitive and booming voices of opportunist and charlatans compete for constituencies. But the old failed institutions of the past do not provide meaningful solutions for the problems of today or tomorrow. New institutions must be built. Institutions and meaningful ventures designed for the problems and people of today and tomorrow. We live in a time of great expansion of communications and our ability to connect, through the World Wide Web, and yet those new tools have served to undermine our connections and increase isolation as much as they have served as tools of connection.

Isolation in all its forms is the enemy of civilization. Whether it's geographic isolation, cultural isolation, or isolation brought on by some form of advantage seeking and responsibility shifting, the consequences are the same: Isolation and exclusivity lead to weakness, stagnation, and vulnerability. And diversity, inclusivity, and free-flowing exchange leads to adaptability, innovation, strength, and progress. Isolation equals death and diversity equals life. It's true of human civilization just as its true among every other type of life upon this planet.

The class DVD ends. Justice rocks back in her chair and reflects on what she had just watched. That was written almost twenty years ago, she thinks, and yet it seems like it could have been written yesterday. If anything, the conditions have gotten even worse, with the advent of the social media distraction machines. How ironic, she thinks, that new information technologies, which carry the promise of greater connections between people, should first be used to further isolate us.

Justice reaches for her notebook, "TOE Two," and begins to write: "The great potato famine in Ireland was caused by a diminishment in the genetic diversity of the potato. The version of the potato that was most desired gained more and more market share until a single genetic strain existed. And then a disease came along that the single potato strain was vulnerable to, and it wiped out the countries entire crop. Just as Bill said in his perpetuity vs. entropy class, diversity equals life and isolation equals death."

Chapter 9

THE CODE OF CONDUCT FOR WESTERN SOCIETY BY DR. BILL MILLER

Justice opens the box titled "The Code of Conduct." On top is a typed note from Bill:

> Generally, the development of individuals follows a recognized path.
>
> - Childhood, which is characterized by dependence on authority figures and is characterized as having a limited sense of self
> - Adolescence, which is characterized by independence from authority figures and the development of a sense of self
> - Adulthood, which is characterized as interdependence and the ability to maintain mutually beneficial cooperative relationships as the result of a fully developed and secure sense of self.

Do we collectively and culturally develop in a similar way through recognizable stages? Does transformative change conform to an underlying development process? Can we see a development process taking place in our history? Can we look at our history and discern a current location in a development process? Can we tell where we're going next? Does this knowledge inform our understanding of the current problems we face and our capacity to find and apply solutions to them?

Justice takes the DVD and places it in her computer, she immediately recognizes her grandpa Bill's voice narrating.

On a beautiful spring day in a small town in northern Poland, an old man lies unconscious on his deathbed attended to by family and friends. Suddenly the whispered tones of mourning give way to murmurs of anticipation, as a boy appears at the door of the house. The boy is flush from the hurried pace of his journey, and he holds a single book in his hand. The young man is quietly escorted into the room where the old man lies dying and hands the book to an attendant. The attendant carefully places the book into the hands of the old man. Suddenly he stirs, regains consciousness, and opens his eyes. He inspects the book, smiles with delight, and then drifts back into unconsciousness and dies. Those reported events took place on May 24, 1543. The old man was Nicholas Copernicus. And the book was the very first copy of *On the Revolutions of the Celestial Spheres*, which Copernicus had written more than twenty years earlier but was afraid to publish for fear of retribution by the church.

Copernicus was a man of great accomplishment during his life. He was a mathematician, an artist, a politician, an economist, a diplomat, a physician, an astronomer, an expert in canon law, and—with his impending death rendering him untouchable by the power of the church—the author of one of the most important books in history. *On the Revolutions of Celestial Spheres* put forth the first scientifically documented arguments for a geography of the cosmos in which the sun was at the center of things. Prior to this time, all competing theories on the organization of the universe had one very important element in common: they all put the Earth at the center of God's creation. So why was a book on astronomy so controversial or important? And why would the church feel so threatened by it? The answers to those questions have little to do with astronomy. Copernicus's book represented a threat to the philosophical underpinnings—the code of conduct—upon which European society had been built over many centuries and the power structure that had promoted and profited from it.

For millennia, people looked to the heavens and saw celestial bodies of various descriptions moving across the sky in predictable patterns. The Earth was therefore thought to be at the center of the universe and all other heavenly bodies rotated around it, putting our planet at the center of God's creation. And with humanity being the preeminent and unrivaled species upon the Earth, then by extension we were obviously the center and object of God's intention. This was codified in Genesis, the first book of the Old Testament which states that God created human beings "in his own image" and then gave us "dominion" over all the resources of the world. Consequently, the code of conduct for human society (in the West at least) became one of unfettered dominance and exploitation.

It wasn't just that it was all about us—it was that everything was ours. The apparent geography of the universe seemed to bestow ownership of all the creation upon human beings. What economists later came to call negative externalities—including the extinction of numerous species, degradation of natural systems, and the destruction of indigenous "unsaved" human cultures—were of no consequence to us. We enjoyed a special relationship with the creation and its Creator. We could exploit and destroy anything and everything without fear of recrimination.

This code of conduct was so pervasive throughout the West that it became all but invisible. At least until Copernicus's book proposed a new map of the cosmos in which the Earth was not the center of the universe after all. That inadvertently opened the door to big questions concerning man's relationship to the creation and its Creator. If the Earth isn't the center of God's creation, maybe humanity isn't the singular focus of His intention either? Maybe there are other ways to interpret Genesis? Maybe the church doesn't speak for God? Maybe the entire code of conduct is wrong? Controversial stuff indeed. So much so, that ninety years after Copernicus's death, Galileo—a celebrated Italian engineer and physicist—was tried, convicted, and sentenced to life in prison for the heresy of using the telescope he invented to make observations that backed up theories proposed in Copernicus's book.

If you were to diagram the code of conduct in Copernicus's time, it would look something like the diagram below.

Code of Conduct

Who had the right to act?		What could they do?		Under what authority?
Limited elite we, nobility, feudal lords, the church	can act	Act in their self interest permissible to Church & feudal lords	because	God: as defined by His representative on earth, the Church.

To the church, science represented a competing narrative explaining the existence of creation, which undermined the supreme power of God—upon which the church claimed its authority. The church vigorously defended its authority by declaring thousands of people heretics and then torturing, imprisoning, or executing them. Despite the church's brutality, scientific inquiry could not be stopped. The human development process offers a metaphor for viewing this battle between religion and science. The dependency of childhood represents the feudal age before Copernicus and the assertive independence of adolescence represents the rebellion of the scientific revolution, which gave birth to our modern age. This metaphor is not meant to render any judgment on the validity of either science or religion any more than the issues parents and an adolescent argue about are valid or not. It simply describes the process of breaking away and developing an independent sense of self. Science provided Western society with the language, methodology, and opportunity for pushing beyond a dependent phase. Despite the challenges to the church's authority, however, the code of conduct for western civilization based on our isolation from and dominance over the natural world remained unaltered.

The Age of Discovery and Colonization of the Americas

Through the Age of Discovery and colonization in the Americas, independence, self-reliance, and the assumption of personal risk were at the center of an ethos that produced both great wealth and rapid development, as well as the unfettered taking and exploitation of natural resources and the heinous practices of slavery of nonwhite people and genocide of indigenous peoples. These practices flourished under a code of conduct that classified non-European non-Christians as simply part of the natural world to which the "conquerors" or "settlers" had been given dominion by the Creator. This unprecedented exploitation by Europeans yielded immense riches and resources, which stimulated and accelerated Western culture's transition from dependence to independence. Just as science fostered a new language and way of thinking about our independence, the colonization of the Americas provided new opportunities to act upon it.

The Enlightenment and Evolving Code

Just like Copernicus and Galileo, Benjamin Franklin was a giant figure of his time. He was an inventor and entrepreneur, a publisher, a scholar, and a diplomat and one of the leading American figures of the era known as the Enlightenment. The principles, values, and ideologies of the Enlightenment really defined the modern age—not just in Europe and North America but throughout the whole world. These Enlightenment ideals including a reverence for science, reason, and democratic self-governance of, by, and for the people; a healthy skepticism of religious authority and the separation of church and state; a system of rights and due process guarantees designed to enfranchise and elevate individual citizens; and freedom to pursue our own self-interest including life, liberty, and the pursuit of happiness. In so doing, the principles of the Enlightenment reduced the power of nobility and the church hierarchy and unleashed the power of human creativity and enterprise. The Enlightenment asserted and institutionalized a culture of independence. It's simple, what made America great was the rights and freedoms given to individual citizens to make themselves great.

Over America's first two centuries, those Enlightenment principles were reinforced and doubled down on time after time. We did so when we extended the rights of citizenship to dispossessed people, including women, racial minorities, and those of all sexual orientations. We did so when we embraced public education for all, which elevated science and reason over dogma and provided access and opportunity for disadvantaged social classes. We did so through economic policies that promote the pursuit of enlightened self-interest and technological advancement. America became great, not despite our multicultural democratic society but because of it. And we defended and strengthened those Enlightenment values numerous times throughout our history. In the eighteenth century, it was the founders Franklin, Jefferson, Washington, and others. In the nineteenth century, it was Lincoln and Frederick Douglass. In the twentieth century it was the Roosevelts. These are considered our best and most influential figures, and what they have in common is the ideals of the Enlightenment. They battled to expand the definition of citizen and to limit the power of special interests.

Code of Conduct

Who had the right to act?		What could they do?		Under what authority?
Limited elite we, nobility, feudal lords, the church	can act	Act in their self interest permissible to Church & feudal lords	because	God: as defined by His representative on earth, the Church.

Post Enlightenment Code of Conduct

Who had the right to act?		What could they do?		Under what authority?
Broader, Enlightened, we. The era of the Democratic Citizen.	can act	Act in their self interest for life, liberty and the pursuit of happiness consistent with the democratic Constitution	because	We the people! Through democratic institutions, the Constitution, and the Bill of Rights.

During the Enlightenment, the code of conduct evolved in terms of who could take action, what could be done, and what authorities could block the actions. The Enlightenment reduced the power of the church, elevated people who were not nobility, and redefined who had what rights. But these changes focused on the rights of those who were considered citizens, so exploitation and genocide of noncitizens continued along with development and destruction of the Earth's natural environment.

In the period between Copernicus and Benjamin Franklin, Western society experienced dramatic changes equivalent to a boy or girl transforming from a dependent child to a willful adolescent seeking independence. The uncompromising embrace of freedom and independence by some of the Enlightenment's leading thinkers is displayed in these quotes:

- *"Freedom is the alone unoriginated birthright of man, and belongs to him by force of his humanity." (Immanuel Kant, German philosopher)*
- *"To love truth for truth's sake is the principal part of human perfection in this world, and the seed-plot of all other virtues." (John Locke, English philosopher)*
- *"The God who gave us life gave us liberty at the same time; the hand of force may destroy, but cannot disjoin them." (Thomas Jefferson)*
- *"Those who would give up essential liberty to purchase a little temporary safety deserve neither liberty nor safety." (Benjamin Franklin)*
- *"God grant that not only the love of liberty but a thorough knowledge of the rights of man may pervade all the nations of the earth, so that a philosopher may set his foot anywhere on its surface and say: This is my country." (Benjamin Franklin)*

After the DVD is over, Justice grabs her notebook, "TOE Two" and makes some notes:

1. Civilization develops through phases analogous to a growing child, including a dependent childhood, an independent adolescence, and an interdependent adult phase.

2. All societies operate according to a powerful code of conduct, which establishes who is authorized to do something, what they're allowed to do, and under what authority they're allowed to do it. The code of conduct for modern civilization has been one stark separation from the natural world and unfettered dominance over it.

3. The pre-Enlightenment battle between religion and science parallels the dramatic emergence of an adolescent breaking out of dependence in search of autonomy.

4. While the Enlightenment represents the triumph of independence, Western society's code of conduct changed as a result—but only in who can act and under what authority. Narrow self-interest still dominates our thinking about how to act.

5. Centuries of modernity and the requisite belief in science and reason have shaped our culture and changed who we are as people. We are no longer a dependent people seeking the approval of an intervening God.

Was the enlightenment dependent on the discovery of America?

Or was it dependent on the development of science? Bill seems to be asserting that the change from a dependent society to an independent society was not likely just because the people were ready to change. That change requires a catalyst. Or even more than one catalyst. That without some form of catalyst change or maturation is not likely.

Could the development of information technology that has the capacity to connect people in such profound ways and the advent of climate change and other global environmental issues be seen in the same light as the discovery of America and the advent of science? As catalysts for a new shift toward interdependence? Reference my section on "Does climate change represent an opportunity?"

Chapter 10

FUTURAMA
THE SUBURBAN AMERICAN DREAM
BY DR. BILL MILLER

The sound of James Brown singing "It's a Man's World" pierces the silence, startling Justice as she's reading an economic treatise by John Kenneth Galbraith. It's the irreverent ring tone on her phone and the ID says "Miguel."

Justice answers, "How's New York?"

"New York is a different environment than we grew up in for sure, but it's a very interesting place. I'm not sure I'd want to live here forever, but I like it," Miguel says. "I miss you though and I think you should come out and spend a couple of days over spring break."

"Well, I'm not sure," Justice stammers.

"Come on, I've got a couch that is very comfortable."

"Aren't you coming home for break?" Justice asks.

"Well, I'll be back some this summer, yes, but I thought maybe I should stay here over spring break and have you come out instead? I mean, you've never been here, right?"

"No, I haven't," Justice admits.

"And there are lots of things to see here, and I'm not very good about going to them alone," Miguel admits.

"Museums, bars and clubs, historic sites, shopping. Just walking the streets here is amazing…come on, you'll love it and we'll have a great time."

"Okay," Justice says, excitement rising in her voice.

They discuss schedules and Justice consults her calendar. "I think the fourteenth through nineteenth could work," Justice says. "Let me check on flights and I'll call you back."

"Okay, but call me back within an hour. Time kills deals," Miguel says.

The least expensive flights from the Twin Cities go to Newark. Then you get on a large bus that goes through the Lincoln Tunnel and right into the Port Authority bus station in Manhattan. To the uninitiated from smaller cities like Minneapolis with lakes and parkways and bike trails, it's an eye-opener.

With her first glimpse of Manhattan, Justice's first thought is, *How does this work? Millions of people living on a single island and many millions more visiting during the day—and every hotdog bun, every paper clip, every copy machine, everything has to get onto this small island through one of a few tunnels and bridges. Wow!*

Her second thought is, *What is that smell?*

Her third thought is, *Never mind, I don't want to know!*

She drags her roller bag through the Port Authority past the George Rhoads's rolling ball kinetic sculpture, past the hot dog and the pizza stands and out onto Seventh Avenue. She jumps in a cab lined up at the curb and gives the driver the address of Miguel's building. She calls Miguel from the cab and he meets her in the lobby of his building.

"Oh my god, it is so good to see you," Miguel says, giving Justice a big hug.

"You're a long way from Minnow territory!" Justice says.

"Yeah, isn't it something," Miguel agrees.

Miguel's apartment is on the second floor of a building full of NYU students. It's maybe five hundred square feet in total. Not really a kitchen but a small refrigerator and a kitchen sink.

"This classic 1950s modernist movement couch upholstered in genuine artificial leather is yours," Miguel says.

"It's perfect," Justice responds. "I bet there's one just like it in the MOMA [Museum of Modern Art] lobby."

"So what do you want to see?" Miguel asks. "It's all going to be new to me too. I've had my nose buried in law books since I got here."

"I think the Guggenheim museum would be my first choice. Then I think we have to see the new World Trade Center construction. I know its several years away from completion yet but just to see it," Justice says.

"Okay, yep, World Trade Center," Miguel says. "What else?"

"Well, it might be fun to take a ferry or a boat ride around the island."

"Times Square, Greenwich Village—oh, and I'd like to see Flushing Meadows in Queens, the site of the 1939 World's Fair," Justice says.

"Where? What? Why?" Miguel quizzes.

"Well, Grandpa gave me some videos of a class that he had done back in the '90s. It was an early distance learning thing. They're almost documentaries. And one of them was about the GM exhibit at the fair, which really set the stage for freeways and shopping malls and suburbia in the 1950s. I think he was thinking they might stimulate some interest in me," Justice says, a little uncomfortable.

"He left me a book on the important legal cases and legislative victories involved in the civil rights movement."

"And here you are in law school."

"And you in economics," Miguel finishes her sentence.

Home from her trip to New York, Justice opens the envelope marked "Futurama" and reads Bill's contextual notes on the Futurama class.

> Suburban development and the all-about-the-auto lifestyle that flourished in the second half of the twentieth century is central to the story of modern culture and our prospects for a

healthy, green, sustainable future in numerous ways.

1. The rise of suburbia represents the last full-scale shift in Americans aspirations and way of life.
2. With boundless personal freedom and growing social isolation at its heart, the suburban dream stood as the high-water mark for an age when independence was revered as a cultural ideal above all others. This does not mean that suburbs are somehow bad or wrong. In fact, the booming auto and home-building industries of the 1950s saved us from another Great Depression.
3. Any serious discussion about the transformation of modern life should begin by noting how quickly change took place in the mid–twentieth century America and understanding the forces that made it possible.
4. Significant unforeseen environmental, social, and economic consequences arose from the rapid suburbanization of the US.
5. The modern environmental movement emerged in reaction to auto-oriented development patterns, and the course of the civil rights movement was affected by massive "white flight" to the suburbs.
6. Any hopes for curbing climate changes and fostering a greener society depends on refurbishing our communities to be more sustainable.

April 30, 1939, New York City. The serpentine line stretched for hundreds of feet, where it intermingled with crowds walking around the fairgrounds. The mood of those waiting was giddy as word of the sights to come spread through the crowd. It was opening day of the 1939 World's Fair in New York City. And the line that was to get into an exhibit in the General Motors pavilion called "Futurama" which promised to deliver a glimpse of the future.

Expectations were high—a simulated airplane ride, futuristic cars traveling at unheard-of speeds, tall transparent skyscrapers built out of glass. But what they saw was bigger still—a vision of the American dream to come. A rosy tomorrow in which they—the working middle class—were going to play the starring role. For people emerging from a long dark economic depression, it fell upon them like a bright white light.

The story of the suburban American dream rose from the despair of the Great Depression. During the '30s unemployment rate rose to more than 25 percent. Trade was cut in half and agricultural crops lost 60 percent of their value. Banks failed and depositors were left with nothing for their years of saving money. People were not just down; they were lost. Around the world, new bold economic and political systems were gaining strength. Communism in Russia and various forms of Fascist authoritarianism in Europe and Japan.

At that time, most Americans lived and worked in compact cities and towns. They walked to work, school, shopping, and entertainment or rode streetcars, trains, and buses because average Americans didn't own cars yet. Families often included three generations living under the same roof. Typically, they didn't own their own homes and most urban dwellers lived in apartments. If they did live in a single-family house, it didn't have much of a yard because buildings were packed tightly together to be near transit lines or within walking distance of a business district.

The 1939 World's Fair, New York City

By the late 1930s the country began to wake up from the economic and social ravages of the Great Depression and get back to work. Optimism was taking hold of the country again, and the World's Fair offered a vision creating machine. Many of America's biggest manufacturing companies created elaborate displays to show the general public a new, freer, more convenient, productive, and satisfying future made possible through the use and enjoyment of their products.

General Motors Futurama Exhibit

To say that the General Motors exhibit at the 1939 World's Fair was successful would be an understatement of gigantic proportions. There were several things that made the exhibit unique and exciting. One was that it wasn't just about them (General Motors); it was about us (Americans). It celebrated a vision of what the future held in store and showed how close we were to achieving it. General Motors' mission was to redefine our expectations and reshape the American dream.

The most popular activity at the fair, hands down, was Futurama. After waiting sometimes for hours, you were seated in one of 322 high-back chairs. Each one was wired for sound and moved up and down to simulate an airplane ride. You looked down at the most elaborate and realistic scale model ever constructed with snow-capped mountains, forests, lakes, and rivers. A shining city of the 1960s featured towering glass skyscrapers, huge vertical parking structures, wide streets flowing with vehicles, and elevated walkways isolating pedestrians from the street for their own safety. Connected to the city by massive highways were new suburbs, where average working Americans could afford a single-family home with a yard and their own private car— once the hallmarks of great wealth. The model contained over five hundred thousand individually designed houses, more than one million trees of different species, and fifty thousand cars, ten thousand of which moved around the model on streets, bridges, and freeways.

Futurama depicted a future in which science, technology and the industrial strength of the United States would transform the life of everyone. The American people took notice, and the American dream was transformed almost overnight.

World War II

On December 7, 1941, the Japanese bombed Pearl Harbor, and four days later the Germans declared war on the United States. The construction of the new American dream would have to wait as the great industrial engine of the United States shifted into high gear to build the implements of war. Factories were hurriedly converted to produce war materials. The Depression became a faint memory as every able-bodied man and many women got down to work.

The United States was transformed into an industrial goliath the likes of which the world had never seen. When World War II ended in 1945, the world's other major powers were crippled by the devastation of war. America stood alone in terms of our economic and industrial capacity. As victors, US soldiers were coming home from the war determined to find the American dream for themselves and their families.

But amid all this joy, some disturbing questions arose. Would the US slip back into depression as the war industries wound down? How could the US economy absorb all those returning soldiers? How could we provide enough high-paying jobs to deliver on the American dream for them? Was it possible redeploy all those factories from making war products to consumer goods in a short enough time? Forward-looking leaders saw the opportunity: Futurama!

A massive push to build suburbs, manufacture cars, and produce consumer goods to go along with all those new suburban homes was the shovel-ready project needed to generate the economic investments and good jobs necessary to deliver the new American dream.

The Great Suburban Expansion

For seventy years, it has been the policy of this country to encourage the development of suburban, Futurama-type communities. The methods of encouraging this growth has come in the form of direct and indirect subsidies to suburban development through programs such as the interstate highway system, GI housing benefits, single-use zoning codes, mortgage interest deductions, municipal bond programs to fund infrastructure such as sewer systems and roads, the FHA, the creation of the consumer finance industry to finance cars, and the creation of the secondary mortgage market (Freddie Mac and Fannie Mae).

Since the 1950s America has been hard at work on the largest public works project in human history, creating the auto-centric transportation system that makes modern suburban life possible. Developers bought huge tracts of land adjacent to new roads and divided them into millions and millions of suburban lots. Each home constructed needed kitchen appliances, furnishings, and all the other necessities of modern life. Each family living there needed two cars or maybe three or four. These new communities needed sewer systems, schools, hospitals, and shopping centers. The building and selling of all this produced enough decent-paying jobs so that most workers could afford cars and houses in the newly created suburbs. *Futurama had been built!*

As was now Justice's practice, she grabs her notebook, TOE Two, and makes some notes:

1. The human capacity to create change is truly astounding. Building a Futurama type American dream transformed the American landscape in thirty years.

2. A unique alignment of events—the Great Depression, World War II, and the need to rapidly convert our economy from war production to consumer

production—stimulated unprecedented construction of suburbs immediately after WWII.

Suburban expansion was encouraged and subsidized by government policies and business practices that are still largely in place today.

3. The suburban way of life was predicated on independence and separation to a degree hardly seen before in human history. We were isolated into single-family homes with wide lawns keeping us apart from our neighbors.

4. Different groups of people were also isolated from each other by zoning ordinances designed to keep races and income classes separate. We lived, shopped, and went to school with people very similar to us.

One of my takeaways from Bill's "Futurama" class is the absolute power of humanity to change and recreate the world when we're all in and together. In the case of the suburban migration it was independent self-interest that was the catalyst for change.

Chapter 11

DAHLTECH MEDICAL

Justice is gripping the mysterious envelope from someone calling themselves Whistle-Blower as she dials Miguel.

"Hi, Justice, how'd the first class back go?"

"You won't believe what happened," Justice says.

"What?"

"Well, when I arrived, the police were there and refusing to let anyone into the building. There were maybe a thousand students at the door. I asked the police what the issue was, and they said my suspension had been reinstated and the class canceled."

"You're kidding," Miguel responds.

"No, so I asked the chief of police to relay a message to President Hogwood that I was going to be on TV a lot in the near future and that I intended to tell the truth, so he was deciding right then what I was going to say."

"Atta girl," Miguel says. "Then what happened?"

"While we were waiting, the students started to chant. Then the chief called back and said it was a mistake and let us in."

"Oh man, the power of numbers!" Miguel says.

"Exactly," Justice agrees. "Anyway, every seat at Northrop was taken. But that's not the end of the story," Justice responds.

"What else happened?"

"Well, after class I was talking to students and answering questions for maybe thirty minutes or so. When that's done and I go back to collect my bag to leave, there is an envelope on my bag addressed to Justice Miller from whistle blower, so I open it. Inside is an article that has been ripped out of a business magazine."

"What's the article about?" Miguel asks.

"It's about some new medical technology that is about to come out that's owned by Dahltech Medical. The article said the technology had recently passed the regulatory testing requirements for FDA approval. Based on the potential size of the market, the technology could be worth billions of dollars, it said. Anyway, on the article is a Post-it note that reads, 'How did Dahltech get exclusive rights to technology developed by the university?' And it's signed 'Whistle-Blower' on the Post-it note.

"Dahltech Medical is owned by Jack Dahl, you know," Miguel says.

"Yeah, exactly, President Hogwood's buddy on the regents and the other no vote on my reinstatement," Justice says.

"Well, we were suspicious Hogwood may have spies in your classes because of the way the protest rally incident happened. But now it looks like your class may also have agents working against your enemies. Man, your classes are like a spy movie."

"Listen, scan and send the article and Post-it note to me and let me nose around a little. I think I've still got some people around town I can ask about some of this. Say, when does this favor stuff start flowing the other way?" Miguel asks.

"Ha, you're still paying off the six tickets I got for you to the NCAA hockey tournament a decade ago!" Justice exclaims.

"Okay, okay, I get it. Just send me the article and note. Sunday night, before the next class on Monday morning," Justice hears from Miguel.

"I'm finding some interesting information," Miguel says.

"What?" Justice responds.

"Well, that Dahltech technology was developed at the university mostly with research grants from the federal government. Typically, technology like that must go through a committee set up to deal with the university's intellectual property. The process is designed to ensure that technology goes to qualified companies, the university receives fair market value for it, and the process is fair and open."

"And did Dahltech go through the process to get the technology?" Justice asks.

"Well, in an abbreviated way that didn't allow another bidder in."

"How did they accomplish that?" Justice asks.

"They declared the technology 'not marketable,' in which case it can be sold cheaply to anyone at the discretion of the director of the intellectual property committee," Miguel says.

"How could that be? The article talked about it being a billion-dollar technology."

"Yes, but there was one study done that didn't replicate the original findings, so the university declared that the technology didn't work and included it in a bundle of patents sold to Dahltech at a fire sale price."

"That sounds like an inside job," Justice says. "I mean somebody had to have known about the promising technology hidden in the package," Justice says.

"Right, well, the punch line is this—the director of the intellectual property department at that time, none other than grandpa's old adversary, then professor and now president Hogwood!

"Oh my god, you're kidding," Justice shouts into the phone! "We need to expose this!"

"No, no, no, not yet, we don't have evidence of any crime or corruption yet," Miguel warns. "It smells bad but that's it. We'd need to have evidence that they knew the good technology was hidden in with the bad and that there was some kind of quid pro quo or payoff of some type. Without that, our accusations could be libelous. I even took the information to some investigative reporters I know, and they said they wouldn't touch it without more evidence."

"So what can we do?" Justice asks.

"It's hard to imagine this type of mistake could happen without someone somewhere committing fraud and falsifying test results somehow. We need to get Whistle-Blower to give us more information."

"How?" Justice asks. "We don't even know who it is?"

"How about if you make a statement in class tomorrow that the Whistle-Blower will recognize as being directed at him?"

"Or her," Justice inserts.

"Right, but it will seem like part of the class discussion to everyone else, including Hogwood's spy."

"Okay, I think I get what you're driving at. What if I say something like whistle-blowers and whistle-blower laws are an early example of feedback loops used for behavior modification? Feedback loops is the term we use to describe Yelp and socially responsible investing and all the rating systems that are changing the economy now."

"Yeah, that could work, and then you say something like 'Whistle-blowers can remain anonymous in most situations, but in order to be effective, they must provide actionable evidence, contact people and discuss the corruption.'"

"Okay, I'll try it tomorrow in class," Justice says.

"Okay, we'll just wait and see what happens. I think we need someone who knows something to help us here," Miguel says.

"Thanks, Miguel, you're getting close to having those tickets paid off," Justice says.

A week later Miguel calls Justice.

"Hi, Miguel, how are you?"

"I'm good. Were you able to get the message out to Whistle Blower in the class?"

"Yes, I did it, just as we planned it."

"I take it there's been no response?"

"Nope, nothing yet."

"Okay, well, I think you should just let it go unless some new evidence shows up."

"I know, but it really makes me mad," Justice says. "This kind of stuff happens all the time. Every day in millions of little ways the public is getting ripped off."

"It could be legitimate, you know," Miguel says.

"You mean that a billion dollars' worth of technology developed by the university and paid for by the public could have just landed in Dahltech's hands by mistake?" Justice says sarcastically.

"Well, I agree some form of wrongdoing is likely involved, but we can't do anything about it unless we have evidence," Miguel says in a firm voice.

"Okay, okay, I won't do anything unless something shows up," Justice concedes. "But this is exactly what WEJ is fighting—economic predators ripping off the public!"

"I know. Maybe someone will show up. If there was wrongdoing, there are people out there who know about it," Miguel says.

"Okay, say hi to Alesha for me. I'll let you know if I get anything else."

Chapter 12

A SINGLE HUMAN CHAIN

Among the handwritten notes in the margin of Bill's "My Big TOE" notebook is a strange message: *"Marble. Golden rule. Women's movement. And Karen Stephens."* No further explanation, just those words. Justice spent quite a while trying to figure out what it could mean. She even googled "Karen Stephens" and searched for her on Facebook, but among many Karen Stephens, nobody popped out with a connection that she could discern. It's one of those things she regretted not having asked Bill when he was alive.

One day while skimming the student newspaper in her office, she notices a series of TED Talks that are going to be filmed at the auditorium. Among the list of speakers was Professor Karen Stephens Tomashevsky, who will be speaking on "The Human Chain." Justice remembers the name. The paper says she received her undergraduate degree from the university in 1999. Did she know her grandpa Bill? Justice decides to attend the event and bring along the "My Big TOE" notebook so she can show her the reference if she gets a chance.

The Human Chain

A short woman in a blue business suit walks out on stage of Northrop Auditorium. The crowd applauds. She acknowledges their welcome with a series of nods and pauses until the room is quiet, and then she reaches in her pocket and pulls out a smartphone, holding it up in the air.

"Who invented this?" she says. As the audiences shouts out answers, she repeats them. Apple Company, yes. Steve Jobs, I heard over there, yes. Apple and Steve Jobs introduced their invention of the iPhone in 2007, that is correct. But how much of the development of the iPhone is Apple actually responsible for? Fifty percent maybe? Thirty? Ten percent? One percent? Let's look. The smartphone is completely dependent on previously developed computer technology, right? There is a direct causal link between the iPhone and previously developed computer technologies. Meaning that the iPhone could not have happened until after that computer technology had been developed. Did Apple develop the computer technology that the iPhone is dependent on? Well, some of it certainly, but probably not all of it. And that earlier computer technology was dependent on previously developed technologies too. On components like printed circuits and processors, hard drives, and operating system software. And those components were dependent on previous technologies as well. On transistors and resistors and before that, on wire and tubes, and before that, on electricity and the work of our friend Benjamin Franklin among many, and on and on and on. And it doesn't stop there either. Every material, every component, every manufacturing process, and every element of basic science involved has a similar history going further and further back in time and involving more and more people. Most of whom are lost to history. And even though all the subsequent developments are dependent on previous developments, none of the original work was created with the smartphone in mind. In other words, they're all reworked or redeployed or recontextualized technologies.

Just as our DNA carries the genetic information from all our ancestors, most human work product of every type builds upon the accumulated knowledge of civilization itself, stretching back thousands of years. So let me ask again: Who invented the smartphone? In terms of the critical innovations and knowledge incorporated into the smartphone, you'd have to say civilization itself is responsible for most of the critical innovations and knowledge that has gone into its development. Innovations and knowledge that go back hundreds of thousands of years and involve

116

WHOLE EARTH JUSTICE

millions of people over time. "Dependent" developments stretch back as far as our ability to control fire.

Matt Ridley in his book The Rational Optimist *describes our process of accumulating knowledge as being like sex. "Exchange is to cultural evolution as sex is to biological evolution," he says. It's not just our knowledge that makes us unique but the sharing and exchanging and recombining and repurposing of that knowledge. The point is this: whether you're talking about biology or cultural development, isolation and homogeneity create weakness, stagnation, and vulnerability; whereas diversity and free flowing exchange creates adaptability, innovation, strength, and progress. We are the only species capable of converting the knowledge gained in our life into a valuable bit of cultural DNA that can be used as raw material by someone else generations later. We will all die, and the credit for our contributions to human culture will likely be forgotten to history, but on a practical level, our contributions will live on. They will remain usable knowledge that can be redeployed within future contexts we could not even imagine.*

This is such a unique and extraordinary process that it really alters the very definition of who we are. Just as our biological DNA carries the unique genetic signature of our ancestors, work and efforts during our lives represent the cultural DNA of civilization itself, and our efforts are added to that legacy and projected into the future. We are not simply one of seven billion individuals living today, but rather we are all part of a single ongoing human chain, both biologically and culturally.

In essence, "life" is not exclusively an "I" story. "We" is a big part of it too. Recognition of "we" as a central element of a single human civilization can be seen all around us every day. Work takes place all around us on projects that are going to outlive their builders. Why? Is it just because we're being paid to do it? [Pause]

Consider this scenario for a moment: Let's suppose a brilliant scientist, after years of study on her own, discovers something very important. A discovery that holds the promise of revolutionizing energy generation. Now, in the process of writing her journal paper where she will reveal to the world the details about her discovery, there is an announcement that a week from Friday an asteroid of immense size is going to hit the planet and humanity will not survive. Would she continue writing her paper?

117

Or would she stop writing in order to be with friends and family? She would probably quit writing, right? [Pause]

Now consider the same situation, but this time, instead of an asteroid wiping out humanity, she is told by her doctor that she has a terminal disease and she has less than two weeks to live. What does she do in that situation? She steps up her efforts on the paper doesn't she! She works harder. In both cases she will be gone, and in neither case will she be paid for her efforts. But in one, civilization will carry on her work and in the other it will not. When Neil Armstrong stepped off the lunar lander in 1969 and said "one small step for man, one giant leap for mankind," we all experienced the accomplishment personally. "We" had landed on the moon!

This notion that "we" is a legitimate way to define ourselves plays itself out in other realms of reality as well. The amazing biological story about "we" is that everything we define as being part of us today will get recycled, when we're not using it anymore. Our atoms and molecules will become the atoms and molecules of others. As a matter of fact, scientists and mathematicians can tell us how many atoms in our body today were once in the body of Thomas Jefferson or Madame Curie, for example. Or how many oxygen and hydrogen molecules in your breath have also passed through the body of William Shakespeare or Gandhi. This same notion of "we" is incorporated into many of our spiritual wisdom traditions as well. At the Last Supper, with his impending demise bearing down on him, what was Jesus's message to his disciples? This is my body, and this is my blood. He demonstrated that he lives in us. In fact, "we" live in each other. Biologically, spiritually, and culturally. "We" is as alive as "I." And it's as legitimate, a way of defining who we are as "I" is.

This observation about humankind was articulated by Adam Ferguson, the eighteenth-century Scottish philosopher, who is considered by some to be the father of modern sociology, this way: "In other classes of animals, the individual advances from infancy to maturity; and he attains, in the compass of a single life, to all the perfection his nature can reach: but, in human kind, the species has a progress as well as the individual; they build in every subsequent age on the foundations formally laid" (An Essay on the History of Civil Society, *Adam Ferguson*).

So I would like to leave you with this simple question: Does this knowledge of who we are, our unique abilities and nature, change your view about our responsibilities toward future generations?

After the event, Justice attends the cocktail reception hoping to solve once and for all the mystery of Karen Stephens. People huddle around the guest of honor, so Justice waits for the crowd to thin before talking to her, worried she might sound silly asking a famous scholar about a reference in some old handwritten notebook. Finally, as people begin to stream out of the event, Justice sees her chance. Walking over, she says in a firm voice, "I loved your presentation, Professor Stephens Tomashevsky."

"Thank you very much."

Justice takes the notebook from under her arm and awkwardly says, "Did you, ah, know…"

"Oh, *My Big TOE,* Stephens-Tomashevsky answers…Did you know Professor Miller?"

Ha. Justice smiles. "Well, yes, I'm Justice Miller and Bill was my grandfather."

"Oh, I'm so glad you introduced yourself. Bill was a big influence in my life," she says.

"Me too," Justice responds, immediately regretting her choice of words. *Of course, he was a big influence—he was my grandfather!* But the professor's attentive gaze calms her.

"Well, I'm here on official academic research business, sort of," Justice says.

"Great, and please call me Karen."

Opening the notebook, Justice points out the handwritten reference to her: "*Marble. Golden rule. Women's movement. And Karen Stephens.*"

"I was hoping you could shed some light on what this means," Justice says.

Karen looks at it and starts to laugh. She pulls her bag off her shoulder and starts searching through it. "I want to show you something," she says. Then she pulls out a large blue marble out of her bag. A brace band is inlaid around the marble and engraved onto the band are the words *"Do unto others, as you would have them do unto you. The golden rule."*

"I've been carrying this marble around with me for forty years," she says.

"There must be a good story that goes with it," Justice says.

"There is, and it involves your grandpa Bill. I am staying at the hotel down the street, and if you've got time, let's have a drink at the lounge and I'll tell you the story."

"Okay," Justice says without hesitation, although she already had plans.

"Perfect, I just need to say thank you to the organizer here and I'll meet you at the coat room and we can walk over?"

Out on the sidewalk, Karen starts by saying, "You know there are a lot of us out here!"

"What do you mean?" Justice says.

"I mean people who had their life changed by your grandpa Bill."

"Really?" Justice says.

"Yes, some of us even continue to meet occasionally."

"You're kidding."

"No. In fact there are a number of copies of 'My Big TOE' still circulating out there as well."

"Wow, I had no idea!" Justice says.

"He was a very influential guy," Karen says. I heard about his passing and was hoping to come to the funeral, but I was in California at the time and it just didn't work out."

"So what's the common denominator among this group that knew Grandpa?" Justice asks.

"Let's just say, he showed us a new way of seeing our journey. By 'our' I mean human civilization," Karen says. "Take my talk tonight, for example. If I had never come across Bill in my life, that talk would never have been made. At least not by me. Bill showed me, and many of us really, the reality and nature of 'we.' How about you, Justice, what do you do?"

"Ha, well, I'm a professor of economics here at the university."

"So you're Professor Miller," Karen says, noting the irony with a smirk. "That's so funny."

"What do you mean?" Justice responds.

"Well, I mean Bill was important to me and I felt like I knew him pretty well, but I guess I never learned anything about his family or really anything else about his life. To me he was just an important teacher, I guess. I really can't separate who I am today professionally, from Bill's influence," Karen says.

"He would be so thrilled to here you say that, Karen," Justice says.

"Thank you," Karen says. "Ha, well, welcome to the group, Professor Miller."

"Thank you, I'm glad to be become a member," Justice says. "Okay, so tell me about the marble and the golden rule."

"Well, my father gave me this one when I was a teenager and told me that I should always keep it with me. That it had magic powers and could protect me. I've carried it with me ever since. Then when I was an undergraduate at the university here, I was in one of your grandpa's classes. Anyway, I can't remember exactly what the context was, but Bill started talking about the golden rule and how interesting it was that that little piece of wisdom had made it into every major religion on earth. So I of course reached into my purse and pulled out the marble my dad had given me.

"'Where did you get that?' Bill asked, carefully studying it.

"'My dad gave it to me when I was a little girl and told me it had magic powers,' I said in front of the whole class. Some of the kids in the class smirked a little at that.

"Then Bill handed the marble back to me and said to me in front of the class, 'I think Karen's dad was right.'

"Anyway, I stayed after class that day and thanked Bill for defending me. 'Not a problem,' Bill said. 'I actually do believe your father was right.'

"'You do?' I said.

"'Yes, it's just that the context is missing,' he said. 'The golden rule is more than we think it is.'

"'How so?' I asked.

"'Well, you know we think of the golden rule as being a simple, even trite, moral platitude. But it's more than that. It's a code, or survival instructions, a life raft of sorts. And it's been hiding in plain sight for thousands of years, waiting for us to mature to the point that we understand it. Waiting for a time when we will need it to survive. Don't run with the scissors! Don't touch the stove! Don't hit your little brother! These instructions came without reasons or context. They were just prohibitions. The reason your parents dictated how you should act—or else!—was because you weren't capable at the time of understanding the reasons why. Only after you matured to a certain point did you understand why you shouldn't smack your siblings. You realized the reasoning for this prohibition. The golden rule is like that,' Bill said. 'A time may come when the fate of human civilization could be at stake. That's when the golden rule will be transformed from a platitude to a deep and meaningful key to survival.'

"He then said there was a small group of students who met for coffee regularly on Saturday mornings to talk about ideas like this if I was interested. So a group of us students would meet with Bill at the coffee shop that's still there over on university avenue."

"I remember a lot of conversations like that with Grandpa," Justice recalls.

"Yeah, your grandpa Bill was an interesting guy. I'm still in touch with some of the coffee shop gang, and I'm meeting with a few of them tomorrow morning at the coffee shop if you'd like to join us," Karen offers.

"I'll be there," Justice says. "I can't wait to tell my parents about this! Do you know why Bill wrote the reference in the notebook to the women's movement, next to the golden rule notation?" Justice adds.

"Yes," Karen says. "Bill believed that women were more naturally wired for cooperation than men and that men were more naturally wired for competition. As a result, he thought that we would see a surge in the women's movement at the same time we were growing into a fuller understanding of the golden rule. Not that they were cause and effect but that they shared a common context."

The next day, the coffee shop was crammed with people when Justice arrived, but she didn't see Karen. Justice looked around at each group wondering if she should go up and introduce herself to see if they were the right group. Just then Karen came in, explaining, "It's too crowded in here so we just moved around the corner to the diner. There's only two others this morning but I've told them about our conversation and they're very excited to meet you."

At the diner, Karen made introductions. Jill is the CEO of a large wellness clinic here in town, and Betsy is an inventor in the tech field and an author. Like Karen, both women were ten to fifteen years older than Justice.

"I loved your grandpa," Jill shares, "he changed everything for me."

"Me too," Betsy adds. "You even look a little like him, and I love the fact that Professor Bill has a granddaughter named Justice!"

"We were talking last night after the conference about the golden rule marble," Karen announces.

"I remember Bill saying that the word 'others' in the context of the golden rule was significant because it included everyone," Betsy notes. "It doesn't say friends or family, for example, it doesn't say allies. 'Others' makes no distinctions between people."

"I remember in 1995, I was working with the UN on a program that was designed to heal communities that had been torn apart by armed conflicts and civil wars," Jill says. "It was just a year or so after Nelson Mandela and the African National Congress, ANC, representing the black majority, had seized power from the white minority apartheid government in South Africa. There were serious questions about whether this transition to a democratically elected majority could resist the impulse for retribution. The ANC decided to create a Truth and Reconciliation Commission to bear witness to the injustice and provide a constructive path to healing. Anyway, during that experience I realized that people don't really want retribution, at least that it's not our primary need. We're actually wired for forgiveness and reconciliation. But we can't achieve that forgiveness and reconciliation unless the injustice has stopped, and been acknowledged, and sincerely apologized for. When those elements are all in place, our nature seems to bend toward forgiveness and reconciliation, even in the case of people we consider 'other.'"

"That's a pretty optimistic view of humanity," Justice says.

"Well, yes, it is," Jill confirms. "I think that's one of the things Bill taught us. Things aren't hopeless. Everything we need is here. It's possible for humanity to meet its challenges and mature and thrive."

"True," Betsy jumps in. "Bill was optimistic about the future, but I remember him also saying that it sometimes takes a lot of motivation to get human beings to acknowledge their common fate. He worried that as our power and technology grew, it was possible we would do tremendous damage to ourselves and the planet before we were able to come together to solve our problems."

Wow! Justice thinks to herself. *My coffee is still so hot, I can barely drink it, and these three women, whom I have just met, have already pulled me into a deep discussion about the very nature of human civilization.*

"I remember many conversations with Bill about interdependence," Justice contributes, "but I don't remember him ever saying anything apocalyptic in any way."

"I don't think he was," Karen says. "He was an optimist, he thought civilization would be able to adapt and make it. But he did think we might get to a point where interdependence was going to be the essential element of our survival, not just a nice idealistic idea. He saw our civilization as being immature but capable of growing up— although the motivation for that growth was likely to be pretty dire. In other words, we weren't likely to mature on our own, short of a cataclysmic motivator. A threat that is universal. I mean different civilizations have come and gone many times in our past because they destroyed the natural environment of the place they lived. Where did they go? They just moved away. Unfortunately, that's not possible anymore."

"And do you see us approaching that cataclysmic time today?" Justice asks.

"Well, the environmental devastation is global, and there's nowhere else to go, that forces us to change—or else…," Karen says, taking a long breath.

"And the women's movement is regenerating again!" Betsy says.

"Ha, yes," Karen says. And she holds up her coffee cup. "To our mentor and teacher, Bill Miller."

The meeting in the coffee shop ends with an exchange of contact information and promises to stay in touch.

Justice rides her bike home while thinking about Bill's legacy.

Upon entering the house, Justice throws her backpack on the table and grabs her "TOE Two" notebook and opens it to the first blank page and writes the following:

> Grandpa, you are so still with us. I hope you know we are still with you. Now, on the way home from the coffee shop, I was thinking about the discussion with some of your other students, and I was also thinking about your class on the code of conduct. Anyway, I see civilization doing exactly what you've said—we're searching for and developing a new code of conduct. A code based on three elements:
>
> 1. Preserving and defending the environment for the benefit of future generations
> 2. Equity among all people
> 3. Economic growth
>
> It's a more interdependent economy and a more interdependent humanity.
>
> Do unto others as you would have them do unto you!
>
> I love you, Grandpa!
>
> Justice

Chapter 13

THOUGHT MARKET

Neal "the Ice Man" Freeman's Lyft ride pulls up to the front door of the headquarters of one of the Twin Cities most prominent Fortune 500 companies. He's met by his old grad school friend Jim "The Master" Bolt, who works for the company.

"Ice, you're late man," Jim shrieks, "we've got one thousand angry executives waiting for you in the auditorium." Neal flashes a million-dollar smile and puts his arm around Jim as they race toward the auditorium.

"Great to see you, Master! Don't worry we're going to make it up to them." Neal's nickname, Ice Man, comes from situations just like this. He's always cool under pressure.

They throw open the doors to the auditorium and race to the front. Jim buttons his jacket and moves to the lectern. "Ladies and gentlemen," he says, using sweeping hand gestures to settle them down. "Please take your seats, we're about to get started." The crowd settles. "Thank you for coming. Because we're a little late getting started, I'm going to keep my introductory remarks brief. I first met Neal Freeman at the university where we were classmates. Some of you might remember Neal from the U of M Gophers' 2005 trip to the NCAA basketball tournament, when Neal was one of the top scorers on the team that year. A season that ended with a game in which the Gophers did not beat the spread, and clock management was an issue as I recall." The crowd laughs, and Neal playfully shrugs.

"You might also be familiar with Neal's father, John Freeman, who is a prominent bishop in the Episcopal Church. After graduating from the University of Minnesota, Neal received graduate degrees from Stanford and Johns Hopkins. One in computer science and one in religious studies. After school Neal spent five years working as a technology analyst with a Silicon Valley Venture Capital firm. In 2016, he became the CEO of a firm the VC firm was invested in, and they launched the Thought Market Company. So without any further ado, please welcome my friend Neal Freeman."

The crowd gives him a polite but reserved applause. "Thank you, Jim. I apologize for our late start, but I can assure you we're going to beat the spread today." Neal removes the microphone from its stand and walks to the front of the stage. He pauses and looks into the crowd silently. Neal is an imposing figure by any standard, who exudes confidence on stage. He's an African American with a bald, shaved head and a 6'2" athletic physique that is unable to be hidden by his clothes, all of which is offset by an attractively self-deprecating sense of humor.

Neal continues. "In 1968 Stanford professor Dr. Paul Ehrlich authored a book titled *The Population Bomb* that predicted that by the mid-1980s, our population would grow to the point where it would overwhelm our ability to produce enough food to sustain us, resulting in major societal upheavals. It obviously didn't happen as predicted. However, his math on the growth of the planet's population, as well as the food production capabilities of the day were correct. What was wrong was that Professor Ehrlich underestimated the pace of innovation and the resulting increases in food production efficiencies. And this is not a unique story. Every industry, every human endeavor has a similar story. Humanity is shockingly creative and innovative. Creativity is at the core of the human experience. But according to many studies done by academic institutions world over, organizational creativity, and innovation happens at a pace that is a tiny fraction of its potential. So if creativity is such a plentiful and universal human quality, why are we so poor at exploiting it?"

Neal lets the question hang in the air as he pauses and walks over to the other side of the stage. Neal is a very accomplished and comfortable speaker. In fact, he grew up as a PK (preacher's kid), thinking he would follow his dad into the ministry. His dad was always Neal's biggest influence and mentor. Even as a child, he would emulate his dad's public speaking patterns and practice.

"The answer to that question is simple and straightforward," he tells the audience. "We choose other values over creativity. For example, we value and choose order and predictability over creativity. We choose hierarchical and accountable management structures and narrowly defined job descriptions and mission integrity over creativity too. And we reinforce these policies by rewarding performance within narrow job descriptions. Stay in your lane! Don't rock the boat! Keep your head down, do your work, and let your boss take most of the credit." The crowd gives up a restrained collective chuckle, given the fact that many of their bosses are also in the room.

"And why wouldn't we choose those things?" Neal continues. "Organizations have missions and goals—which do not usually include fulfilling their employees desires to be more creative, or happier, or more fully human."

Another pause.

"This is really quite puzzling," Neal continues, "because creativity and innovation can measurably enhance an organization's ability to reach its goals. Creativity is a dramatic force multiplier! The truth is," Neal continues, "in today's competitive world, we need both. Today, organizations must innovate and remain competitive, and they also need to do so without loosening their mission integrity or predictability or reliability. And if an organization can accomplish both of those things, they will thrive, and so will their employees.

"This is what Thought Market is—a strategy to help organizations achieve both. Mission integrity and enhanced creativity. *Both* and," he emphasizes, "not *either-or*. To help describe for you how Thought Market works, let's look at this animation." On the screen behind Neal, a cartoon character appears of an executive sitting at his desk pouring over data of some kind.

"Welcome to the fictional Great American Cereal Company."

It's 8:00 p.m. on a holiday weekend and diligent Dan, an executive at the Great American Cereal Company (GACC), is still at his desk pouring over sales reports.

Now thankfully GACC has a Thought Market program. So Dan signs on and posts a message: "Sales of Weirdo cereal is down again this month with our core constituency group."

Now that message will be received by everyone in the company who signs onto GACC's Thought Market program, but they won't be able to see who wrote it. It's all semianonymous, so it records who makes the comment, but it's not visible to the participants in real time.

"Okay, let's go on," Neal says. A second cartoon character pops onto the screen, but this time it's a woman sitting with a young girl. "It's now Saturday morning and Alice, a data management person in the HR department at GACC, is doing math homework with her daughter. While waiting for her daughter to complete some problems, Alice signs onto the GACC Thought Market program, and she reads Dan's post. She of course doesn't know who placed the post, but reading it causes her to have a comment of her own and she writes: my kids only like cereals that are sweet."

A third character appears on the screen behind Neal. "This is scout leader, Sarah, a part-time employee of GACC who works as a demonstrator at trade shows and various functions. Sarah signs on to the GACC Thought Market program and reads the first two anonymous posts: Sarah wouldn't have had a thought except the first two caused her to think of something and she writes, 'My kids seem to like crunchy things in their cereal like nuts.'"

A fourth character appears on the screen behind Neal and he continues. "It's Sunday morning and Marketing Mark is at the golf course waiting for his buddies to get there. While waiting he signs onto the GACC Thought Market and reads the chain of comments: 'Sales are down.' 'Kids like sweet.' 'Kids like crunchy.' Mark thinks about that for a minute and then writes, 'How about if we make Honey Nut Weirdos'?

"So at the core of Thought Market in its simplest form are several elements or features, designed to improve collaboration between people:

1. Semianonymous threaded conversations, designed to let people from all stations in the organization contribute in meaningful and strategic ways. We don't often see a CEO having a discussion with a custodial staff person about the company's products or the direction they should go, but that doesn't mean they don't have something to contribute. In fact, innovation often comes from outsiders because insiders may be to close, to see the solutions.

2. Second, Thought Market is an easy to navigate online bulletin board or database of organizational development subjects. It's a library or database of strategic conversations and threads designed to stimulate contributions as well as provide a simple searchable map of the strategic enterprise within the organization. As we demonstrated in the mock-up conversation, people often need to be stimulated to be able to contribute. Its only when our employees saw the posts from their colleagues that they had something to contribute. This is important for several reasons: first is that people in your organization have contributions to make outside their official job descriptions, and second, because a sense of ownership or belonging happens when people have an ability to contribute to the strategic enterprise. And this is why we use semianonymity—because we want to be able to track down the contributors and reward them when something productive happens. People given access and permission to contribute to the strategic apparatus of the organization, and people who are appreciated with rewards for doing so feel like they belong. Like owners, not mere employees. And people who feel like they belong will give a lot more of themselves to the organization. One of man's prime needs is to feel like we belong to something bigger than ourselves.

3. The third part of the Thought Market program is professionally trained online facilitation by organization employees. These are trained employees who are tasked with keeping the conversations moving forward, keeping them from getting redundant, or screening out inappropriate comments or keeping them from getting stopped by unmanaged judgments.

4. The fourth part of the program is classes and instruction designed to encourage participation. By the time your employees have gotten here, they've endured five, ten, twenty, thirty, forty years of people telling them *no*. We're socialized and conditioned to see our lane and only our lane. If we have opinions outside our lane, we suppress them in order to get along and be a team player. We need to be invited and encouraged to participate—and shown how to do it without taking social risks.

5. Fifth, a reward system that tracks participation and rewards innovations. Napoleon Bonaparte once said, 'A soldier will fight long and hard for a bit of colored ribbon.' If money is what the enterprise is about, then the rewards must include a form of money to have value. But in addition to money, recognition is what Napoleon was referencing. Recognition, ownership, membership, belonging—these are the things we live and fight for.

6. Sixth, right time conversation. How many times have you left a meeting and thought of something you should have said on your way down the hall afterward? These conversations don't take place in real time; they take place in right time. Right time for the contributors.

Neal, pauses and looks at the audience and asks if there are any questions so far. A voice from the middle of the auditorium says, "This whole thing seems a little like snake oil to me. I mean, you're promising to both release employees from bondage and saying they will stay at their desks and do their jobs! I don't see any evidence you can do that! It just doesn't seem grounded in a reality."

The confrontational spirit of this comment casts a pall across the plush seats. It's the kind of moment that explains why more people fear public speaking than fear death, according to opinion surveys. But Neal stands up tall, takes a deep breath, and then…smiles. When he was young, he and his dad would go fishing and talk for hours on end. Neal's father would use sports metaphors to get his points across with his adolescent son. When it's in the fourth quarter, and there's two seconds left on the clock, and the game is on the line, you will find that there are two types of people out there on the court, his father said: the guys that want the ball and the guys that want nothing to do with the ball. He would continue, "Of the guys that want the ball, there are two types as well. Ego-deluded people, who, if they fail, will blame everyone but themselves. And the second group, people who know themselves, know their limits, know their God, and know they will survive no matter the outcome. These people can perform despite the challenges because they're secure in themselves and able to remain calm and able to perform."

Neal lets the silence hang in the air for a few seconds longer. He looks intently into the audience and says, "Who wants to be next to speak?" More uneasy silence. "Of course, you don't," Neal calls out. "This gentleman just registered a judgment, which is the same thing that happens every time someone speaks of new ideas. This shows us why speaking up feels risky. Its why people don't ask questions in class. Somebody is going to shoot you down, and you're going to look stupid or be embarrassed." Pause. "But the truth is, these judgments are right sometimes. Judgments are important. But the downside about judgments is that they stop creative chains of collaboration from happening. They stop brainstorming dead in its tracks. So one of the things that Thought Market does is manage these judgments. They aren't considered until the brainstorm is completed. At the end of the process, not during it. So I would like for you to do the following: make a note about this gentleman's concern and judgment. At the end of your exploration of this presentation, after you've had a chance to ask your questions and after you've had a chance to review the materials and studies about our history and success, I think it would be appropriate and wise for you to consider this gentleman's concern and judgments, as well as your own, and those of others. If you find these judgments credible at that time, I strongly recommend that you not pursue the Thought Market program."

The Master couldn't help but smile. He'd seen Neal do it hundreds of times in many different settings. Just as things seem bleak and the pressure is on, the Ice Man turns the situation with a serene gaze and few calm words. Neal continues through the rest of the presentation, going through each element of the Thought Market program, then he concludes with this: "There is no magic provided by the Thought Market program. All the creativity resides in the people using it. People are the magic ingredient. What Thought Market does is provide specialized communication channels that helps facilitate collaborative, creative communications. It surfaces potential. Potential that is within every one of us but is often hidden from view.

"If I was to say to you, write down everything you know about the mechanics of a car, or physics, or space flight, or computer science, you might say 'I don't know anything about those subjects,' and you'd write very little in response. But if I were to ask you questions about those subjects, you would likely be able to answer far more questions than you would have guessed. That's because our knowledge is like an iceberg. Only a tiny fraction of what we know is visible above the waterline. We call that explicit knowledge. Explicit knowledge is the information we know we know. It's part of our identity or expertise for example. But below the surface is where the bigger portion of our knowledge resides. This is called tacit knowledge. This invisible knowledge is not only invisible to others, it's also largely invisible to us as well. Its only available to us in a reactive form, like if a question is asked or someone or something stimulates its appearance or recognition. This tacit knowledge is said to represent 95 percent of all the knowledge we possess. Thought Market is a program that is designed to surface this potential knowledge and organize it so it can be used more efficiently.

"I'd also like to say something about the efficacy of networked information sharing, which is how I would categorize Thought Market. Networked information sharing as a category includes most of the shared or collaborative economy systems like Uber and Lyft, or Airbnb, or all the others. Many of which have proven to be highly productive and efficient. The category also includes sites or programs we call social media. And some of us have become disillusioned by some of the consequences of social media in general. There certainly is plenty of evidence that despite early speculations, and the best of intentions, it has caused more isolation and alienation rather than cure it. But unbridled cynicism like its cousin unbridled optimism are rarely right. My personal view or analysis might be something like this: When people who are motivated to get or share information for a productive purpose, it's productive. But when the actions or information sharing is of a nonproductive nature, it can have different consequences, depending on what the people are bringing to it. In any case, however, learning and trying things and doing the work to understand how to make it perform is the creative path. At Thought Market we've been doing the work to make our program perform. We know for example, that creative innovation is derivative in nature. Meaning our creative insights typically don't come as random out of the blue inspirations but rather are derived from some stimulus. Changing the context of another thought, experimentation, and hard work. We know that people in organizations can stimulate each other and help the process of pulling tacit knowledge out of each other. We know that people who are invited to participate in the strategic enterprise of an organization feel a greater sense of belonging. We know that people who have a sense of belonging in their organization bring more of themselves and work harder. And we know that there are all kinds of cultural and personal barriers that get in the way of people contributing, unless they're ameliorated through process controls and features." He pauses again, then continues.

"There are almost a thousand people in this room right now. The potential present in undiscovered fragments of knowledge between us is astounding. You probably know some of the other people in this room. And some are not known to you. Each of us represents an amount of combined tacit and explicit knowledge that might be analogized as a large public library let's say. The people in the room that we know well or work with daily, maybe we could say we're aware of an amount of knowledge they possess and analogize it as being the equivalent of a book or two perhaps. The rest of the library about them is unknown. Likewise, there are people you know little. Maybe just their name, or what department they work in, or maybe nothing at all. So this group represents a huge library of information, only a tiny fraction of which is known. Now imagine you could ask that vast library of knowledge, that includes both explicit and tacit knowledge from all of us combined, for help with what you're working on.

"The secret sauce is us, the unrealized potential is beyond calculation, and Thought Market is simply a tool to help us see it and act upon it. Thank you and I'd be happy to try and answer any questions you may have."

The crowd stands and gives Neal an enthusiastic applause. People come down and stand in line to ask Neal questions or make comments. Some of them of course are local basketball fans who want to talk about Neal's playing days. At the very end of the line, waiting patiently, is a woman who introduces herself as Dr. Alice Voss. Dr. Voss looks to be in her forties.

"I enjoyed your talk very much, Mr. Freeman," Dr. Voss says.

"Thank you, and please call me Neal."

"Oh, okay," Alice says a little uncomfortably, not wanting to drop the *Dr.* off her name just yet.

"What do you do here?" Neal says.

"Well, I'm actually a consultant here, my regular job is a psychology professor at UW-Madison. I'm here consulting in the area of organizational development and particularly creativity development. I have read most of the articles and materials on your Thought Market program, and I think this organization is a perfect fit for it. If you'd be interested, I'd be happy to meet with you and discuss putting together a specific implementation plan that could be evaluated by management here."

"Fantastic! Thank you, Alice, when can we do that," Neal responds as he brings his calendar up on his phone.

"Well, I live in Madison with my wife and kids, and I'm only here in the Twin Cities maybe once a month."

"Well, let's meet in Madison then," Neal says.

Alice has never been very comfortable around guys like Neal. Good-looking, heterosexual, athletic, and Christian. The big-man-on-campus types. But nonetheless, Alice says, "That would be great, that makes it much easier, thanks."

They set a date and time for a follow-up meeting in Madison and exchange cards. They shake hands and Neal says, "Thank you, Alice."

"You're welcome," she responds.

After Alice leaves, the Master walks up smiling and puts his arm around Neal. "It never gets old, does it?" the Master kids him.

"What's that?" Neal responds.

"Hitting grand-slam home runs to win the game!"

"Hey, we all get lucky occasionally," the Ice Man says. "Let's go get a beer."

Chapter 14

A NEW TYPE OF MOVEMENT

The international attention devoted to the university divestment protests and Justice's jailing helped launch the Whole Earth Justice movement, or WEJ (pronounced "wedge"). While successful at capturing people's imaginations, the movement struggled to finance and implement programs worthy of the attention they were receiving. They were disorganized, in a constant struggle for funding, and found it difficult to manage volunteers and contributors. The bright spot was the sales of thousands of "sustainable hero briefs," T-shirts, and the like. They were also successful in getting celebrity endorsements and got millions of views of their video clips playing on YouTube. But the big asset they had was the press coverage they received every time students showed up at protest rallies wearing a pair of briefs on the outside of their pants.

The WEJ movement's message is about fostering interdependence. That economic practices based on being fair were far more productive than practices based on laissez-faire. But it's a cumbersome message in some ways, more suited to elites than the mainstream. About a year after the divestment protests sparked the movement, Justice received a life-changing phone call.

"Professor Miller, we've never met but my name is Dr. Alice Voss and I'm a psychology professor at UW-Madison, but I also work as a business consultant, that works in the field of organizational creativity development. My understanding is that you and I also have a mutual friend in Betsy Johnson."

"Oh yes, I know Betsy," Justice responds.

"Well, I've been following your WEJ movement for some time now and I have to say, I see it as a very important and timely development."

"Thank you," Justice responds.

"I also have an idea concerning WEJ I'd like to discuss with you."

"Okay, can you give me a little idea of what you're thinking about?" Justice asks.

"Sure, one of the strategies we've been implementing lately for companies and organizations is called Thought Market. It's basically a program designed to mine tacit information from within loosely affiliated groups and foster greater collaboration," Alice says.

"Hmm, okay, can you say that one more time using different words?" Justice asks.

"I apologize for the jargon. It's a program designed to identify common thoughts and ideas within a group and then facilitate productive collaboration among the group," Alice says.

"When I saw you on the *Oprah* show," Alice continues, "and you were talking about interdependence, a lightbulb went off in my head. The Thought Market program is basically an interdependence-generating machine. It identifies and surfaces thought fragments and then combines them into productive ventures. What we're doing right now is an example," Alice says. "I mean, you have this movement about interdependence, and I have experience in how to foster interdependent relationships and practices. If we combine those fragments together, we make a bigger and better whole! That's interdependence in action," Alice says.

"That sounds interesting, let's set up a meeting. Can I ask Betsy to join us?" Justice asks.

"Of course, I'd love that, I haven't seen Betsy in a while," Alice says. "I'll also invite a colleague I've been working with on the program, Neal Freeman. He's the president of the firm that owns the Thought Market program."

"Hmmm…that name sounds familiar," Justice says.

"He was a basketball player at the University of Minnesota at one time," Alice responds.

"Maybe I remember his name from that, although I was never that big of a basketball fan," Justice says. "But I did make it to a few games over the years. Anyway, I'll talk to Betsy and we will come up with a few dates and times to consider. Does Neal live in the Twin Cities?" Justice asks.

"No, he lives in the Bay Area, but we're both in the Twin Cities frequently because we've got several clients there," Alice responds.

"Okay, well, Betsy and I will get back to you soon," Justice says.

"Perfect, I'm so looking forward to this," Alice responds.

Hanging up, Alice immediately calls Neal.

"Neal, I just had a discussion with Justice Miller of the WEJ movement."

"The WEJ movement?" Neal says.

"Yeah, you know, Whole Earth Justice!"

"Oh, sure, okay, I think we've discussed them a time or two," Neal responds.

"Anyway, I had this flash when I was watching her talk about interdependence on the Opera show and how all these social and environmental justice movements could benefit from a network that tied them all together."

"Interesting," Neal says. "So the Thought Market platform becomes a social and environmental justice network? Interesting… what would the goals be?"

"Same as typical applications," Alice answers. "Identification of people and thought fragments. Networked ideation and resources. Feelings of belonging and ownership and interdependent collaborative development!" Alice exclaims.

"I get it," Neal says. "It's brilliant!"

Then Alice says, "A little tongue in cheek, that's the nicest thing a straight man has ever said to me!"

"Ha, well, in the event that's even a little bit true, I apologize on behalf of all male heterosexuals."

"Oh, okay then, based on your apology, I guess I forgive all straight men," Alice says.

"Nice!" Neal responds.

Likewise, after Alice's call, Justice calls Miguel.

"Miguel."

"Hi, how are you?"

"I'm good. What's up?" Miguel asks.

"Do you remember a guy named Neal Freeman from the university?"

"You mean the basketball player?" Miguel responds.

"Yeah, the basketball player."

"Sure, I remember him. We were in high school I think at the time, but he was one of the stars that went to the NCAA tournament, maybe five or six years ahead of us or so. Why did you meet him?" Miguel asks.

"No, not yet, but I'm going to meet him I believe. He's working with a UW professor who has an interesting proposition for WEJ."

"Interesting," Miguel says. "Well, he was a star on that team. I think I might have gone to a game or two with grandpa during his playing days. Grandpa was as big of a Gopher basketball fan as he was with hockey."

"Yeah, I remember that. Okay, thanks," Justice says.

The Thought Market meeting begins with introductions in a university conference room Justice had reserved.

"Justice and Betsy, this is my colleague Neal Freeman," Alice says.

"My grandfather Bill Miller was a professor here at the university and was a big fan of your basketball career," Justice says.

"Well, actually," Neal says, "your grandfather Bill was friends with my father, John Freeman, who is the bishop of the Episcopal Church in Minnesota. I think your grandfather was even over to our house a few times when I was growing up. I remember him well," Neal says. "He was a very interesting guy as I recall."

"You're kidding, thank you, what a small world we're living in," Justice says. "Oh my gosh, Bishop Freeman. I remember Bill talking about him!"

"Small world. I'd love to catch up some more, Justice, but while we've got all these people assembled here, maybe we should wait until a more appropriate time," Neal says.

"Perfect, let's go," Justice says.

Neal walks over to the table at the front of the room and clicks the remote. A picture appears on the screen behind him of a smiling father and son (maybe from India or Pakistan) fishing at a river. There is a wicker basket filled with maybe a dozen fish that they've caught. Neal says nothing, letting them look at the picture.

Then he says, "'Give a man a fish and you feed him for a day. Teach a man to fish and you feed him for a lifetime.' That's from Maimonides, the twelfth-century Spanish philosopher.

"Let me try and put that in a more relevant context: If you give volunteers a task to do, they may do it, and feel good about their contribution for a day. On the other hand, if you teach them how to find partners, how to locate and use resources, how to develop ideas and implement them, you've given them the opportunity to be leaders in the changing of the world, and that comes with its own energy and power," Neal says.

Neal clicks through his presentation describing how in corporate settings they've been successful in making organizations more creative and innovative while at the same time maintaining mission focus. Alice has heard the presentation many times before, so she watches the prospective clients and makes notes as Neal talks. She's particularly attentive because Thought Market hasn't been implemented into a social movement setting before. Neal is about halfway through the presentation when Justice stops him and says, "What would a program like Thought Market do for Whole Earth Justice? How does it get used by our membership?"

Karen jumps in and says, "Since this was kind of my idea, let me take a stab at that, if you don't mind, Neal. Social justice movements like WEJ typically get people to sign up to be on the mailing list, they get them to show up at rallies, they get them to vote for legislators or politicians in support of the cause perhaps. And maybe they get them to support petitions or other messaging campaigns. But membership involvement is typically a sporadic thing. They agree with the movements purpose so they participate in these activities if they can, but the activities are external to their lives. What a program like Thought Market can do is to facilitate members bringing interdependence into their daily lives. Not just at rallies but every day. When they're at the grocery store and buying paper towels, there might be a good choice and a bad choice. By good and bad here we mean there might be a paper towel supplier and brand that supports interdependent values well, and one that doesn't. Thought Market can provide an easy to use tool to determine that information. It's the difference between supporting change and being the change. And it can work because corporations are incredibly risk-averse," Karen continues. "My father was a plaintiff's lawyer who did personal injury work on unsafe product lawsuits. This is an anecdotal story, but it makes the point well. You know those rubber or plastic guards on the backs of power mowers that prevent people's feet from slipping underneath and cutting toes off?" The group nods. "Well, the reason all mowers have those isn't because of regulations, it's because of liability. Some manufacturer was sued and lost because it was deemed to be an unreasonable risk to the user given the fact that the preventative measure is so inexpensive. So building the product in an unsafe manner became a liability risk, so they voluntarily changed the product.

"It's about creating consequences for bad behavior and holding them more accountable to the public," Karen replies. "Let me give you another example. Consumer Reports started testing and reporting on safety issues and product quality in 1936. They were instrumental in demonstrating the effectiveness of seatbelts in cars as well as operational and longevity issues. Testing showed that American cars were inferior to foreign made cars in terms of quality. As a result of Consumer Reports testing and reporting, the American car companies responded and greatly increased quality. But they didn't make those changes because of regulations, they changed because of the marketing problems caused by the reporting."

"So Thought Market can work like a boycott?" Justice asks.

"Yes, boycotts are done to impose a market consequence on a company's bad behavior. As a matter of fact, Consumer Reports now has a new environmental review process called GreenerChoices.org that evaluates environmental sustainably issues related to products and processes. There's also the LEED process that applies to architectural design and the sustainability of buildings. Why shouldn't consumers also be able to access information that ranks a company's interdependence? It's about raising the risks associated with a supplier's predatory behavior, done at the expense of others. When corporate executives are making decisions on whether or not they're going to walk away from the pollution they've caused, or offshore their income so they don't have to pay taxes, or pay their CEO one hundred million dollars, we want them to think about the market risk of that action. The truth is corporations are very risk averse. It doesn't take much to change their behavior if they think there's a potential for market consequences.

"Though Market is a tool to inform members how they can apply interdependent pressure in the marketplace through the actions of their daily lives. But that's just one side of Thought Market, the behavior-modification side. Thought Market also has a developmental side that allows members to bring more interdependence into their lives. Neal is much better to speak to this because it's closer to what Thought Market does in a corporate setting."

Neal picks up where Karen leaves off. "Yes, Thought Market provides a development collaboration tool for members to connect and network with neighbors so they can do things together, buy and operate a carshare car for instance, develop an energy microgrid, improve a vacant lot. Coming up with good ideas is one thing, but how to connect with others who might be interested is another? How do they find the expertise they need? Has anybody ever done it? Can we locate the resources we need to make it work? Should we share a new environmentally friendly lawn mower or snowblower? Those are the types of things that a collaboration network can do. It can also provide benchmarking for example. What are other neighborhoods doing? How are they doing it? What have the problems been?"

Neal takes the group through the differences between tacit knowledge and explicit knowledge and how that relates to a collaborative ideation process. He then talks about membership and belonging.

Neal continues, "In corporate settings one of the issues we deal with is people who are unmotivated. They don't feel like they belong to something. They're just employees doing a job. In the case of WEJ, it's a little different. People come to you because they believe in the cause! They're already motivated enough to become members. The question is, can you take them from being members to being owners? Can you make them feel like they belong? Can you take them from caring about WEJ to living it?

"So, we started out with a question—what can a networked collaboration system like Thought Market do for a movement like the WEJ?

"What if the system provided members with tools that can help them distinguish between suppliers based on interdependent guidelines?

"What if the system provided tools so neighbors can collaborate and ideate over interdependent development initiatives and activities?

"What if the system provided them with a resource hub that can identify expertise and services or benchmark with a national or international network?

"What if the system provides people with ways to bring interdependence into their daily lives rather than just being an outside add on activity.

"What if the system provides people with a sense of belonging to something bigger than themselves?

"And lastly, what if the system facilitated them growing as individuals and helped them become more fully human?"

As Justice listened to the presentation, she feels excitement mingling with something else. A feeling she hadn't felt much since she was young, before she pushed so hard to finish grad school, launched her career at the university, and then got swept up in the movement.

"The key to getting participation is success and meaningful actions," Neal continues. "As I understand Whole Earth Justice, it's not just about collaborating for the sake of doing it. It's about defining and pushing a new interdependent type of economy. The WEJ brand and strategy is about bringing an end to predatory economics and give a new justice-based economics a chance to take hold and thrive."

Justice thinks about that statement for a second as she's listening to Neal describe the WEJ mission. Neal has a way of saying things that sound big and shocking but are just true. *He's exactly right*, she thinks. It's simple and true. It reminded her of something her grandfather Bill would have said.

"The Thought Market program is about interdependent systems, and we believe the WEJ movement is about that as well. Liberating people to rise to their potential and solve our environmental and social justice problems. To become the realization that we, humanity, have everything we need, to make it on this good Earth, if we reach for our higher selves, together.

"So now," Neal guides, "if you would all open the three-ring binders in front of you. In these binders you will find detailed sections on the specific elements of the program we're proposing. It's the same as what I e-mailed you last week." Neal went over the highlights of each section. "Let's take fifteen minutes to refresh ourselves with material, and then I will try to answer any questions." His gaze lingers on Justice for just a tad longer than he thought professional.

As they reassemble after their break, one of the WEJ board members asks, "I think what you're saying is we will get more out of our supporters and volunteers because we've stimulated them by giving them more opportunities?"

"Yes, that's right," Neal responds. "We start from the premise that people want to be creative. To use their skills and talents in a cause that they believe in. We find that it kind of creates a feedback loop of energy. As people become more involved in the strategic apparatus of the organization, the more energy they feel and the more they can put in. Or want to put in."

"And I get that this network and program acts as a sort of clearing house for people's ideation."

"Yes, that's right," Neal nods.

"But how do we, how did you put it...maintain mission integrity?"

"Great question, thank you. To be honest we've never implemented this type of program in this type of organization before, but having said that, the two biggest innovations that have spurred the shared or collaborative economy have been first the ability to network information, like we've been discussing, and second, the development of a feedback system. With Uber, for example, and any of them really, both the driver and the passenger are subject to ratings or feedback. Within a network that information is powerful. Feedback and rating systems are really a new way of fighting back against predators and gougers without going to court. It uses the power of the market to shape behavior. I would see developing a system like it to shape behavior inside the network as well as outside the network. But I might also add, the people you're talking about inside the network are independent operators. You're really in some ways like a library or database or maybe a consulting firm is the better analogy. These people come to you with their own causes, energy, and desires. You help them by providing them with networked connections to partners, collaborators, resources, and know-how! The network has to be concerned about maintaining mission integrity and alignment, but it isn't to centrally plan the future. I think in this case, one of the differences with a corporate environment is that you are helping the participants do their own thing, provided it is aligned with your goals and methods."

As Neal closes his presentation, Justice stands up and says more quietly than usual, "Neal, you have certainly given us a lot to think about and discuss. I have to say, you really seem to understand the importance of trying to create an interdependence-based society for the future."

Betsy seconds that view and suggests they all go out for dinner at a family-run taco place just down the street.

Alice immediately answers, "Sounds great! But I'd like to stop by my room at the hotel for a few minutes first if that's okay? Where is the restaurant?"

"University Avenue and Oak Street," Betsy says.

"Sure, how about if we meet about seven," Alice says.

Neal and Justice both nod, each looking off in different directions.

"I'll get a reservation," Betsy says.

Chapter 15

ALLIES EMERGE

When Neal and Alice arrive at LaFiesta Tacqueria, Betsy and Justice have already arrived and greet them with margaritas in their hands. While Alice and Neal had traded business attire for casual, Justice had raced home to put on a little black dress.

"So, Neal, organizational development seems like a long way from religious studies," Justice opens as soon as Neal's and Alice's margaritas arrive.

"Yeah, I was headed for the cloth," Neal says, choosing his words carefully.

"What changed your mind?" Justice asks.

"Humm, good question…well, in one of my religious studies classes, we went through the process of writing our own creeds. Mine didn't quite mirror the one written in Nicaea."

"Yeah, Nicene Creed is a little exclusionary for me," Justice says.

"Exactly," Neal responds with a little surprise at her response.

"Anyway, rather than end up as a member of the clergy with nonconforming beliefs, I decided to look for an alternative path. That's when I moved toward computer technology. Then after college I ended up working at a Silicon Valley venture capital firm. Anyway, the Thought Market business was a start-up the VC firm was involved with. The owners decided to take it public, and they asked me to sign on. In some ways it feels like a ministry to me that is a little closer to my actual beliefs than the church did."

"Interesting," Justice says. "So what do you remember about my grandpa Bill?" Justice asks.

"Not that much really, he would be with my dad occasionally. I knew him as Professor Miller. Nice guy. Always wanted me to stay and join in the conversation with himself and my dad. I remember sitting with them one time for a moment and they were talking about the golden rule."

"Yeah, a common theme with Bill," Justice offers.

"How did you end up in economics?" Neal asks.

"Well, it had to do with influences from Bill. Bill was of course an anthropologist who really focused on human civilization now and into the future," Justice offers. "And while I think it was Bill's influence that caused me to want to go to grad school, I wanted to study something that was relevant and applicable to today's struggles and changes. Economics just seemed like a way to influence the world in real time," Justice continues.

"Did you try to go pro as a basketball player after college?" Justice asks.

"No, not really. I had some injury issues and wasn't likely to get much of a look in the NBA. I think I could have gone to Europe and played for a while, but truth be told, I was ready to move on."

"I remember going to a game or two when you were playing," Justice adds.

"Overall it was a great experience for me, but I'm really just as excited about what I'm doing now," Neal says.

"How about you?" Neal asks. "I understand I'm not the only one at the bar whose been to the big NCAA show?"

"Yeah, well, we had a good run and it was fun," Justice says.

"You were the goalie, right?"

"Yep."

"Is it true what they say about goalies?"

"I don't know, what do they say?"

"Don't get in their way!" Neal responds.

Justice laughs and then says with a flirty smile, "Yes, it's true!"

"Tell me more about creativity development," Justice says.

"Okay, creativity development, well, it's almost like a ministry to me," Neal asserts.

"How so?"

"Well, I just think creativity is how were made in God's image. It's what distinguishes us from other life. So being involved in stimulating that part of people is like helping them to become more fully human, to reach for their potential," Neal adds. Human development, creativity development, and spiritual development are all the same thing."

"Not to pry," Justice says, "but are you still a member of the Episcopal Church?"

Completely left out of the conversation, Alice and Betsy share a knowing smile.

"Well, yes, I would say I still consider myself a Christian and Episcopalian, but I'd say I'm not really on board with all the church's teachings, I guess," Neal confesses.

"I hear that," Justice responds.

Just then the food arrives, and Alice announces, "The magic moment has come." Tacos become the dominant topic of discussion for the next quarter hour.

Justice then thanks Alice and Neal for reaching out to them. "I feel like the Thought Market program could make a big difference in the WEJ movement. While it seems funny, we'd use the same tools as a breakfast cereal company. But your work is certainly aligned with us philosophically! I think it can help us practice what we preach."

"What you're really doing at Whole Earth Justice, as I see it, is shifting the economy away from predatory capitalism and toward the golden rule," Neal says.

After dinner, Alice says, "It's getting on to my bedtime, so I'll excuse myself and say how excited I am we got to meet."

Betsy also jumps up and says, "Me too, I'll walk Alice home. I want to get her advice on a project."

Neal says to Justice, "You interested in a nightcap?"

Without hesitating, Justice says, "Yes, there's a quiet, cozy bar just down the street."

Neal and Justice walk down the street toward the bar. At 6'2" Neal is significantly taller than Justice. Trying to make light of it, Justice comments on how funny their shadows look as they walk under streetlights. The bar is quiet with only a few patrons and they sit at the corner of the bar.

"We should trade creeds someday," Neal says.

"Yeah, that would be interesting I'd love to do that," Justice responds. "I'll see if I can find mine and send it to you."

"Me too," Neal responds. Do you remember any of your grandfather Bill's thoughts about the golden rule?"

"Yes, I remember some, and I've also heard from other students of his about their remembrances of it. He saw it as a type of code or cypher, I think," Justice says.

"What do you mean?" Neal asks.

"Well, it goes well beyond Jesus's Sermon on the Mount. Bill found a version of the golden rule in every major religion and every language going back to 2000 BCE. The idea of reciprocity is as close to a universal ethic as we have in civilization."

"That's interesting," Neal says. "And what is the code of?" Neal asks.

"Well, Bill was a big believer that civilization would develop a more interdependent ethos, but he was also a believer that civilization would not necessarily do it without global consequences developing first."

"It would appear he's right about that unfortunately," Neal says.

"Well, Bill thought that at that moment, when we were dealing with all those global issues, the golden rule would somehow change from a simple platitude about getting along with others, to something else."

"What?" Neal asks.

"It would emerge as a survival instruction so to speak. A universal operating system. A life raft for civilization."

"Wow, that's interesting," Neal responds.

"I really miss him," Justice says.

Neal nods knowingly and puts his hand on her back.

The next morning Alice comes down to the hotel restaurant at 9:00 a.m., rolling her suitcase behind her. To her surprise, Neal is already there.

"Well, I'm not sure I really expected to see you this morning," Alice says.

"Ha, well, I don't kiss and tell, Alice, so you're going to just have to guess."

"Well, based on the size of your breakfast there, I'd say you must be in a refueling mode."

"Circumstantial evidence, Alice, very flimsy."

"Okay, okay, did you at least get any insight into her thinking on the project?"

"Well, we didn't talk about it directly after you left, but my sense is we are in a strong position to get the project, so we better start worrying about delivering what we promised."

"Yes, but before I start worrying, I'm going to celebrate with a pancake. They've been off my list for a long time."

"Good idea," Neal responds, "get the blueberry."

Chapter 16

ATTACK OF THE ESTABLISHMENT

Within two weeks of the Thought Market presentation, the WEJ movement, formally informed Alice and Neal that they wanted to move forward with the project. Neal and Alice both saw it as an important step to show that the Thought Market program could make an impact outside the business world. But they were nervous too. Although the new partnership was under the radar right now, Thought Market could alienate some corporate clients not wanting to be associated with a controversial political movement like WEJ. And if they failed with WEJ, it could be damaging to Thought Market's future sales and marketing efforts. Further complicating the issue was the fact that Neal was becoming very enamored by the WEJ movement and its leader as well. He saw the WEJ movement as spontaneous and authentic—a nonpremeditated reaction to the times they were living in. He also saw Justice in similar terms. Those authentic and spontaneous qualities, however, were both an asset and a liability for both the movement and its leader, he believed.

Feeling awkward about their interlocking personal and professional lives, Neal and Justice did their best to keep their relationship under wraps, though no one was fooled. The two of them made an unlikely couple in some ways. Neal was a basketball hero, a business success, and from a prominent Twin Cities African American family. He was a big presence in any room he entered and prided himself as a man of action who could get things done. He was tall, good-looking, and relaxed and had a disarming personality and smile.

Justice is an accomplished athlete herself, but her persona is completely different from Neal's. Justice is 5'6" and maybe 120 lbs., dripping wet. She has an unreserved laugh that is infectious but was somehow slightly naïve seeming. She's whip-smart and gives off a feeling of anxious energy. Where Neal has the presence of the classic American hero, Justice comes across as the slightly awkward challenger or underdog but one you might be reluctant to bet against. Where he shows confidence and grace, she shows grit and determination.

Justice was highly competitive and had a reputation for aggressive play on the ice. She wanted to win at everything she did. During her senior year, while she was the starting goalie on the hockey team, a picture of Justice appeared in the campus newspaper. She was in the street with her biking gear on fighting with a guy who appears to be twice her size. The caption of the picture says, "Goalie!" The story explained that the driver of an SUV almost hits her as she's riding her bike. Rather than stop and take inventory, she pours it on and chases the car for over a mile through traffic. She finally catches up with him at a stoplight, pulls her bike in front of the car, gets off yelling at the driver, walks over to the driver's door, and reads him the riot act. A giant of a man gets out of the car, calls her a vulgar name for a portion of the female anatomy, and pushes her away. But she punches him, right in his beer belly. Someone in the car behind caught the whole thing on his phone. Nobody got hurt in the incident and legal charges were dismissed in both directions, but the incident burnished Justice's reputation around campus as feisty and formidable.

Neal was several years older than Justice, and he had never lacked for feminine attention, starting with cheerleaders in high school and sorority coeds in college. Justice, on the other hand, never made much time for dating or romance. She often felt insecure around men except on a frozen pond or hockey rink. On the rink growing up, she could skate circles around most of the boys and loved being able to do it.

Justice was unlike anybody Neal had ever dated before. She didn't possess classic features or beauty, but she wasn't the least bit entitled or self-absorbed either; in fact, she had grown into her name well and was determined to fight for what's right. He admired how driven she was to change the world and was drawn to Justice's energetic and optimistic fighting spirit and saw her occasional social awkwardness as part of her charm.

Unknown to Justice or anyone else at WEJ, the Choke Group, a large conglomerate owned by the prominent conservative Choke brothers, whose father made a fortune in the oil business, put Justice and other members of WEJ under surveillance through one of their many front organizations. They wanted to know who Justice was and where she might be vulnerable if the movement picked up steam. When Neal and the Thought Market company entered the scene, they started secretly buying stock in the publicly traded Thought Market Company through a number of surrogate firms. As soon as it started to look like WEJ would purchase and adapt a Thought Market program, the Thought Market board receives a letter from a group of stockholders demanding information from the company about the deal, a restraining order preventing it from going forward without a court order, and a claim of negligence and willful violations of his fiduciary responsibilities by Neal, the company's president. The opposition came as no surprise to Justice, but the nature of it was. The Chokes obviously had sources inside WEJ, they had money to spend to buy stock in Thought Market, and they were willing to do whatever they needed to, in order to protect their interests.

Justice pulls her bike into the garage of her small bungalow in the Prospect Park neighborhood on the edge of the University of Minnesota campus. Neal has his own key and stays there when he's in town. Neal's car is in the driveway and is in the house waiting for her when she pulls in. Justice embraces Neal and says, "I'm so sorry to get you mixed up in all this."

"Nonsense," Neal says, "but I think we do need to change our thinking about what we're dealing with."

"Okay, how so?" Justice responds.

"Well, for one thing we should assume, this house may be bugged."

"You think so?" Justice says, looking around.

"Yes," Neal says. And the phone and your car, and they have someone in top management at Wedge. And they clearly have that, and more, at Thought Market as well," Neal says.

"What can we do about it?" Justice asks.

"Well, were just going to have to be more aggressive about security," Neal responds. "And it's going to cost money. Let's go for a walk and talk outside, I don't like talking in here."

As they're walking down the sidewalk, Justice says, "I feel like a mob guy."

Neal places his hand over his mouth imitating a mob guy and says, "FAGITABOUTIT!"

Justice laughs and says, "Maybe we should play cops and robbers tonight!"

Neal smiles and says, "Okay, but I get to be the cop."

"A corrupt cop maybe."

A few minutes later and Neal says, "I've located a security company who we can work with. They will come in and sweep everything for bugs and then set up procedures to ensure we're not being overheard."

"So what about the situation at Thought Market?" Justice asks.

"The Thought Market board received another letter from a lawyer representing activist stockholders' group who had had the injunction filed. I'm going to meet with them next week to discuss their intentions and demands," Neal says.

"Do you think they have enough shares in their group to gain control of the company?" Justice asks.

"We don't know, but it looks possible," Neal responds.

"So what will you do?" Justice responds.

"I don't know. We could rebrand the program for WEJ? Thought Market could pull out entirely? I could resign?"

"Could we build a whole separate system?" Justice asks.

"That's a good question," Neal says.

"Would you rather just walk away from the idea of working with WEJ?" Justice asks.

Neal stops and turns to Justice and says, "No, I'm in this with you. I just want to be realistic and I want us to win in the end. Fight the fights we can win. We may know more after the meeting. In the meantime, I'll give the idea of building a specialized version of Thought Market some serious thought."

It was the perfect "I love you" moment, met with silence from both of them. Neal wanted to say it, but he was unsure where the relationship was going. Justice wanted to say it, but she just felt awkward; she hadn't ever said it in the context of a relationship like this before.

What Justice did say was, "I'm afraid."

Neal turned and drew Justice in close and said, "We'll be okay. We're doing what we should be doing."

But that isn't what Justice meant. She meant she was afraid for them, as a couple.

Neal noticed they were standing on the sidewalk in front of an old Eastern Orthodox church they had passed on the street many, many times before.

"Have you ever been in there?" Neal asks.

She shakes her head no.

Neal takes her hand and leads her up the front steps. They push open the giant doors and enter the empty church. It's majestic inside. A large dome overhead and walls filled with old icons in gold of the Holy Family.

In the center of the main aisles is a fountain with holy water. Neal dips his thumb in the water and makes the sign of the cross on Justice's forehead. Then they sit down in a pew toward the back and silently look around. There is a lingering smell of incense in the air and candles are burning. Justice feels choked up and struggles not to cry. She grips Neal's hand tighter and leans her head on his shoulder.

"Look," Neal says, pointing to a stained-glass window.

"What is it?" Justice asks.

"And over there." Neal points at another window. "And over here," he says as he points at another.

"What are you pointing at?" Justice says.

"The golden rule," he responds.

The place is full of stained-glass and icon paintings depicting the golden rule.

"You're right," Justice says, walking over to get a better look.

Her footsteps echo through the sanctuary as she walks.

"This one is 'do unto others.' And there's 'love your neighbor as yourself.' That makes me feel the presence of Grandpa Bill," Justice says.

They sit speechless, entwined for ten minutes, and then they get up to leave.

Walking out of the church, they're met in the narthex by a young Eastern Orthodox priest. He has a long beard and is dressed in black vestments.

"May I help you?" he says in a broken English.

"Oh, thank you," Justice says.

"No, we're just admiring the church, we're not really members or even religious, I guess," Neal adds.

The priest smiles. Then he says, "Did you grow up in a church of some type?"

"Yes, I grew up Episcopal," Neal says.

"Me too," Justice adds. Neal looks over at her, surprised.

"And do you believe anything today?" the priest asks.

Neal thought what a weird question, but then Justice responds, "Yes, I think I believe in some sort of spiritual realm but not necessarily Orthodox Christian."

"Ah," the priest says, "then you are on a spiritual journey, and it is my mission to help if I can."

Neal starts to tug Justice toward the door and says thank you but we really need to be going now.

"But," Justice stops and says, "we have made some very scary people angry with us and we're afraid of them!"

The priest looks at her and then at Neal and says, "Please…a twenty-minute cup of tea."

Neal offers a halfhearted okay.

The priest leads them to an office lined with books. They sit in big comfortable chairs. The priest pours hot water into cups and places a basket of tea bags on the table.

The priest looks directly at Neal and says, "Thank you for staying." And then he says, "Tell me what you can, I want to help you in any way I can."

Neal is thinking, *Okay, he'll agree to pray for us, and we're out of here.*

Justice says, "We're part of a social justice movement called Whole Earth Justice and this movement is becoming perceived as a threat to some very powerful people."

The priest's face lights up with recognition and says, "Justice Miller...Whole Earth Justice...underwear on outside!"

"Yes," Justice chuckles.

"And you are named?" he asks Neal.

"Neal Freeman."

"And you're son of the Episcopal bishop?" the priest asks.

"Yes," Neal acknowledges, wiggling in his chair.

The priest gets up walks over to a desk, opens a drawer, and pulls out a Whole Earth Justice colored bracelet.

"WEJ very good ministry," he says, laughing, but then grows serious. "What's the difficulty, who are the scary people?"

Justice apparently feels comfortable telling everything to this guy. Neal doesn't quite understand, but he recognizes she needs to tell him.

"Mostly oil and gas interests," Justice says. "Wealthy people who own oil and gas companies," she explains. "They're spying on us and doing everything they can to disrupt our plans and intimidate us," Justice adds.

"What plans?" the priest says.

"We were planning on implementing a program called Thought Market that would allow people who believe in greater interdependence to network and collaborate better," Justice says, talking rapidly. "Neal is the president of the company that owns Thought Market. Anyway, these oil and gas people have been buying up stock in Neal's company and are threatening legal actions to stop us from implementing a network."

"Hmm," the priest says. "I understand social media and collaborative communications networks," he says. We used to communicate with oppressed people in Russia and Ukraine and other eastern countries. I am Father Dimitri Valaskyov, I also have a master's in computer science from MIT."

Neal laughs and says, "I can't believe it. I have a computer science master's from Stanford!"

Father Dimitri looks at Neal and smiles and says, "Stanford is a pretty good school too."

"What do you mean when you say you operate a collaborative communications network?" Neal asks.

"We have some friends and supporters in Silicon Valley."

"I can't believe it!" Neal repeats.

Father Dimitri says, "Mysterious ways, my friend, mysterious ways!"

"We are familiar with petrochemical mob types from our ministries in Eastern Europe. Very difficult!"

"What should we do?" Justice asks.

"We start by asking for help and wisdom," Father Dimitri says. He reaches out and the three of them join hands.

"Lord, help us to understand and accept your will. Grant us the peace, strength, wisdom, and resources to carry it out. Protect us and our adversaries on this our journey. We are filled with gratitude for your ever presence. Amen."

Then Father Dimitri says, "Come to church any time. We will stay in touch."

"Thank you, Father," Neal says giving him his hand to shake and then gives him a business card with his closely guarded personal e-mail address.

"Yes, thank you, Justice," Father Dimitri says. "The WEJ mission very important for whole world. By the way, I couldn't help noticing your interest in our iconography," Father Dimitri says.

"My grandfather was a believer that the golden rule is a vailed message, and that when the time comes, it will provide civilization with a roadmap to safety," Justice responds.

"Humm, that is an interesting idea," Father Dimitri says.

"I think both as a person of faith and as an anthropologist, he thought it was very strange that the golden rule had made its way into so many religions and languages and cultures," Justice says.

"Say more," Father Dimitri says.

"Well, he thought that when universal or global problems were threatening us, it would provide a message on how to survive and move forward," Justice adds.

"Yes," Father Dimitri says. "Thank you for coming, and I hope you will come back again soon."

"Thank you, Father."

Chapter 17

OPEN SOURCE

Walking back from the church and their chance meeting with Father Dimitri, Justice's phone rings.

"Hi, Miguel, how are you?"

"I'm good and I'm in town for the night and wondered if you're around for dinner or a drink or something?"

"Well, I'm with Neal, but I'll ask him."

Neal looks at her and shrugs. "Sure."

"How about if we meet you in an hour at Murphy's bar?" Justice says.

Murphy's is a quiet neighborhood bar and grill, famous for its Caesar salad that replaces anchovies with smelt. When Justice and Neal arrive, Miguel is seated at the corner of the bar, talking to the person on the stool next to him about the prospects for the year's Gopher hockey team. Justice introduces Neal and Miguel and Miguel says, "Should we get a table?"

"This is fine with me," Neal says as he grabs the other side leaving Justice the coveted corner seat in the middle.

Neal and Miguel immediately see a bit of themselves in the other. They discuss Neal's basketball career, Justice's hockey career, Sugar Lake and the Miller clan, Neal's father the bishop, and the Minnesota Twins, all with exuberance that attracts curious attention from everybody in earshot.

"You guys better check and see if you've got the other half of each other's amulets!" Justice jokes.

After they're seated in a booth for dinner, the conversation shifts to WEJ and Thought Market and what was going on with the Choke family.

"Ya know, one of the problems I'm having is that I don't know who I can trust at Thought Market," Neal says. "I mean, I'm sure the Chokes have someone inside," he continues. "I'm afraid it might be someone in the legal department, given the information the dissident stockholders seem to have."

"Man, that complicates things, doesn't it," Miguel says.

"Yeah, I almost feel like I need to have outside legal counsel helping me with this since I'm suspicious there is a mole inside the Thought Market legal team," Neal offers.

"You know, I think I've got a lawyer if you're interested," Miguel says. "He went to law school with me at NYU. After graduation he went with an M&A [mergers and acquisitions] firm in the Bay Area. I'd be happy to call him for you if you'd like me to," Miguel says.

"I think that's a good idea," Neal responds.

A few days later and Miguel and Neal are standing together in front of a large window on the fortieth floor of one of San Francisco's most expensive skyscrapers, at the offices of Daily and Grundell, attorneys at law. Neal grabs the binoculars sitting on the window ledge and looks through them, adjusting the focus. "The Oracle America's cup catamaran is out on the bay practicing," he says. He hands the binoculars to Miguel and says, "You know that sailboat can go fifty miles per hour!"

"Amazing," Miguel responds.

Neal turns and takes off his suit jacket and drapes it on the back of a conference room chair.

Two men enter the conference room.

"Miguel, how are you?"

"Great, Neal Freeman, meet Joe Batt."

"Nice to meet you."

"And this is Jack Daily. Jack is the senior partner here at D&G and an expert in hostile corporate insurgencies."

"Nice to meet you, Neal," he says as they shake hands.

"Are you a sailor, Neal?" Jack asks.

"No, not really, I was out on Minnesota lakes a few times with friends, but no, I'm not an experienced sailor. But I'm fascinated by those big flying cats they run in the America's Cup races though. I've been told they can go faster than the speed of the wind that's propelling them," Neal says.

"Yes, amazing technology," Jack says. "Listen, Neal, I understand you've managed to piss off the Choke brothers?"

"Apparently," Neal responds.

"I've read the briefs provided by Joe and Miguel on your situation. I've reviewed the demand letter from the rogue investor group, and I've also reviewed the Thought Market articles and bylaws, and I understand that we believe Thought Market isn't really the target of the Chokes, that a client of yours named Whole Earth Justice is the real target," Jack states.

"Yes, it appears to be the case," Neal responds.

"And we also understand that there is a personal relationship between yourself and the leader of Whole Earth Justice?" Jack asks.

"Yes, that's true, Justice Miller is her name, but how exactly is that relevant?" Neal asks.

"Well, it's not relevant from a legal point of view, but it supports the idea that you could be motivated to take an action that would be harmful to the stockholders of Though Market," Jack responds.

"I see, sure," Neal says.

"I think we're speculating about several assumptions here in gaming this thing out, so let's discuss those," Jack says. "First, we're assuming that the Chokes' real target is WEJ! Second, we're assuming that they want to disrupt WEJ in any way they can and prevent them from growing and becoming more effective, right?" Jack says.

"Yes, that's right," Neal responds.

"And how would WEJ affect the Chokes' business?" Jack asks.

"WEJ is really about trying to organize and leverage consumer demand, to make business more responsive citizens," Neal offers.

"And how do they do that?" Jack asks.

"Through a specialized Though Market program that connects social justice groups and individuals," Neal says. "The program allows people to organize and consolidate their economic footprint, giving them more leverage in the marketplace. That consolidated economic power is then expressed in the marketplace in support for companies and organizations that are good citizens and as resistance or negative for companies that engage in predatory behavior in some way. It's also a tool that can be used to help people form and pursue new ventures bringing new choices and alternatives to market," Neal says.

"But you've never successfully done this before, right?" Jack asks.

"No, the Thought Market program is a corporate creativity enhancement program that utilizes networked information sharing," Neal responds.

"Well, the Chokes sure seem to have confidence in it," Jack says.

"Maybe they'd endorse us?" Neal quips.

"Here's the bottom line of our analysis," Jack says. The only way I can see this thing ending with the Chokes leaving Thought Market intact would be if you left the company and the company doesn't sell or license its program for use at WEJ," Jack says.

"How about if I leave and WEJ develops a program themselves that is similar but not the same?" Neal asks.

"See, that's the issue. If they can claim it's Thought Market technology, they can assert they were harmed. Either because they should be getting a royalty for it or because its being misused and as a result it will have a negative impact on the value of the asset. I'm sorry, Neal," Jack says. "It's a tough box to be in, particularly given that Thought Market isn't even the target."

Neal gets up out of his chair and walks back to the window, picks the binoculars again, and looks out and repeats the line Jack just told him, "As long as they can claim its Thought Market technology."

Then Miguel says, "What if Thought Market abandoned its intellectual property and went open source?"

"Say more," Neal says.

"Well, I mean what if you declared your patents public art?" Miguel says.

"They're mostly just source code anyway and most of our revenue comes from implementation services," Neal says.

"They'd still attack you for selling out the stockholders," Jack says.

"Not if sales and the stock price go up as a result," Miguel counters.

"How would that happen?" Jack responds.

"Greater sales, more services," Neal says.

Then Miguel says, "It's like the Linux open source operating system and that company that services them called Blue Hat!"

"Okay, let's game this out a little," Jack says with a hint of excitement in his voice.

"Suppose the Thought Market board votes to make their intellectual property patents public and available to anyone for free immediately," Miguel poses. "Then they announce it to the public and finish off their deal with WEJ."

"Then the Chokes will sue, WEJ, Thought Market, and me as they threatened."

"What does their case look like in each instance?" Jack says.

"Against WEJ, I don't see much of a case," Jack says.

"Against Thought Market and you, I think those cases hinge on the validity of the marketing strategy involved and on what happens to sales and the stock value in the aftermath."

Thinking out loud, Neal says, "If we were to open source the Thought Market program code, it still doesn't get potential customers the semianonymity aspect of the program, it doesn't get them the facilitated collaboration aspect, it doesn't get them the searchable database of conversations, the creativity stimulation classes—those things are really implementation services. Most of Thought Market's revenues come from implementing the program with those important elements, not from royalties on the code itself," Neal says.

Then Miguel adds, "But it might get Thought Market more customers!"

"Can we get some market research on this to validate it?" Neal says. "In the meantime, can we have Daily and Grundell do some due diligence on the plan and put some thought into planning defenses for Thought Market and myself and the entire board?"

"Yes," Jack quickly answers. "In fact, I will oversee this myself. This could have big ramifications throughout the information industry."

A day or two after the meeting, Neal gets a call from Alice. "Hi, Alice, how are you?"

"I think I should be asking you," Alice responds.

"Yeah, things are complicated, I'm afraid," Neal says.

"Well, unfortunately, I'm not going to help matters much, I'm afraid. Apparently, a company controlled by the Choke brothers has made an offer to my consulting firm for our Thought Market shares."

"Do you know what the offer is?" Neal asks.

"It's about twice the trading value. My guess is, management is likely to take it," Alice responds.

"Okay, well, I guess the good news is they wouldn't be offering a price like that if they had the controlling shares they needed. Try and get management to delay as best you can. We may be able to match or exceed the offer on the table," Neal says. "Thanks, Alice."

Within several weeks of the planning meeting, the Thought Market team had worked up a revised marketing plan based on the idea of open source and conducted research that confirmed its efficacy, and the law firm of Daily and Grundell had written detailed briefs on the process and defense strategies required.

They met one more time to review the plans and strategy, then called a press conference and announced the plans.

The stock dipped significantly after the news came out.

The Chokes, through their dissident stockholder group, sued Thought Market and Neal personally.

Much of the business media was covering the story.

A month after the announcement, however, and inquiries and presales of the Thought Market product had increased significantly. The price of the stock rebounded and surpassed the price on the day of the announcement.

Within six months of the announcement sales had grown by 50 percent over the previous year and the stock price had doubled.

After a year, the Chokes sold their shares back to the Thought Market company and dismissed the lawsuits.

Chapter 18

BECOMING AN INTERDEPENDENT ACTOR

Justice frequently brings her lunch to work in a brown paper bag. A sandwich, a yogurt, and a piece of fruit. When nice outside she goes and sits on one of the benches on the pedestrian mall connecting some of the university's most prestigious-looking buildings. Over years of conditioning, some of the wildlife that lives in the canopy of giant old trees that populate the mall earned a pretty good living approaching snacking students and teachers. Justice was a regular dining companion with a chipmunk she referred to as Professor Kelp. The chipmunk is named after Dr. Paul Kelp a leading American economist, a recipient of Nobel Prize in Economics, and a professor emeritus at multiple Ivy League schools both in the US and Europe. He is also an outspoken critic of the conservative, libertarian, small-government approach to the economy and a regularly featured syndicated columnist and on-air guest on economic matters.

Just as Justice sits down on her regular bench just outside the grand staircase and columns of Northrop Auditorium, Professor Kelp jumps onto the bench next to her. "Well, good day, Professor, she says as she opens her bag. What do we have here today? Well, you'll have to share my apple, I guess, because I neglected to bring something especially for you." Justice takes an apple slice and puts it down on the bench next to her. It's maybe a foot or so away from her leg. The professor shows no hesitation, as he moves on the apple and begins to eat it. Justice unwraps her sandwich takes a bite, looks at the busy chipmunk, and says, "So, Professor, have you noticed a difference since the university grounds crews switched to natural fertilizers? I was a little worried about you and the rest of your neighbors last year when we found out what they were spreading. At least they didn't put up a fuss when we asked them to switch to a less harmful product." The sound of Prince's song "Purple Rain" emanates from inside Justice's purse. Justice fishes around for her phone in her bag. The professor continues undeterred.

"Hello," Justice says.

"Justice, it's Marcy." Marcy is Justice's agent for TV punditry gigs and the like.

"Hi, Marcy, what's up?"

"You aren't going to believe this," Marcy says excitedly. "Can you get out to the KARE 11 studio's out on Highway 55 by four thirty this afternoon? They said they'd send a car for you."

"Ah, today...well, I...," Justice stammers.

"You'd be part of a panel discussion on MSNBC with Paul Kelp."

"What?" Justice says, shocked. "But how...I don't understand."

Marcy continues, "The producer of the show thought it was too many white men arguing over dry materials, so he suggested they find a woman economist they could include on the panel as well. Apparently, it was Kelp who suggested you!"

"What, you're kidding," Justice says. "I've never even met him. I'm a big fan."

"I know. So will you do it?" Marcy asks.

"Four thirty in Golden Valley—yeah, I think I can do that!"

"Excellent, I'll let them know," Marcy says. "Where do you want them to pick you up?"

"Here at the office, I guess."

"Okay, I'll get them the address and specifics."

Justice hangs up the phone, looks at the happy chipmunk working on the apple slice, and says, "I'm going to meet your namesake today. But I'm not going to tell him about you, you know, the rodent thing and all."

Justice then calls her mom, and Neal, and WEJ headquarters to inform them of the show.

The show is *The Beat* with Ari Melber as the host. They establish the link before the show to make sure everything is working, and it also allows the host to introduce himself.

Ari Melber suddenly appears on the monitor in front of Justice. "Professor Miller, this is Ari Melber, nice to meet you and thank you for coming on *The Beat*."

"Please call me Justice, and I'm very glad to be here, thank you."

Just then Paul Kelp appears on the monitor as well. "Ari, this is Paul, can you hear me?"

"Yeah, we've got you, Paul, say I'd like to introduce you to Professor Justice Miller with the Whole Earth Justice movement."

"I'm very glad to meet you, Justice, I've been following your work at Whole Earth Justice for some time now," Kelp says.

Justice laughs. "You have no idea how ironic that is that I would get to meet you, and you would tell me you're a fan of my work! I read everything you write!"

"Well, thank you, Justice, I'm delighted, and I'd love to talk to you further about the WEJ movement offline sometime?"

"I'd love that," Justice says.

Justice has a kind of natural sincerity on TV that the cameras love.

Then Dr. Steve Sack of the Cato Institute pops onto the monitor. The Cato Institute is a Washington, DC, think tank started in the midseventies by the Choke brothers to promote and facilitate a more libertarian political agenda and economy.

"Hi, Paul, how are you?"

"I'm good, Steve, thank you. Steve, meet Professor Justice Miller, she's going to be joining us today."

"Yes, hello, Professor Miller, nice to meet you. When you agreed to be on the show, the producer sent over some information on you and the WEJ movement. Your work to change the dress codes is very impressive, but beyond that, the only theme I could discern was an opposition to success!"

Justice pauses for a moment and then says, "Please call me Justice, and no, we're only against successful economic predators. Success that comes at the unfair and unnecessary expense of others. Like price gouging through monopolies for example."

"Well, good, I look forward to you enlightening me."

Then Ari Melber jumps back in.

"Okay, you all know the drill, we're going to discuss the economic implications of what we're calling progressive capitalism, on the one hand, characterized as providing an expanded social safety net and increased government regulations and interventions and cost, versus what we're calling libertarian capitalism, on the other side, characterized as smaller government and minimum government intrusions into the economy and life of citizens. We're looking for a lively debate that will get us some ratings, so we expect you to be strong advocates for your positions, but don't talk over each other and no profanity. See you all in about twenty minutes." Then he signs off.

The light goes green and they are on the air.

Ari Melber introduces his guests and the subject. Immediately Professor Kelp and Sack are off arguing their points. Professor Kelp leads with the statement, "If libertarian capitalism is all about producing greater economic benefits including higher returns, which is what we here every time the conservatives propose a new tax cut, then why are we so poor in this country, particularly when compared to more progressive countries?"

"First of all, we're not poor, we're the leading economy in the world. Second, if there is an unfair distribution of wealth, it's because of the failures in public education and other government programs. The last thing we should do is double down on the parts of the economy that are causing the problems. The way to make those government activities more efficient is to privatize them and get some entrepreneurial spirit and competition into them. Listen, respectfully.

"One company controls 80 percent of the soybean and corn seeds.

"Four companies control 82 percent of beef packing.

"Four companies control 85 percent of soybean processing.

"Two companies control 70 percent of all the toothpaste.

"One company controls 80 percent of sunglasses and sunglass retail.

"One company controls 100 percent of plastic hangers.

"Two companies control pet foods.

"Two companies control travel bookings.

"Four control cable TV.

"And drug companies are able to pay generic manufacturers to not produce generic drugs.

"And on and on and on. We don't live in a free-market economy, we live in a monopolistic economy," Professor Kelp shoots back.

The debate gets a little testy as Kelp and Sack struggle to gain control of the narrative and the facts. Justice listens intently but doesn't know how to get into the debate.

Then Ari stops the two combatants and asks Justice for her thoughts.

Justice says, "Listen, the debate about what should and should not be a part of the commons that we all own and what the rules and regulations should be that control economic activity is a good and certainly timely debate. But that debate misses some of the immediate opportunities present."

"And what are those opportunities?" Ari says.

Justice looks in the camera and says, "Five minutes from now, every one of our listeners could be networking with other like-minded people from the right or the left who are interested in wringing out the abusive aspects of our economy. It doesn't require one philosophy to prevail over another. It doesn't require another penny be raised in taxes, and it doesn't mean you have to stop being a liberal or a conservative.

"In five minutes, your viewers could be in discussions with their neighbors on fighting back and challenging the economic predators, with market forces. They can be in discussions today, in just five minutes, about supporting interdependent and cooperative entrepreneurs and how they can fight back against economic predators and monopolies.

"In some ways the economic arguments give people an excuse to sit and do nothing. What I'm saying is this, creating a more interdependent economy is available to us right now through the choices we make as consumers and citizens in this economy and nation. New networked information sharing has revolutionized our ability to focus and concentrate our market power. But it's only going to happen if we take it on ourselves and decide we want a fairer, less predatory interdependent economy and abandon laissez-faire, which means, buyer, be aware and move toward being fair, which is accomplished by making supplier's feel the judgment of the consumer. Listen, getting ripped off is neither a right nor a left value. Nobody wants to pay more than is fair or be treated unfairly. Go to wholeearthjustice.org right now and sign up to receive information on how we can concentrate our market strength and have an impact today!"

Ari Jumps in and says, "I'd like to thank our guests for this lively debate, more to come on this topic in the future." And they go to a commercial.

The local director gives Justice a thumbs-up and says, "Good job, I think you stole the show!"

As Justice is removing the wires for microphones and stuff, an assistant walks in, hands Justice a note, and says, "Mr. Kelp would like you to call him."

Oh boy, I hope he isn't mad about something I said, Justice thinks.

Justice dials the number on the paper.

"Professor Kelp," Justice says.

"Yes, is this Justice?"

"Yes."

"Well, I just wanted to tell you that I thought it went very well. I think your pragmatic, no-nonsense message about participating was an important message and brilliant."

"Oh, thank you, Professor, I was worried I had stepped on the two of you a little."

"Nonsense, I think your absolutely correct we should stop talking so much about what we should or shouldn't be doing in the future and focus more on what we're doing right now," Kelp says.

"Well, thank you, Professor."

"Please call me Paul. I'd like to participate in Whole Earth Justice somehow, but I think my support should not be publicized. I have a lot of enemies out there, and my visible support would prevent some of them from participating. But please consider me a resource and call me whenever you think I can help you somehow."

"Well, thank you, Paul, I will certainly do that," Justice says.

"Neal and the rest of the WEJ movement people were excited by Justice's performance and both donations to WEJ through the website and people signing up for participation in the network spiked. Perhaps the earliest important development was the ability of people to find like-minded neighbors in their area and start interacting together. Local chapters were being set up through the fledgling network all over the country. Even in deeply red states and districts. As soon as WEJ passed the five-hundred-thousand-membership mark, other social justice movements focused on other causes began to form their own sites or pages on the network. This exposure to people in other social justice causes increased the pace of sign-ups and increased the utility of the site, in the sense that people could get useful information through it. The facilitation aspect of the Thought Market program became very important as people and groups dedicated to fighting social justice groups like gun rights advocates or white supremacists all tried to put up pages or sites on the network. These were immediately taken down. Unlike other social media sites the WEJ network was policed and dedicated to causes and people interested in social justice."

Neal gives a presentation to the WEJ board on the launch and effectiveness of the new network.

"The network is growing fast," Neal says. "But we're being hacked every day by groups trying to do us harm. We should expect a legal fight about our ability to restrict membership. We need to prepare for the fight."

"Don't we have people sign a statement when they sign up?" one board member asks.

"Yes, but my experience is that those are pretty light in terms of teeth. I think in the end we will be okay because of all the trouble other social networks had when they didn't police and let anybody use their networks. We've never seen it the same way because we grew out of private settings, not public settings," Neal responds.

"And I wouldn't really call us a social network either, at least not like other public social networks that are designed for personal use. We're more like productive networked information sharing. The platforms that got in trouble for being conduits for political subversives were seeing themselves as generic not as news sources with editorial responsibilities. We're the opposite we embrace our editorial responsibility.

"Another effect of the growing network was the ability to get people to show up at rallies all over the country. Not just in places like NY or DC but places like Shingle Creek and Mayberry as well. Through the network people were able to find and participate with others in their areas. When Earth Day rolled around, it was easy to see. The rallies in NY and DC had gotten bigger, but there were also far more rallies all over the country as well. It also started to become clear that the participants in the WEJ movement represented a broad demographic swath of America. There were just as many chapters in wealthy white areas as there was in poor minority neighborhoods."

A few weeks after the MSNBC panel discussion, Justice gets a call.

The voice on the other end says, "Is this Justice Miller with the WEJ movement?"

"Yes," Justice responds.

"Please hold for Mr. Michael Bloom."

Michael Bloom is a self-made billionaire philanthropist who has spent hundreds of millions, if not billions, of his own money on climate change issues.

Elevator music.

"Ms. Miller, this is Michael Bloom."

"Yes, hello," Justice says in a soft unsure voice.

"Ms. Miller, I like what you're doing with the WEJ movement and I'd like to help."

"Please call me Justice," she says, regaining her composure.

"Sure, fine, thank you, Justice, and please call me Michael. Well, the thing is, Ms.…. Justice, I believe your movement has a real chance to carve out a viable space in the middle and get us past this whole polarization thing that has happened in our politics. It's gotten so bad that every time something is either labeled a conservative thing or a liberal thing, it's finished. It just can't go anywhere."

"Yes, we—"

"Well, the thing is, Ms.…Justice, we think you could use some professional help with your branding and explanation of what you're doing."

"Well, we—"

"So what I'm proposing is that you get some professional help with those things and I will pay for it. If that sounds okay to you, I will have an assistant of mine contact you and you can work out details with him."

"Thank you, Michael."

"Ha-ha, well, actually people usually call me Mr. Bloom."

"Well, thank you, Mr. Bloom, and can I say I think the work you've been doing on climate change is wonderful and very important," Justice says.

"Well, thank you, Justice, I'm looking forward to working with you."

"Thank you," Justice says. And he was gone.

Justice rocks back in her chair and smiles. *People aren't going to believe this.*

About ten minutes later, her phone rings again.

"Hello, this is Justice."

"Please hold for Mr. Bloom's assistant."

Elevator music.

"Hello, Ms. Miller?" the voice says.

"Yes, this is she."

"Ms. Miller, my name is Ben Stevens and I'm an attorney and assistant to Mr. Bloom."

"Okay, sure, I didn't expect your call so soon," Justice says.

"Yes, well, Mr. Bloom has a unique relationship with time," Mr. Stevens says.

"Ha, well, I think I get it," Justice says.

"So, Ms. Miller—"

"Please call me Justice."

"Oh, okay, very well, Justice, thank you. As I understand the situation, you have spoken with Mr. Bloom and he indicated to you that he would like to help you with branding and marketing of the WEJ movement, do I have that right so far?"

"Yes, that's what he said."

"Okay, so here's how I think this could work," Mr. Stevens says. "I will e-mail you a list of possible consultants who Mr. Bloom respects. There will be several who have previously supported Democratic candidates, several who have supported Republican candidates, and a couple who have worked with independent candidates. You should contact them all, go over your situation with them, and get them to write you detailed proposals on what they think needs to be done and how much it will cost."

"Okay," Justice says.

"Then you pick out the two or three that you like the best, and you send me there proposals along with your rankings. Then we will look over the contracts and give you our opinion. If we agree, you will finish off the contract with the consultant and Mr. Bloom's foundation will contribute to Whole Earth Justice in that amount. Does that work, Ms. Miller?"

"Yes, that's wonderful, thank you," Justice says.

"Okay, great, now here's my contact information and I will send you an e-mail with details before the end of business today."

"Thank you, Mr. Stevens."

"No reason to thank me. It's all Mr. Bloom and I know he is excited to be working with you."

"Wow!"

"Yeah, I get that from people sometimes," Mr. Stevens says.

Within an hour Justice receives an e-mail from Mr. Stevens at the Bloom Organization. As was discussed, the e-mail contains contact information for six consultants—two who have worked mostly with Democrats, two who have worked with Republicans, and two who supported independent candidates, including Michael Bloom.

Justice shares the letter and story with the other members of the WEJ team. There is tremendous excitement at the prospect of an association with Bloom.

Justice discusses the conversations with Neal as well. Neal is also very excited about the prospect of working with Bloom and says, "We need to do this right."

"What do you mean?" Justice says.

"Well, I think what we should do is put together a presentation and notebook describing WEJ and its history, philosophy, people, everything, and then present them to each of the consulting teams. My guess is, they will already know about Bloom's involvement. We want them to be as impressed with us as we are with them. I mean, I'd assume they have a channel to Bloom and will be talking to them," Neal says.

"Could you help organize it and coach us through it?" Justice asks.

"Yes, absolutely," Neal says enthusiastically.

Neal and Justice pull together a team at WEJ to make what amounts to a small documentary about the movement. They decide to use Bill Miller's old format for his distance learning classes. The digital multimedia presentation includes news clips of the divestment protest that got out of hand and the hopes and problems associated with the Thought Market program. All of which has voice over narration explaining what they're looking at. The interviews on MSNBC where Justice is describing the WEJ movement and philosophy. Background information on interdependence versus independence that is in Justice's Futurama 2.0 class and information on membership and revenues, etc. At the conclusion, Justice shows up on camera and solicits questions they may have and describes what they're looking for. Whole Earth Justice wants to get to the next level of involvement with the American people. We want to be change agents and advocates for changes we believe are necessary for humanity to survive and thrive.

In each case, Neal talks with the consultant group on Bloom's list. Then a copy of the digital presentation and request for proposals is sent. The RFP asks that proposals are due in two weeks on a specific day and time. A copy of the presentation RFP is sent to Mr. Stevens at Bloom's office as well. All six proposals come in, within a couple of hours of the deadline. No declines, none early, and none late. Apparently, people know how to work with Bloom.

In each case these small consulting groups have put in a lot of thought and time and effort into the proposals submitted. Justice is also blown away by the amount of work and money being proposed. Hundreds of thousands of dollars in each case. They include research into past related developments, both qualitative and quantitative research, a creative and branding portion and a marketing planning guide. None of them include any actual marketing money, just research, planning, and branding. Justice and Neal and the rest of the WEJ team select two proposals, rank them, and send them to Mr. Steven's at Bloom's office as instructed.

Within two hours Justice gets a response from Mr. Stevens. "Mr. Bloom accepts your choices. Please proceed. WEJ will receive a contribution from the Bloom Organization in an amount sufficient to cover the selected consultants' fees, within ten days' time."

Several hours later Justice and Neal are together and celebrating a little bit when her phone rings. "Bloom," it says on the ID.

"Hello."

"Justice, this is Mike Bloom."

"Hello, sir, and thank you so much for your help."

"Don't mention it, I'm glad to be a part of it. Say, I just want to say that was a marvelous job you did on getting that RFP together. Very impressive!"

"Thank you, sir, but the credit really belongs with Neal Freeman. Neal is on the board of WEJ, and he's also the president of the Thought Market company."

Neal smiles and gives Justice a thumbs-up.

"He's standing right here if you'd like to tell him yourself, sir."

"Yes, I'd like that."

She hands the phone to Neal.

"Hello."

"Well done, son, I was very impressed with what you put together in that RFP."

"Thank you, sir."

"I look forward to working with you and Justice and the whole WEJ team. Oh, and by the way, the consultant you selected is Zip?"

"Yes," Neal says.

"Well, I guess you'll find out soon enough."

"What do you mean, sir?" Neal responds.

"Well, Zip is a genius for sure, but he is also one eccentric dude."

"I'm looking forward to meeting him," Neal says.

Dial tone.

Neal looks at Justice and hands her the phone and they both begin to laugh.

"What did he say about Zip?" Justice asks.

He said, "He's a genius and a bit eccentric."

Chapter 19

SXSW

Justice, Neal, and Karen arrive at the Austin Bergstrom International Airport at noon on a Wednesday in the middle of the South by Southwest (SXSW) festival. Knowing the festival was on during this time they had suggested that Zip travel to the Twin Cities for the initial meeting, but Zip insisted.

"I've been involved with this festival for a decade, I can book rooms for you and get you passes to the events you'd like to attend," he said. "That way we can get to know each other a little bit too."

The airport is packed with people and large digital displays of performing acts are everywhere, adding to the chaos as people abruptly stop to look at the show ads. As they head to baggage claim, the crowd only intensifies. At the entrance is a large group of people holding up signs trying to connect with travelers arriving. In the middle of the crowd, an Apple iPad is being held up with the letters *WEJ* written on it. Justice identifies herself to the person holding the sign.

"Oh, good, I'm glad you found me," the woman says in a falsetto voice. "I'm Mia, I'm Zip's assistant."

Mia is an attractive, obviously transitioning woman, who at six feet towers over Justice.

"Mia, this is Neal and Karen, and this is Mia. She has thankfully come to rescue us," Justice says.

They all walk through the parking ramp, put their luggage in the back of the gray sedan Mia points at, and pile in.

"Zip asked that I take you to your hotel first so you can dump your luggage and stuff, and then I will pick you back up in an hour or so, if that works," Mia says.

"Zip is expecting us about three at the gallery."

"Gallery?" Neal says.

"Yes, Zip owns and operates an art gallery. In the back of it are his offices for his consulting business."

"Interesting," Justice responds.

"What kind of art?" Karen asks.

"All kinds really, but currently we're featuring a new contemporary artist from Prague. Paintings with small sculptural elements blended in. Quite interesting stuff really," Mia says.

Mia pulls the car into the portico of the Driscoll Hotel. "You're already checked in," Mia says, "just stop by the front desk and sign the register and they'll give you your keys. I'll pick you up right in front here at two forty-five, if that's okay," Mia says.

The Driscoll is a four-star hotel near downtown Austin that dates to 1887.

"Wow, are you sure this is for us," Justice says to Mia.

"Yes, it's where Mr. Bloom stays when he's in town too."

"Dress casually and comfortably," Mia says, "you'll probably go to dinner and a concert or something before getting you back to your hotel tonight." Then she gets back in the car and drives off.

When Mia picks them up the second time, she's dressed a little differently herself. She's wearing a casual western outfit that says "I'm going out on the town" as opposed to the business attire she had on the first time. "I'm going to join you tonight, if that's okay with you," Mia says.

"Yes wonderful," Justice responds.

"Okay, this is it," Mia says as she pulls up in front of a contemporary-looking building on a retail street. The gallery looks like an Apple store with tall glass front and big glass doors. Inside lining the walls are some large and wildly colorful art pieces.

"Hello, welcome," a jovial gentleman says as they enter the gallery. He's wearing cowboy boots, jeans, a giant belt buckle Elvis would be proud of, and a Hawaiian shirt. "I'm Zip, I'm so glad to finally meet you all." He extends his hand to each of them.

"I know it's a little awkward coming down here during the festival and all, but I think it's important we get to know each other a bit, for the sake of the project," Zip says.

"Sure, well, we're glad to be here, I've never been to South by Southwest, so I'm looking forward to it," Neal adds.

"Me too," Justice says. "This is really interesting art by the way."

"Yeah, I think so too," Zip responds. "The artist is a young guy from Prague, in the Czech Republic."

"It's interesting how he uses sculpture and painting together," Karen says.

They walk over to a large piece that depicts a large field of sunflowers in bloom, with the foreground containing a sculpture of a large bloom and a sculpture of a bee the size of softball suspended above the blooming flower.

"The artist likes to play with perspectives and mediums all at the same time," Zip says. "In this case, he wanted to create the reality of the scene from the perspective of the bee."

"What are the sculptures made of?" Karen asks.

"They're papier-mâché over carved Styrofoam and then attached to the painted background with coat hanger wire, I believe. The painted canvas is stretched over a wood backing so the sculptural elements can be attached."

"They're really fun," Justice says.

"Well, the artist is giving a little talk tonight if you're interested in meeting him," Zip says. "He's an interesting guy, and he's going to talk about his art of course, but I think he's also going to talk about what it means to be in a once-communist country like the Czech Republic. Should be interesting," Zip says. "Okay, follow me." He turns and walks through a doorway at the back of the gallery space.

It looks like there are two or three office spaces, an administrative area, and conference room. As they enter the conference room, you can't help but notice the head of a giant wild boar hanging on the wall. Underneath is a small plaque with a photo of Zip with his gun and his foot on the dead beast.

"That there is Hugo van der Goes the Boar. He's named after a Flemish Renaissance painter. Hugo and I had a profound encounter with each other about twenty years ago in which only one of us was going to walk away unscathed. Luckily it was me," Zip says.

"Wow, he looks like quite a vicious animal," Karen says.

"He was vicious that's right, and he would have killed me had I not been able to kill him first, but it wasn't personal, it was his nature. He was going to hide from me if he could, and then when he was discovered, he was going to try and kill me. He charged right at me full speed. If I had panicked or dropped my gun, I might be hanging on the wall in his conference room. Okay, here's my agenda," Zip says. "I thought we'd spend a couple of hours talking about the WEJ project, then we can go and get some dinner someplace, then if you're up to it, we can see something at the festival?" Zip says.

"Perfect, sure," they all respond.

"So let's dig in," Zip says.

"I've read everything and reviewed all the materials you sent in the RFP, and as I understand it, this is what you're saying with WEJ." Zip is writing on the white board.

"First, Whole Earth Justice is in the business of trying to bring about greater environmental and social justice!" Zip says. They all nod affirmatively.

"Second, you're saying a lot of the social injustice and environmental injustice in the world today has a common cause, and that cause is an independent competitive culture!" They all confirm the statement.

"Third, WEJ is saying the way to attack all these social and environmental justice issues at the same time is to support and foster a cultural shift to a more interdependent culture and economy?" Zip says.

"Yes, the whole economy is rigged in a million little ways as a result of an independent culture and mind-set," Neal says.

"Okay, give me some examples," Zip asks.

183

"Okay," Neal responds, "when executives of public companies pay themselves hundreds of millions of dollars at the expense of stockholders and other stakeholders because they've got the leverage to do so. Or when organizations go to great lengths to rake in profits for themselves and leave the public sector stuck with the costs of cleanup for example.

"I mean, we're living in a culture where a person who is successful making billions of dollars by shifting responsibility and costs to others is placed on the cover of business magazines and hailed as a genius and hero. We're living in a zero-sum, predatory economy that is based on the independent idea that we're in competition with everyone for everything. Scarcity and competition.

"Take the effects of specialization upon our culture, for example. I mean specialization has certainly been one of the gooses that laid the golden egg in terms of societies progress. But it has a down side as well. For example, doesn't specialization relieve us from responsibility for the whole? Our limited role in the systems turns issues into 'not my responsibility' problems. None of us get up in the morning and decide to pollute the air. We're just trying to get to work. None of us decides to pay criminals to enslave children in sweatshops, we're just trying to buy a shirt we can afford. None of us are deciding to kill bees. We're just trying to buy some fruit. We don't feel the pain or consequences of our choices because our specialized culture says it's not our responsibility to worry about those things. It's somebody else's responsibility, some other expert, maybe the government—but not me."

"Okay, I get it, but how!" Zip asserts. "How are you going to affect the culture? It feels like throwing a stone into rough waters—no ripples!"

"That's the thing," Justice says, "it's happening on its own and it's likely to continue because global existential issues require us to cooperate with each other, in order to solve them. We can't cooperate without a sense of justice, and we can't achieve a sense of justice without changing our hearts and our ways. We have to grow up and become more interdependent in order to survive and thrive. But it's not just doing the right thing for the right thing's sake. There is money and opportunity on the table too. Big opportunities and big personal benefits."

"Okay, well, if it's happening on its own, what is the WEJ role?" Zip asks.

"Good question," Justice says, "it's to make it visible. What the feminists of the early 1970s called consciousness raising. So people can see it and choose it. To see the costs associated with the selfish, independent actions and see the benefits of the interdependent actions."

She picks up steam. "It's to facilitate and reward positive interdependent actions and to identify and penalize predatory or independent behavior that has a consequence to others. Its win-win— economic activity without unwitting victims. It has to be seen and recognized as a viable alternative solution."

"So it's providing a visible alternative to the frog in the pot with slowly rising temperature? He will sit there and do nothing unless an alternative is presented," Zip says. "WEJ is making an alternative visible?"

They all nod.

"What's the difference between now and say one hundred years ago or a one thousand years ago?" Zip asks.

"No refuge," Neal says.

"What do you mean?"

"Well, it doesn't matter if some country switched to renewable energy if other countries continue to burn fossil fuels, for example," Justice says.

"I agree," Neal says, "one hundred years ago we could still move away from a problem, today we can't, but more importantly, we can't solve them without the cooperation of others. And there are many more tools that can be used today," Neal asserts.

"Look at the growth of socially responsible investing, SRI, or Angie's List, or Yelp, or Uber, or the rest of the shared economy strategies. They're all dependent on networked information sharing. Productive feedback loops. In addition to the feedback scenario's networked information sharing has the potential to help consumers concentrate their market power by organizing and by using the technology to resource new developments and initiatives. Local initiatives that affect them personally. Think of the efficiencies like-minded neighbors can generate if they cooperated and work together? It's not just sharing a lawn mower. What if a community developed a motor pool they could join, and they all got to reduce their dependence on individually owned cars? What if they got together and created their own microgrid utility? What if as consumers people could distinguish between suppliers based on their good or bad behavior?"

"So what are the core activities that WEJ engages in to inform people and bring these changes about?" Zip asks.

"Well, we assert our messages in traditional ways and in some nontraditional ways, I'd say," Justice offers.

1. We rally and protest and march and fight and convene in conventions, and write books and magazine articles, for attention and to get our message out in all the traditional ways. The underwear thing has been very successful in drawing attention and participation I'd say.
2. We act in support of positive actions and candidacies, and we act in protest of negative actions, negative companies and industries, and candidates.
3. We try to get our message out through media punditry and blogging and column writing.
4. We try to confront politicians and economic predators and win their support for our goals or publicize their bad behavior. We've been called blackmailers by some, but exposing their bad behavior is not blackmail, provided we've done the due diligence and can defend our actions.
5. We want to act as a resource to other social justice or environmental justice groups. We should cooperate and help each other in every way we can. We're all on the same team as far as we're concerned. If we can help them, it helps us. Whole Earth Justice!
6. We provide an opportunity for celebrities and others to express their support and declare their intentions and make them real and operable. We're a decentralized resource that

helps people to be leaders themselves and live the life they want to live. Be the change!

7. We use networked information sharing technology to allow people to connect with other like-minded people in their community and worldwide, to form action groups.

8. We use networked technology to add resources and expertise to people's actions.

9. We use networked technology to educate each other as to what suppliers do a good job and which are not, creating feedback loops.

10. And we think we can license our brand to operators willing to operate in positive ways through operating agreements and covenants. Like creating a public option in health care, we would do a similar kind of thing in businesses where suppliers would have to up their game in order to hang onto market share.

11. Oh, and lastly, we think we can provide a nonaligned movement. In other words, neither right nor left. People from both sides who want to act.

"At least those are the things we do or want to do, off the top of my head," Justice says.

"That's a great list, Justice, but with respect to the technology, what's different between what you're doing and say Facebook, for example?"

Neal jumps in. "We're monitored and facilitated by people. We provide editorial review. We're different in a couple of ways. Facebook and Google and others see themselves as neutral platforms and provide no editorial review. We provide editorial review. Second, we're supplying focused productive mission centric information. We're closer to Uber than we are to Facebook, I'd say!"

"And you developed this program as a creativity development tool for organizations?" Zip asks.

"Yes, exactly—productive, targeted, professionally facilitated, networked information sharing!" Neal responds.

"I wonder if we could shorten it and simplify it?" Zip asks. "Would you mind if I gave it a try?"

"No please," Justice says.

"Okay," Zip says.

1. We create belonging for ourselves and others with related causes!
2. We message, educate, and act upon convictions.
3. We network and share information to support the above!

"Okay, isn't that basically it?" Zip asks.

"Yes," they respond.

"Okay, well, all of that makes sense," Zip says, "but people don't change because of thoughts! Change is hard to do! People do it for emotional reasons. People are really apathetic about doing the right thing, unless there is an emotional driver," Zip asserts.

"I would agree with you on that," Neal asserts. "That's our experience too with the Thought Market program in corporate settings. We operate on the assumption that people are naturally creative and want to have a sense of belonging, but they have been conditioned to not participate. To not take the risks necessary to participate. The same situation exists in the culture more broadly as well, I believe."

"So the emotional reward is belonging?" Zip asks.

"To participate in something meaningful that is bigger than ourselves," Neal says.

"Humm." Zip nods. "Okay, that's starting to sound emotional. It's starting to sound like love," Zip says.

"Ha, yes!" Neal confirms. "Yes, love of others, love for our descendants in the future, love of self," Neal says.

"I love the message, but I've got to tell you, culture is a hard thing to change," Zip says.

Justice jumps in. "It is but as we already said. It's already changing. We're just facilitating it so it can speed up!"

"Humm, good point, good point," Zip says. "I think one of the things that is truly unique here is the nonaligned aspect. The truth is, people vote against their own interests all the time because they follow their party or tribe. If additional market pressure can be applied without it being aligned with one side or the other, it would be a good thing."

Neal adds, "To be clear, our program isn't a replacement for environmental or labor regulations of any type. I personally come from a progressive background, we're just saying that this program doesn't subscribe to any ideological point of view—WEJ information sharing doesn't require any alignment. We're basically doing what Consumer Report does when they rank cars on performance and resale factors. We're just reporting different information. And we're speculating that progressives will see the benefits of it because it provides consumer benefits. And we think conservatives will like it because it delivers consumer benefits and it doesn't require any government support. It's really a market response."

Mia enters the room and goes over and whispers in Zip's ear.

"Oh my god," Zip says, looking at his watch.

"I should have asked this earlier, but we got caught up and time got away from me, are there any dietary restrictions in this group? Any vegans or vegetarians?"

They all shake their heads.

"Well then, we've got to go right this second because we're about to miss our reservation at one of the best restaurants in Texas. And believe me, they won't hold it for a minute. Let's go, just leave all your papers and stuff out. We'll be back and everything is locked up."

Chapter 20

ZIP AND MIA

Just as they're walking into the restaurant, they hear, "Dodson, party of five! Dodson!"

"Here!" Zip shouts.

"Wow, perfect timing," Justice says as they're shown back to their table.

"This place is owned by friends of mine, but that wouldn't have helped us had we missed the bell. At least not during the festival," Zip says.

As they take their seats, Zip explains, "This place is owned by a partnership between two James Beard Award–winning chefs. One owns an award-winning Japanese restaurant in town called Uchi, and the other partner owns an award-winning BBQ place called the Franklin Barbeque. The Franklin BBQ you might recognize, it has a national footprint really. It's been featured in every major food magazine in the country, and the chef owner has been on many TV food shows, and he's written a number of cookbooks."

"I think I saw something about it in the flight magazine on the way down," Justice says.

"They call this place Loro and is described as an Asian smokehouse and bar," Zip says. "Everything is really good here, but I usually get the smoked brisket. I don't know what they do to that brisket, but I'll say this about it. You find yourself thinking about it the next day," Zip says with a smile.

Mia jumps in and says, "Oh, Zip, it sounds like crack when you describe it that way."

Zip laughs and says, "Well, I doubt crack cocaine is the secret ingredient, but it would explain some things."

They all order drinks.

Through dinner, the conversation remains focused on WEJ and its opportunities and challenges.

A couple of drinks later, however, as they're finishing their entrées, the conversation loosens up.

"Neal, isn't your father the Episcopal bishop in Minnesota?" Zip says.

"What?… What?" Neal responds.

Justice looks at Neal. "Zip asked about your father," Justice says with a little elbow jab.

"Oh, sorry…I was thinking about the brisket I just finished."

Everybody laughs.

Zip says, "I know."

"Did you ever think about going the clergy route yourself?" Zip asks Neal.

"Yeah, I was all in on it up until the end of college and I needed to make a decision about seminary."

"What changed your mind?"

"Well, it was a religious studies class at the end of my under-graduate work. I had this class where we studied the Nicaean Creed and then toward the end of the class, we wrote our own creed. Anyway, the process was enlightening, and it showed me that my beliefs weren't really compatible with the church I was going to end up representing, so I decided to go another direction," Neal says.

"Do you still have a copy of your creed?" Zip asks.

"Yeah, I do," Neal responds.

"I have one of my own that I did too Justice pipes in, and I've asked Neal to share his with me, but it's never happened," Justice says.

Neal jumps back in and says, "I'd share it but it's written in Latin!"

The table laughs.

"I grew up a PK myself," Zip says. "My dad was a Pentecostal preacher. We moved around a lot doing revivals throughout the south. There was dancing with snakes, laying on of hands, casting out of demons, and taking money from people who were so poor, they didn't have shoes. When I was sixteen, my father and mother ended up in trouble with the law because I wasn't attending school. They were charged with child abuse and the settlement was that I had to go and live with a foster family in Austin, Texas. Anyway, both of my natural parents are dead now, but I still have contact with my foster mother. My foster father died six and a half years ago. Those people changed my life in a big way. They enrolled me in high school and tutored me up to the point where I graduated on time at eighteen. They helped me through college and graduate school. Wonderful people. I owe them everything," Zip says.

"Wow, that's quite a story," Justice says.

"Well, your comments about writing your own creeds made me think," Zip says. "My foster parents recognized I had a fragile relationship with religion because of my childhood. But they themselves were Southern Baptist. They always told me that when I was ready to take another look at my spiritual life, I'd know it. Anyway, those discussions kind of flashed through my mind when you were describing writing your own creeds," Zip says.

"Well, I think it's a really good process to every so often try and figure out what you actually believe," Justice says.

"Yeah, I should update mine in fact. How do you spell *brisket* in Latin?"

"And did you grow up in Austin too, Mia?" Justice asks.

"No, I grew up in Dallas," Mia says.

She looks at Zip for reassurance; he nods.

"Well, I obviously grew up a man. My name was Michael. I was married and have two sons. Anyway, when I started to transition my wife was supportive at first, but we still broke up. It was hard for her and I understand. Anyway, she married someone else, and he didn't want me around. He convinced her that I was a bad influence on our sons. They didn't want me around. It was tough for the boys too, being teenagers and all. So I moved away to Austin because I thought it was a little more accepting kind of place," Mia explains. "I didn't really know anybody in Austin, but there is a trans community here, so I connected with some people that way."

Mia looks at Zip again for reassurance and he nods.

"Well, I was out one night, maybe a few months after having moved here. I left the club about midnight and headed to the parking lot to get my car. A group of young men started to taunt me and shove me around on the street. They were obviously drunk, homophobic, and violent," Mia says with some emotion starting to creep into her voice. "They punched me very hard. I went down and they began to kick me. One of them grabbed me by the hair and dragged me, kicking and screaming to an isolated corner of the parking lot. They lifted my skirt, ripped off my underwear, pulled out a knife, and said they were going to cut off my genitals."

In a restaurant with the decibels of a rock concert, you could have heard a pin drop at the table.

Mia checks Zip one more time.

"I was terrified," Mia says. "Then from out of the blue, a huge fight breaks out. Zip was walking past and saw what was going on. He jumped in and started fighting the assailants. After a few minutes, the assailants ran off. In the process of saving me, however, Zip who I did not know at the time was stabbed badly and bleeding terribly from his wound. I had had some training in the military, so I had an idea of what to do. I took off my blouse and wrapped Zip's knife wound. Just prior to jumping into the fight, Zip had dialed 911 on his cellphone and set it down on the sidewalk. Just as we were getting to our feet an ambulance arrived. The doctors said if they would have cut my genitals off, I could have bled out very quickly. And had I not been there to restrain Zip's knife wound, he could have bled out quickly too. And we've been together ever since," Mia says.

The story is obviously very emotional for Zip. He looks choked up and unable to respond. Mia reaches over and places her hand on his.

Everybody at the table is just frozen by the story.

The waitress comes by and Zip says, "I'll have another bourbon please…make it a double."

"Yes, me too," Justice says.

"Me too," Neal says.

"Yes, me also," Karen says.

"Thank you, but I'm the designated driver," Mia says.

The drinks come and Zip holds his glass up and says, "Justice, Karen, Neal, I'd like to thank you for choosing us to be part of your project. We are both flattered and excited to be a part of it. To changing the world for the better!" And they all say yes and take a swig. "Now let's finish up here. We've got a bunch of offerings we could choose from," Zip says, pulling out his SXSW program guide.

Karen says, "I'd be interested in seeing the Czech artist from the gallery!"

"Me too," Justice says.

"Good, I believe he has a late presentation tonight at ten so we can stop in at something else first and then make it to his presentation at the gallery."

Karen looks at Justice and says, "It's been a while since I've been to a ten o'clock show of any kind!"

Justice smiles and then says, "Me too."

"Not to worry, we can get you back to the hotel at any time, so don't be shy about speaking up."

They arrive back at the gallery at ten on the dot. Twenty people or so are seated on folding chairs waiting to begin. Zip directs the WEJ group to three open seats and then places his sport coat on a fourth and stands in the back. When Mia arrives after a trip to the restroom, he directs her to the seat with his jacket on it.

"Thank you for coming at this late hour. My name is Evzen Eckert, I am from the Czech Republic, and this is my art on display here today." Evzen is about thirty years old and speaks English with almost no trace of a foreign accent. He's wearing a black sport coat over a black T-shirt and blue jeans. He presents as a young urban artist you might find in any big western city.

"I would like to thank my host, Zip Dodson, who is the owner of this wonderful gallery." Evzen claps and the crowd follow suit with polite applause. "I have several subjects to speak to you about tonight in addition to my art. One is I'd like to spend a minute talking about what it's like to do creative work in a country where creativity was once restricted under communism. And second, I'd like to spend a minute talking about America and what it has meant to people in places like the Czech Republic.

"You as the viewer, of course, get to decide for yourself what the art means but to me, our reality is dependent on our perspective. Therefore, truth is a matter of perspective as well. In college I had a teacher who played for us a famous piece of classical music. We all recognized the piece of music although I've forgotten what it was now, perhaps a famous piece by Beethoven. He played it at the correct speed first. Then played it at 50 percent speed. It was still recognizable but very different. Then he played it at 10 percent speed. At that speed, it was just random sounding noises. He did it again but this time going up in speed. First twice the speed, and then ten times the speed. In each case it was the same effect. The point is this, our reality depends on our perspective. It's true for bees, for example, as well as for us. As people our perspective depends on a lot of factors. Our country and circumstances of birth but also what happens to us along the way. Our reality is shaped by our perspectives. But unlike the bee, we have some modicum of choice over our perspectives. We can forgive or not. We can be afraid or not. We can love or not. Those choices shape our perspectives and in turn shape our realities.

"Now, I'd like to give you my 'perspective'—ha-ha—on the state of Prague and the Czech Republic. First, Prague is a beautiful city. I invite you all to come see for yourselves. You will not be disappointed I assure you. Second, I am thirty-five years old and really part of the first generation to have grown up in a free Czech Republic. Me and my friends, we do not have a direct memory of the time under Soviet domination. Our view of it is indirect. We can see the effects of the oppression all around us, but it sits in contrast to our own experience. What I can tell you is that oppression robs people of their humanity. Oppression means hopelessness, and people cannot live with hopelessness, at least not very long or very well. The signs of hopelessness are very clear in the people who are of the generations before my own, who lived under communist oppression.

They accept their fate as a horse accepts his and stays put if the rider drapes the reigns over the rail.

"My generation is full of hopefulness and ambition. And as a result, Prague is a vibrant city and exciting city. But there are also a great many broken people who cannot escape the hopelessness of their oppression. Poverty, war, starvation, homelessness, illiteracy, mental illness, disease, climate change, pollution, immigration—these are the causes of oppression and hopelessness, not only in Prague but over the entire planet we call home.

"Lastly, I would like to give you a bit of an outside perspective of the United States of America. To much of the rest of the world, the very presence of the United States of America has provided hope-fulness to oppressed people everywhere. I can tell you that my gen-eration in Prague lives in hopefulness because we live in the shadow of America. We listen to your music, watch your movies, use your technology, and emulate your unrestrained energy and ambition to act. America has acted upon the world as a young, strong, ambitious adolescent of good character acts. Heroic, altruistic, and generous of spirit, mind, and treasure. But at times America has also acted with impetuousness and been self-serving and arrogant. Like any good teenager perhaps. But today we live in difficult times. The bad guys don't wear black hats or swastikas on their lapels. Today the enemies live within. Hate, prejudice, greed, domination—these are the true enemies of our time. And our old friend America is right on the front lines again. The first and longest-lasting multicultural democracy in the world. Engaged in a titanic struggle within for her soul. And the world waits, and watches, and hopes.

"Thank you, and now I would be happy to answer any ques-tions you might have on my art or anything else."

"Wow!" Karen says. She looks at Justice and Neal and says, "After the Zip and Mia's story and now this. I need to go to my room and get into a fetal position and suck my thumb for a while."

"I hear that," Justice says. "I hear that!"

Chapter 21

WHAT IF COURAGE

Karen wakes to the sound of the alarm on her phone. She gets out of bed, turns on the shower, and fills the paper coffee cup with water to start the in-room coffee maker. Forty minutes later, she shows up at the hotel café where Neal and Justice are already there eating breakfast and reading the paper.

"Good morning," Neal says as Karen sits down.

Karen looks at Neal and says, "Don't start with me."

Justice laughs.

"I woke up fully clothed on top of the bedding and one shoe missing!" Karen says. "That hasn't happened since...I don't remember that ever happening."

"Yeah, well, you must admit it was fun," Neal says.

"As I recall, we had dinner and a couple of Manhattans at that great Asian smokehouse, then went to a music venue, then to the gallery presentation, and then I think we hit another music show, at what I think was a gay bar, and then had even more drinks at the hotel bar where we argued about what the best TV series is since the beginning of the binge-watching era, I still stand behind *The Sopranos* by the way," Karen says.

"Ha, it sounds kind of shallow when you describe it," Neal responds.

"Shallow but lots of fun," Justice adds.

"Have some breakfast, you'll feel better," Neal says. "By the way I told Mia not to come for us this morning that we'd either walk or take an Uber. Its less than a mile and I figured we could use the exercise."

Karen looks at Neal and says, "Easy for you maybe, you've got legs that are a block long. Justice and I probably have to take three steps for every one of yours," Karen complains.

"Don't include me," Justice says, "I'd rather walk too."

"You know after you guys went up last night, I stayed up with Zip and had one more," Justice says. "Mia had gone home too, and Zip decided he was going to stay and then take an Uber home. Anyway, I told Zip how moving and dramatic a story it was about his and Mia's meeting."

Zip instantly became emotional again, paused, and then said, "Mia is the bravest and most courageous person I've ever known. I love her with every fiber of my being."

Wow, Justice thinks to herself.

They arrive at the gallery on time, and Zip greets them with large glasses of fizzing liquid. "What's this?" Neal asks.

"Trust me," Zip says. "This will chase away the remnants of last night."

"What's in it?" Neal says as he looks into the fizzing glass.

"Old family recipe, I'd call it, that involves a trip to an Asian grocer," Zip responds.

Karen says, "That artist Mr. Eckert, he really knows how to get you thinking, doesn't he?"

"Yeah, I met Evzen in Prague about a year ago," Zip says. "After the show I walked up and introduced myself and asked him if he would have any interest in doing a show in Austin during the SXSW festival. Anyway, I think a lot of him. He's the deep end of the pool for sure!"

"I think there's a whole community of young talented, educated artists in Prague right now."

"Okay, let's get back to work, we've got a lot to do today," Zip says.

"As you can see, I left all the materials and comments from yesterday up on the whiteboard. Let's spend a minute looking at them and going through them.

1. We rally and protest and march and fight and influence leaders and write books and magazine articles to get our message out in all the traditional ways. The underwear thing has been very successful in drawing attention and participation I'd say.
2. We act in support of positive actions and candidacies, and we act in protest of negative actions, negative companies and industries, and candidates.
3. We try to get our message out through media punditry and blogging and column writing.
4. We try to confront politicians and economic predators to win their support for our goals or publicize their bad behavior.
5. We want to act as a resource to other social justice or environmental justice groups. We should cooperate and help each other in every way we can. We're all on the same team as far as we're concerned. If we can help them, it helps us. Whole Earth Justice!
6. We provide an opportunity for celebrities and others to express their support. We're a decentralized resource that helps people to be leaders themselves and live the life they want to live. Be the change!
7. We use networked information sharing technology to allow people to connect with other like-minded people in their community and worldwide to form action groups.
8. We use networked technology to add resources and expertise to people's actions.
9. We use networked technology to educate each other as to what products and companies do a good job and which are not, creating feedback loops.
10. And we think we can license our brand to operators willing to operate in positive ways through operating agreements

and covenants. Like creating a public option in health care, we would do a similar kind of thing in businesses where suppliers would have to up their game in order to hang onto market share.

11. Oh, and lastly, we think we can provide a nonaligned movement. As the German Green party used to say, we're neither right nor left but in front. People from both sides want to act.

Underneath Justice's list of eleven things, Zip had written his three summary points:

- We belong.
- We message.
- We network.

"And what are we hoping to get from the network?" Zip asks. "I mean, what are the desired effects we're trying to bring about."

Justice responds,

- Behavior modification: We'd like to see people and businesses change their behavior.
- Development: We want people to see or be presented with opportunities to act. To become interdependent actors and leaders themselves.
- Resources: Locate the resources we need. Teach each other!

"This is mostly thinking stuff," Zip points out. "People act with emotional triggers. Greater efficiency, more from less, these are all rational things. We need connections to emotion. *Why!*" Zip shouts. "Why are people going to join and participate in WEJ!"

Then Justice says, "Courage! It takes courage to change! In 1850 when those young people were standing on the dock in Ireland, waiting to get on the boat that would take them to the new world, they knew, they would never see their loved ones again. It was a courageous act. Done for love of self, love of family, love of adventure, love of life. When a family went west seeking opportunity in unsettled territory, it took courage. When a person starts a business and invests his life savings, it takes courage. Courage to change, courage to risk, courage to love, these are the central tenets of the human enterprise. Just like you said last night, Mia is the most courageous person you've ever met! And what makes her so courageous—her willingness to seek the truth and change. I'm sure it would have been a lot easier for her to live the life society and her friends and family wanted her to live. But she sought and accepted the truth—no matter what! We're an adventurous species and we love life. WEJ needs to be the boat, the facilitator, the connector, but they're still going to supply the courage and the love."

There is a silent pause in the room.

Then Zip starts to applaud. "Exactly right! Well done, well done. We are selling passage on a boat to a new world. They're bringing the love and courage. I LOVE IT! And what do we call this new world we're taking them to?" Zip asks. "I'm talking about the destination, not the boat."

Forgetting their headaches, the three of them begin throwing out ideas with ever-increasing enthusiasm. They brainstorm about the destination the promise land so to speak.

> The Educated Economy
> Good Citizens
> Interdependent Free-Market Economy
> Interdependent Market Economy
> Interdependent Response Economy
> Interdependent Consumer Response Economy
> Enlightened Response Program
> Enlightened Response Network
> Enlightened Response Economy
> Enlightened Consumerism
> Demand Response Economy
> Community Feedback Economy
> Free Market Economy
> Feedback Market Economy

Response Market Economy
Commons Market Economy
Social Market Economy
Creative Cooperative Economy
Progressive Capitalism

"We don't want this destination to include blatantly political terms, like the word *progressive* or *conservative*. Those things just alienate potential constituencies," Zip says. "It's really about educating consumers so they can make more informed choices," he says. "In the end, they all agree on *Enlightened Consumer Market*. That's it, the new world," Zip says. "It's trans-ideological and can appeal to a broad constituency. Its lofty and simple. Idealistic and pragmatic. It requires no new government action to bring it about. Every individual is a decision maker. It's where we need to go."

Then Zip writes,

> Free-market capitalism = laissez-faire = buyer beware!
> Enlightened consumer market = being fair = supplier beware!

"Okay, so we have *Whole Earth Justice*, they're selling the vision. They provide messaging and education and membership and opportunities to participate. They're like the passage company selling the opportunities in the new world. And the *Enlightened Consumer Market* is the destination…the new world. A world where predation and abusive behavior are discouraged through the concentration and application of market forces.

"So the collaborative networking program is the ship. The vehicle that takes us there. I don't think we should call it Thought Market because that is a corporate creativity program. It may utilize a lot of the elements from Thought Market, but I think it's different," Zip says. "We need something that reflects an emotional response again."

Again, they wrestle with many ideas.

Justice looks at Neal and says, "I loved it when you were wrapping your first presentation to us and you used the term 'What if'! What if people could do this, what if they did that? And I liked it when you used the term *courage* when you were describing Mia and the immigrants coming to America."

Then Zip says, "How about if we call it 'What If Courage'!"

"The *What If Courage* program." Everybody agreed it said the right things and was a provocative and memorable brand. So an organization called *Whole Earth Justice* is promoting and encouraging and educating the public and organizations to book passage to a new world. A world called the *Enlightened Consumer Market,* in which predation and abuse is partly controlled by market forces and new development is not only the purview of the wealthy. And passage to this new world is upon a vehicle named *What If Courage!*

"Okay, that's a wrap. Let's go celebrate," Zip says.

"Ah, sorry, Karen and I are booked at the hotel spa. A steam, some healthy, light food, and ten hours of REM sleep is what's on my agenda," Justice says.

Then Karen adds, "I'm going to try and sleep without street clothes on and underneath the blankets tonight. Baby steps."

"Well, we're going to miss you, how about it, Neal? Mia?"

"Actually, there is a presentation right down the block from the hotel on new emerging technologies. AI, autonomous vehicles, that sort of thing, you interested in a little dinner then the conference?"

"Yeah, that sounds good," Neal says.

"We can drop you girls off at the hotel," Mia says.

"Actually, I'd rather walk," Justice says, looking at Karen for confirmation.

"That's okay with me," Karen adds.

Zip suggests to Neal that they bike to the restaurant and presentation.

"Mia and I have our own bikes and we can get one for you at the bikeshare rack."

"Sounds good," Neal says. "We bike almost everywhere back in Minneapolis."

Neal and Zip and Mia pedal past Justice and Karen just as they're arriving at the hotel. "Last chance," Neal shouts.

Justice and Karen wave and say, "Have fun."

At the restaurant Zip, Neal and Mia order drinks and talk about the project.

"I have to say, Zip and Mia, this has been quite an experience," Neal says.

"How so?" Zip asks.

"Well, I just feel like we made progress in positioning the WEJ project. Prior to this week, Whole Earth Justice was simply a brand that held people's hopes and maybe their own ideas about what needs to be done. Now I think it's more. It's a set of principles and strategies and promises. Things that can help it move forward. The WEJ movement just kind of happened organically, so the work of pulling together a cohesive strategy and message never really happened. Anyway, I feel like we made progress on it the last couple of days."

"Well, thank you," Zip says.

Then Mia says, "What you're doing is hard! It's hard because people don't want to hear the truth and they sure don't want to change. Idealism, creativity, change, these are difficult things in our shallow mass merchandise culture. Change is uncomfortable! You must deal with it every day at Thought Market too?"

"WEJ is lucky to have someone like Justice leading the way," Zip says.

"That girl is a warrior at heart," Neal says. "The only thing she's afraid of is being on the wrong side of her conscience."

"If it's right, it's right, consequences be damned."

"I think her faith kind of revolves around the idea that you do what's right no matter what, and let the world, or God, or whatever, deal with the consequences. She's not particularly religious, but she has a deep sense of mission and a strong spiritual core that gives her strength and a capacity for idealism."

"Well, idealism and passion are also the special sauce necessary to changes the world," Zip says.

"Yeah, with a smile of recognition, Justice's passion and idealism can be kind of addictive," Neal says. "And it's not always comfortable either. People get sucked in by her idealism and passion and fearlessness and her beautiful almost naive unencumbered nature, and then before you know it, she's changed you. You suddenly find yourself walking an unfamiliar and challenging path, but you feel more alive than you've felt in a long time. I guess she's given me the experience I've been talking about and promoting all these years with Thought Market."

"And what's that?" Zip says.

"That using your creativity, and participating in something bigger than yourself, and accepting the risks necessary to pursue those things will make you more fully human, and that comes with its own energy and rewards. Anyway, I feel like the two of you have helped WEJ, and I myself personally find some needed clarity, and I thank you both." Neal holds up his glass and says, "Whole Earth Justice!"

Both Mia and Zip hold up their glasses.

Zip says, "What if we had the courage to seek Whole Earth Justice!"

And then Neal adds, "And the courage to let love and Justice into our lives!"

Chapter 22

A GOLDEN RULE FOR OUR TIME

Justice sits down at her office desk and taps in the code to release her voice mail. "Justice, this is Father Dimitri at St. Mary's. I have something for you and Neal, and I hope you could find the time to call me back or stop by the church for a short chat?"

Justice intends to call him back but the rest of the day flies by and she forgets. After work, however, Justice and Neal are out for a walk. As they're approaching the church, Justice smacks her head and says, "I was supposed to call Father Dimitri back."

"He called you?" Neal asks.

"Yes, he said he had something for us, and we should call or stop by the church."

"Well, let's stop and see if he's around."

The church is quiet and seems empty. They ring the bell at the desk and wait. In a few minutes Father Dimitri appears.

"Justice, Neal, how good of you to come," he says.

"You said you had something for us," Justice says.

"Indeed," Father Dimitri says with a big grin on his face. "Please let's go sit for a moment."

They enter the office. Neal begins examining the books on the shelf. Father Dimitri pours the hot water for tea into mugs.

"Here, Justice, Neal, handing them each a mug of hot water." On the table is a basket full of tea packets. "Well, as I had mentioned before, we have a network of religious clerics and lay people all over the world who help people who are oppressed by bad governments."

"Yes, I remember that," Justice says.

"Well, it's an interfaith network. It's comprised of over a million members worldwide. They speak every language and are members of most faith traditions, I would say," Father Dimitri explains. "We use this network, to help oppressed people, but we also use it to explore theological or ethical questions and dilemmas," he says.

"Like game theory?" Neal asks.

"Well, no, not exactly, but along those lines," Father Dimitri says.

"Interesting," Neal responds with increased interest.

"We do use algorithms, and language conversion, and analysis to pose our questions and to interpret the responses."

"So it's like a survey with language and cultural analysis over-lays?" Neal asks.

"Yes, I think that's a pretty good interpretation of it," Father Dimitri says. "Well, here's the thing, I was fascinated by your grand-father's interpretation of the golden rule," he says, nodding at Justice, "so I came up with a methodology to use the network to reinterpret the golden rule, given our current global issues. I included climate change, the immigration and refugee crisis, the issues of economic disparity, racism, and education."

"Wow," Justice says with excitement.

"And what happened, what did you find?" Neal asks.

"Just to be clear," Father Dimitri says, "this is not a consensus statement. Nobody said this or chose this from among statements. It's a values consensus written by the algorithm from many languages and cultures and then put into English."

Justice and Neal are both on the edge of their seats.

Father Dimitri flips over a piece of paper on the table in front of him. On it is written:

To save ourselves, we must save the others.
To save the others, we must free ourselves.

Justice gasps, places her hand over her mouth, and begins to cry." It's beautiful!"

"It's exactly what your grandfather thought," Neal says. "A survival message. A life raft. An instruction on how to survive."

"Yes," Father Dimitri says. "And translatable into every language and supported by every culture and religion on earth."

"I imagine that the first part of the statement means just as it says—like with climate change, for example, we must cooperate and solve the problem for everyone?" Neal says.

"Yes," Father Dimitri responds.

"And the second sentence means in order to do this, we must first free ourselves of the injustice and prejudices and predatory actions that prevents our cooperation?"

"Yes," Father Dimitri says. "To save ourselves we must shed our complacencies to the things that make the injustice."

"So what's next?" Neal asks. "I mean, what will you do with it?"

"We begin to teach it," Father Dimitri says. "We teach it in every language and religion and culture on earth. Simultaneously! And we do so as a reference or reinterpretation of an existing meme they already accept. Justice, this is quite a legacy for your grandfather's work and insights," Father Dimitri exclaims.

"Thank you, Father," she says with a quiver in the voice.

Progress

As the birthplace of Whole Earth Justice, the Twin Cities had the most members, active chapters, and activist strategies. In fact, WEJ Minnesota led to new business enterprises and branding deals with private operators who agreed to certain operating covenants and a split of the profits in exchange for identity affiliations. Some of the branded products included a growing rideshare operation called WEJ Rideshare that competed with Uber and Lyft on a local basis. A line of commuter clothing for people who don't own a car. A group of members decided they would start a new type of carshare operation called Neighborcar that allowed a group of neighbors to own and operate a car together. Another group started an electric bike subscription service called Moov Commuter that provided for reduced barrier access to electric bike technology. One of the most popular items was "Briefs for your feet." They were advertised as sturdy, comfortable footwear for people who regularly walked for transportation. You could stride through puddles and snowdrifts in them, but they still look presentable at your job or on a date.

A WEJ group in Iowa developed a line of cleaning products, WEJ Clean. Not everybody was able to make cash contributions to a cause they believed in, but everybody buys soap, so everyone could support the movement that way, the creators figured. The WEJ movement's revenues started to grow. It went from pennies and volunteer time to millions. WEJ was gaining traction and becoming a force in the marketplace

On the activism side, they seized upon the idea of the rating system or feedback loop and applied it to corporate elites. It evolved into a powerful and sometimes controversial set of activities designed to discourage bad behavior. Targets included large companies that were exploiting people and the planet and those moving assets to other countries to avoid paying their fair share of taxes at home. Most of these predatory practices were perfectly (and ridiculously) legal although harmful to others. Dedicated WEJ activists publicize the bad behavior and draw attention to it, and that raised the risks associated with it. It was Socially Responsible Investing on steroids, except the ratings went beyond companies to include the managers and board members who made these decisions. Some executives who got bad ratings found it difficult to get new jobs because companies didn't want the liability that went along with a poorly rated management team. It would put too much downward pressure on the stock value. WEJ did small commercials for TV and radio and produced a line of greeting cards called Greedy Cards that highlighted executives of companies who were raking in millions in salary while plundering the planet and their workers. People did mass mailings of these cards to shareholders and institutional investors. It was all controversial because it really amounted to a form of public shaming, but public opinion polls showed a vast majority of Americans supported these efforts to put a face on the problems bedeviling us.

Local WEJ organizations were sued many times but had the support of volunteer legal counsel and consistently won these court battles. The lawsuits usually backfired on the executives in terms of bad publicity, and WEJ chapters would often receive a surge in donations and volunteers.

As the WEJ movement grew it also became a de facto resource hub and coordinating committee for social movements focused on everything from environmental causes to civil rights to community revitalization. Many of these groups formed their own chapters in the What If Courage network. Everyone from organic farmers to carpenters to venture capitalists wanted to express solidarity with the WEJ movement and offer their services to movement groups or members. The interconnected capabilities of the What If Courage platform made it easy to root out insincere groups trying to scam activists for easy money, just like Yelp or Airbnb.

Chapters existed in most of the country and some were also being formed in Europe as well. And the What If Courage platform tied it all together. It both localized the movement and internationalized it at the same time. After several years of rapid growth, WEJ decided it was time to have a large convention. The idea was to make membership and belonging mean something. Bring home the message that they aren't alone. The networking program was great for connecting people and resourcing, but it was also important for creating belonging and being a part of something bigger than themselves. They also wanted to send the message to the predators out there that this group was formidable and not going away easily. WEJ decided to model their convention on the famous Apple conventions where app developers would come and show and sell their ideas. At the WEJ convention, however, it was chapters and members who set up booths and would show or sell the projects they were working on. The first convention was held in Minneapolis at the convention center downtown, but it was clear they were going to need a larger space for future conventions.

At the first convention, participants approved a proposal to create a national governing collaborative known as the wisdom council, drawing on Native American traditions of governance, and Justice and Neal were both elected to be part of it. With the success of the What If courage network, Neal's stature within the movement grew to the point where no one voiced concerns about nepotism.

Justice remained the movement's most recognizable figure other than the battalions of celebrity supporters from the realms of film, television, music, literature, art, technology, and business.

Justice's course on interdependence called Futurama 2.0 became popular around the world, available through MOOC online service. She published a book on the emerging interdependent civilization that became a best seller and was translated into eleven languages. The University of Minnesota, who had had her jailed and fired for her activities with the divestment protest, not only divested their endowment from fossil fuel and other dubious industries, they were in the process of establishing a new college focused on sustainability and interdependence.

The weight of WEJ work forced Justice to stop teaching, but the university made her an honorary chair of the new school. She also became a convenient target for interests upholding the status quo and was often confronted by right-wing activists in a way similar to how WEJ supporters challenged corporate executives and politicians. For personal support, she counted on her family and Betsy and Karen and Neal. In some ways WEJ had become part of her extended family. Justice's grandfather Bill was always with her too, providing inspiration and guidance, as she remembered their many conversations growing up.

With his heavy involvement with the WEJ movement, Neal stepped down from his role in the Thought Market company and handed operations of it to Alice Voss and the Master. Neal also moved back to the Twin Cities from the Bay Area. He continued his regular round of speaking engagements, however, both for income and to promote and educate people on the value of collaborative networking. Occasionally, Justice would come along on some of Neal's speaking engagements, depending on the location to get a little R&R.

Despite Justice's tremendous strength and energy, she would occasionally run out of gas. Neal had learned to recognize the symptoms, which could be cured by a few days of biking, hiking, climbing, and seeing the local sights.

One morning, Neal wraps his arms around Justice and says, "How about if you come with me to Iceland on Friday?" I've got a conference there and you could sit in the geyser hot springs for a couple of days?"

Justice gives him a sudden kiss and says, "Yes, yes, yes! I won't even think about work," she declares.

Neal rolls his eyes and laughs, and Justice scowls at him. "Oh, did that escape my head?" he asks. "Sorry, no work! Got it."

Chapter 23

MISSION

Several days later in Reykjavik, Iceland, Neal returns to the hotel from the conference seminar and spots Justice sitting in the coffee shop reading a book. Neal bends down and kisses her.

"See, no work!" Justice proclaims. Holding up the book, she says proudly, "It's a trashy novel." Despite Justice's good intentions, a short time later the conversation turns to Bill Miller.

"I wish you would have gotten to know my grandpa Bill," Justice says. "One of the best things about him was that he always stayed so calm and positive, never casting people who disagreed with him as enemies. I think about him in times like this and try and imagine what he would tell me."

Neal walks away and then returns with two cocktails. Justice confesses, "I am worried about the momentum of the movement."

"What are you talking about?" Neal says.

"WEJ is one of the most successful social justice movements in history! I know that's true, at least on paper, but I feel it losing stream," Justice says. "We're so busy fighting about the way forward. Fighting with the predatory capitalists. Fighting to keep the activists everywhere engaged. We're getting worn out. We're falling into ruts."

Neal says, "I didn't know Bill, but based on what you've told me about him, he was a long game player. I think he'd tell you, you'll be much happier if you accept that you're only human and can't hold the whole world up all by yourself."

Justice hugs Neal even tighter and says, "Thank you, Neal, I love you." Then in typical Justice way, she adds, "You know we need to do something dramatic to capture people's attention."

Neal laughs. "Let's go."

Justice ignores the laugh. "We need to directly challenge these adolescent ideas that people and the culture still hang on to. What we're looking for is something that represents the truth about interdependence that makes more sense to people than what they believe now. I'm thinking about the human chain, for example," Justice says. "Did you ever see the TED Talk that Karen had done on the human chain?" Justice asks.

"Yes," Neal responds, "you showed it to me the morning after we first met."

"No, I didn't," she says indignantly—then remembering it, blushes.

"Well," Justice continues, "if we were to take the truth of the human chain and develop a policy perspective around that, what would it look like?"

"I don't know," Neal says, not wanting to talk about it anymore. Then a look of "aha" flashes across Neal's face. "How about a method for productive enterprises to compensate society for the public equity and public intellectual property that is invested in private ventures? I mean, the capital gets a return on investment, the people who provide new intellectual property get a return on investment, why shouldn't civilization get a return on investment for what they invested? Why shouldn't civilization receive some of the proceeds or benefits from those investments?"

"You mean, like the commons?" Justice asks. "My grandpa used to talk a lot about that. He'd always say what belongs to all of us together is just as important to our lives and livelihood as what we own privately. The natural environment, the accumulated knowledge of humanity, the educated workforce, the capital markets, the infrastructure—all of which are integral to the success of every venture."

"Yes," Neal says, "yes!"

"I get it," Justice exclaims, almost knocking over Neal's martini with a sweep of her arms. "When people use their ingenuity to build an enterprise based on the foundations laid by previous generations of past workers, they owe something back for this commons equity invested in their business. They didn't create that commons equity. It was invested in their enterprise by civilization. They've incorporated those civilization equities into their business, but they don't pay anything for them. Following up on Karen's Apple iPhone example, why should Apple stockholders be the only beneficiaries of that public equity that was invested in their products? So how do we establish a system that compensates everyone for the important treasure we all own together?" Justice says.

"How about...," Neal says.

Justice finishes his sentence, "An estate tax?"

"I mean, the reason people think they're against the estate tax is because they're sold the idea that it's taking money from the rightful owners of a successful venture," Neal says. "The people who made the money! This argument turns it around. It says the developers and businesses that captured and privatized the benefits of past work are the ones that are unjustly taking public benefits without compensating society for those investments."

"I love it," Justice says, "humanity as a whole is a silent partner in their enterprise and deserves a share of the profits. So how do we press the case for an increased estate tax when the current government is all about cutting taxes?"

"Good question!" Neal says.

They both sit silently, finishing their drinks.

"What if we proposed it as a constitutional amendment!" Justice says.

"Yes. That's it," Neal answers, triumphantly slapping the table with his hand.

The Convention

The next Whole Earth Justice convention takes place at the Las Vegas convention center on the strip. The auditorium is packed with people the first evening. On a giant screen at the back of the stage is

"Whole Earth Justice." A pulse of clapping hands, stomping feet, and whooping voices begins to rumble. It gets louder and louder.

Justice Miller is standing in the wings of the stage with Neal.

"This is not my favorite part," she says.

"I know." Neal pats her backside. "You always say that. But you're really good at this."

Justice walks out onto the stage and the crowd erupts. She claps herself and points at the crowd, then pauses until the auditorium is dead quiet.

"They said nothing could be done about climate change and extinction of animal species! They said nothing could be done about predatory capitalism! They said this couldn't happen," she said, pointing at the crowd. "But we've proven them wrong! Our numbers are growing, our creativity is growing, our sustainable and socially just projects are growing, and our impact is growing. But we're not done yet! We didn't set out to be a footnote in the history books. We set out to change humanity and make the earth a better place to live."

The crowd starts in: "Justice is the only way, that is why we're here today! Justice is the only way, that is why we're here today!"

She quiets them down again with her intent gaze. "It's true we are doing some amazing things together. But what we're about to embark on is even bigger still. It's bigger, bolder, and riskier and will be harder than anything we have yet set out to do. But as a movement, we haven't just done what's easy. We define our actions by what's necessary. And what needs doing is we need to change the government of the United States— and every other nation around the globe. We need to change government so that it better reflects the will of the people! We need to change it, so it's more sustainable and less beholden to the predatory capitalists. We need to change it so that in one of the richest countries in the world, health care and education are not rationed based on how much money you have. And we need to make changes that are permanent—not easy to flip every four years. And that means, we need to change the US Constitution.

"So Whole Earth Justice is hereby announcing its intention to mount a sustained campaign to pass three constitutional amendments:

"The first is called the fair elections amendment and is designed to get big money out of politics once and for all. It simply states that money

is not speech as defined by article one of the Constitution. And secondly it says that corporations are not citizens eligible for protections under the Constitution.

"The second new constitutional amendment proposed is called the just compensation amendment. The idea behind this amendment is that the wealth of all financially successful individuals and businesses depend in part on an inheritance of natural and human-made assets that are owned by all of us. These include a publicly educated workforce, government-enforced patent protection, numerous laws and regulations that ensure a free market, and much more. So it's only fair they compensate us with some kind of dividend for our generous equity investments. And the best way to collect that debt is through a progressive estate tax.

"The third new constitutional amendment is called the right to education and health care amendment. It establishes the right of all citizens to affordable education and health care regardless of financial ability. It doesn't stipulate these things need to be free but that they cannot be rationed based on ability to pay or social status. The reason for this amendment is that education and health care are fundamental to the ability of people to succeed in society, which in turn is fundamental to the ability of this country to succeed in the world.

"These three amendments are all closely connected, although they will be enacted separately. The just compensation amendment provides a way to pay for the health care and education amendment without huge tax hikes for lower- and middle-income Americans. Indeed, numerous economic studies show estimate that Just Compensation would pay for critical education, health care, and urgent environmental measures without raising the average family's taxes at all. The fair election amendment will remove the grip of the special interests, which over time would make government far more efficient and cost effective and better able to tackle the social and environmental problems ahead.

"Now, some people may question the wisdom of such bold steps at democratic reform when so many bright people over the past sixty years have failed to enact much-less-daring versions of these ideas. I believe we can for one reason: We have to! And we have to do it now! It promotes the ideals of interdependence—the fact that all Americans are in this together—and that creates new political alliances. Many people across

217

the country who have been suspicious of environmentalists and liberals and people who didn't look or talk like they do are beginning to see what's at stake. At stake for them and for their children and grandchildren. Together these amendments will restore the promise of America. Restore our ability to lead the world into a new era of environmental and democratic progress and justice!

"But this will not be easy to accomplish. Predatory capitalists will fight us at every turn, and in every corner of the country. But ultimately, I believe, they will not succeed in stopping us. Because we will keep going until the job is accomplished.

"Thank you and God bless you, the people of Whole Earth Justice."

Chapter 24

BIG GOALS

Having become one of the recognizable faces of the fast-growing movement, Justice is frequently invited to take part in key organizing and fundraising events around the country. A bit of an introvert by nature, these are not Justice's favorite duties although she recognizes they are essential to the cause. On one such occasion she finds herself at the Beverly Hills home of Rob Krinner, a well-known actor and director, among a group of A-list Hollywood movers and shakers. Despite her apprehension, Hollywood celebrities are important to Whole Earth Justice financially, as well as being influential carriers of the message. In the past few months, it has become fashionable to ride up to one of LA's hottest restaurants or clubs on a bikeshare or carshare vehicle emblazoned with the WEJ logo.

Upon arriving at the party, Rob and his wife, Erin, meet Justice at the entrance and tell her how grateful they are for WEJ and how important a cause they think it is.

"Well, thank you for having me," Justice responds. "Your support of WEJ has been very generous from the very beginning." Despite her apprehension about these Hollywood events, the truth is, she and the WEJ movement have always been very well treated by Hollywood celebrities.

"I have someone I'd like you to meet as Rob leads her into the backyard." He walks up to a tall woman with high cheekbones and bigger-than-life sunglasses. "Svetlana, this is Justice Miller, one of the leaders of the WEJ movement."

In a strong Russian accent, she extends her hand to Justice and says, "Svetlana Kazakov. I'm a big fan of WEJ and I'm very pleased to meet you."

Then the host says, "Svetlana is a member of an activist Russian rock band called Pussy Riot."

"Oh my god! I know who you are," Justice says. "As I recall, Putin sent you and your bandmates to prison for your outspoken performances?"

"Yes, that's right. I did about two years in a prison outside Moscow."

"Wow, two years! I did two hours in an American jail and felt oppressed by the whole experience," Justice says and then thinks how stupid that sounded.

Svetlana says, "When I heard you may be here, I asked to meet you because I want to discuss how we may support each other. I see us as being engaged in a single struggle."

"Okay, I think I agree but say more," Justice says.

"Pussy Riot finds itself with a power to recruit and deploy young activists. Activists who are angry and willing to brazenly confront the power structure. We want to help train and position these activists in the service of a cause greater than tearing society apart. And the WEJ movement looks like an example of a cause that can make a difference."

"That makes sense," Justice says. "So how can the WEJ movement help Pussy Riot? And what can Pussy Riot do to help the WEJ movement?"

"First," Svetlana says, "I can tell you that the fight you're engaged in is probably bigger than you think."

"How so?" Justice asks.

"Poland, Hungary, Russia, Turkey, Philippines—there is an authoritarian, nationalist, antiglobalist movement emerging all over the world. They are all using fear to pull people back to a dependent insulated hierarchical type of society. The message of the WEJ movement is to move society in a more interdependent direction."

Svetlana grasps Justice's hand, removes her glasses, and looks deep into eyes and says, "You should realize authoritarians like Putin, and those in the US too, will do anything to win. The only reason I'm alive today is because the beast determined my celebrity represents a problem for him if something were to happen to me." Svetlana says in a matter-of-fact voice that relays no fear, "You might think you are insulated from such things here in beautiful Beverly Hills, but remember, power is power, and if you represent a threat to them continuing to have it, they will consider you an enemy. Justice just looks at Svetlana studying her."

"That's a sobering message," Justice says. "Thank you."

Then Svetlana says, "Let's talk at another time, in a quieter place, about how we can help each other."

"Sure, that's fine," Justice says.

"I think we can be of help to each other. I'll call you," Svetlana says as she walks away in the direction of a Hollywood leading man who has been trying to get her attention.

As the WEJ movement was preparing to announce its plans for the constitutional amendments campaign, the public accountability strategy (referred to by opponents as the public shaming campaign) they had been using seemed to take a more ominous and potentially violent tone. A group of activists wearing briefs on the outside that say Pussy Riot on them began confronting and shaming petrochemical executives from some of the most polluting companies in the world, along with some of the politicians who take money from them. They would confront them in restaurants or at their homes. The activists would identify themselves as Pussy Riot, but by wearing briefs on the outside implied an association with the WEJ movement. Several incidents occurred where a person wearing Pussy Riot briefs was beaten by bodyguards.

Vigorous opposition to the WEJ movement seemed to appear overnight. In trials stemming from these beatings in New York, Washington, Houston, Aspen, and St. Paul, it came out that a group of billionaires had hastily founded a group to spread false propaganda about the WEJ movement. WEJ leaders were said to be linked to Latin American drug gangs, Iranian terrorists, wealthy abortion doctors, and most ridiculous of all, Vladimir Putin. The movement put together a nonviolence messaging campaign, stating, "The WEJ is a nonviolent movement seeking sustainability and social justice for all. We do not condone violence of any kind, by any side, at any time. However, calling people out for their bad behavior at the expense of others in a civil manner is not violence, it's education. We practice peaceful, educational engagement."

At three in morning, the phone rings at Justice's home. She's sound asleep and it startles and awakes her. The caller ID is unknown. She would normally let such a call go but in her barely awake state she answers it.

"Hello."

"Justice, it's Svetlana, sorry for the late call."

"Svetlana, is everything all right?" Justice asks.

"Well, no, I must leave the country in a few hours, but I wanted to see you and finish our discussion before I go. Can I come over to your house and talk for a few minutes?"

"Ah, okay, where are you?"

"I'm sitting in a car in front of your house."

"I'll be down and open the door in a few minutes."

Justice opens the door and Svetlana walks in.

"Are you in danger? Would you like some tea?"

Svetlana smiles. "Yes, and yes, that's why we all love the Midwest of America."

"You mean showing up in the middle of the night with cryptic messages doesn't work for you everywhere," Justice says with a sarcastic tone.

"I'm very sorry for the late-night intrusion Justice. But I'm on my way to the airport. There's a chartered plane waiting for me there."

"What is it?" Justice asks.

"I've had a secret benefactor in Russia. An oligarch who is connected to the Putin government. We had a secret affair and he has helped me at many points along the way," Svetlana says. "We were apparently found out and he was killed. I don't know for sure, but I'm assuming they may come after me as well."

"Oh my god, do you have resources?" Justice asks.

"Yes, I do, thanks to my friend," Svetlana replies. "I will be fine. But I did want to finish our conversation before I leave. You are, of course, aware of our involvement in the public-shaming program," Svetlana says.

"The public accountability strategy," Justice corrects with a smile.

"Ha, yes that," Svetlana replies. "What do you think of our involvement?"

"Well, I must admit your people know how to stir the pot," Justice says.

"Yes, we are good pot stirrers," Svetlana replies.

"The thing is, we're a nonviolent group," Justice says.

"So are we!" Svetlana replies. "You're just a little more nonviolent than we are. Look, our people are never armed. They've been coached in how to handle delicate situations, and they know how to get attention," Svetlana says. "And you have deniability with us. We identify as Pussy Riot nothing else. The kids just like the underwear thing, Svetlana says with a smile."

"Look, Svetlana—"

"Just call me Lana, all my friends call me Lana."

"Okay, thanks, but the thing is, we do a tremendous amount of due diligence on our targets and plan these things very carefully. If something happened and somebody got hurt or if we get sued and are found to be violating somebody's rights, or there is collateral damage somehow. Our movement would be at risk."

"You seem to be saying that your movement is legitimate and ours is not and your association with us will damage you," Lana says.

"No, I'm not saying that, Lana, we're both fighting the establishment, but I get the impression that some of your people are more interested in the fight than the cause," Justice says.

"I see," Lana says. "How has fundraising been going since we've been involved?"

"Well, I must admit, pretty good," Justice says.

"And how about recruitment of activists?" Lana asks.

"Not that good," Justice admits.

"Don't you see, Justice, we have more people than we can vet," Lana says.

"You vet them?" Justice asks.

"Of course, we do, we don't want a bunch of barbarians running around claiming they're Pussy Riot," Lana says.

"Ha," Justice begins to laugh. "Pussy Riot is worried about its brand?"

"Of course, we are," Lana says. "We want to be part of the solution, not the problem."

"Well, we do recognize the value of your people," Justice says. If WEJ decided to help, what would that look like? What could we do to help you?"

"I would like you to set up a defense fund to support them in the case of any problems. And I'd like you to pay for their medical, life, and disability insurance," Lana says. "I don't care how you do it. It can be secret offshore accounts, or you can get a benefactor to do it. But these kids are risking a lot by being out there and they need support if something happens to them."

"Humm." Justice stirs and then takes a drink of her tea. "Well, no guarantees, Lana, but I can discuss it with the board. My guess is, they will suggest that you get your own insurance for your members and we can figure out a way to pay for it," Justice says.

"Thank you, Justice," Lana says.

"Okay, now let's talk about how you can help WEJ," Justice says.

"What do you have in mind?" Lana replies.

"Well, I'm just thinking off the top of my head here, in the middle of the night, but I think we want to place some operating procedures and rules on your activists' activities when they coincide with ours," Justice asserts in a forceful way.

Lana pauses and stirs her tea. "It's not all that easy to control these kids, you know!" Lana says.

"I know, but that's the deal—rules of engagement for insurance and a defense fund," Justice says.

"Look at the adults we've become," Lana says.

Justice laughs. "Deal. I'll discuss it with WEJ and get a proposal on the engagement and how we can handle the insurance and defense fund."

"I should have anticipated a champion hockey goalie would drive a hard bargain," Lana says.

They shake hands.

"Where are you going?" Justice says.

"Best if that is just between me and the pilot for now," Lana says.

"Oh sure, but how will we communicate?" Justice asks.

"I'm afraid I'll just have to be in touch with you," Lana says. "Maybe I can use other people. Do you have a deck of cards?" Lana asks.

"Yeah, sure." Justice pulls one out from the drawer of an old desk that belonged to her grandparents.

"Okay, pick one," Lana says.

Justice shows it to Lana

"Okay, if it's me, I'll know the card," Lana says, buttoning her coat and hustling out the front door.

Wow, Neal is not going to believe this, Justice thinks as Lana drive off.

WEJ began its constitutional amendment campaign by setting up offices and hiring personnel in every state in the union. They then set out to identify the positions of every politician in every state on the proposed constitutional amendments. The process to pass a constitutional amendment is a high bar and involves several steps. The first step is winning a super majority of 66 percent in both houses of congress. The second step is getting a presidential signature before sending it to the states for ratification. The President's signature is not actually required, however as the leader of a major party an amendment is unlikely to pass over the Presidents objection. The third step is getting a super majority of 75 percent of the states to ratify the amendments.

The WEJ campaign plan operates on several levels. On a national level it involves TV commercials, celebrity endorsements, and merchandise with messages, and social media campaigns. The plan also calls for a priority or a phasing schedule. Rather than spread resources thin over the entire country, all at once, the plan is designed to win the support of congressional members in more sympathetic states first and then build pressure on holdouts. This process also allows WEJ to focus its resources in a more productive way. The state delegations that were being focused on at any given time were referred to as being in the focus zone. The strategy inside a focus zones includes four main parts they called (1) the playing field, (2) the targeting plan, (3) the shakedown, and (4) the replacement plan.

The playing field section is about surfacing information within the delegation members districts. Research includes attitudes and demographics and messaging effectiveness studies as well as voting records down to the census track level. The playing field also includes analysis of each congressperson's strengths and vulnerabilities in their districts. Which constituency groups support them, and which oppose them and why? Lastly, the playing field includes forcing the congresspersons from within the focus zones to take unambiguous public positions on the proposed amendments. Politicians are good at hedging, so this is accomplished through unrelenting asking and reporting and applying of pressure to get them to commit.

Once the playing field has been developed inside a focus zone, a targeting plan is developed in each congressional district where a congressperson is a "no" vote on the amendments. The targeting plan is a campaign strategy to erode the congressperson's support among his constituencies and increase support for the amendments. The targeting plans go down to specific demographic and psychographic groups of constituencies in specific census tracts. Tailored messages and strategies for this group of voters and that group of voters.

The third portion of the focus zone strategy is called the shakedown. The shakedown is designed to get the targeted congresspersons to change their position by showing them portions of the targeting plan, the resources that the WEJ forces have to spend against them or for them if they switch, and the possible primary opponents the group may field against them if they don't switch positions.

The last portion of the focus zone strategy is called the replacement plan. The replacement plan is just like it sounds—a plan to get the congressperson replaced by a more favorable politician. This could include a primary challenger from within their own party, or it could be a candidate from the opposite party or an independent, or it could be both. In several circumstances WEJ supported both a primary challenger as well as an opposition party candidate in the general.

The opposition was well funded and organized as well. They had a detailed plan to stymie the movement. They identified states and members of congress they thought could block the WEJ movement. It was all over if the amendments couldn't first pass out of congress with a super majority.

Some of the people running the WEJ campaign were veterans from previous campaigns including for LGBTQ rights, Black Lives Matter, Me Too, 350.org, climate justice, and human and civil rights campaigns.

An experienced member of the team put it this way, movement politics is like the straw that broke the camel's back! You build pressure and build pressure and it sometimes seems like nothing is happening, and then you place the last straw on the camel's back and change happens all at once. It's a matter of strategic focus, concentration of resources, and picking off delegations one by one. The WEJ campaign planners knew it would take multiple cycles, and they had plans that were at least a decade in duration. If they can't convince delegations to switch, it meant getting opponents voted out of office and proponents voted in. It was a monumental task. The equivalent of war in its scale but hopefully much less costly in terms of life.

Chapter 25

THE RALLY

The Rally

After a year of organizing, the WEJ wisdom council decided it was time to have a rally in Washington, DC, to kick off the constitutional amendment campaign publicly. It was a risky thing to do because if the rally didn't go well, it could shower the campaign with apathy before it even gets out of the box. On the other hand, if they didn't have a rally, it would seem weak as well. As the weekend for the Whole Earth Justice rally for social justice, environmental sustainability, and government reform approached, they began to get indications that it might be okay. In fact, it turned out to be historic, ranking alongside some of the biggest events Washington has ever seen. The crowd stretched from the Capitol to the Lincoln Memorial, filled with hundreds of thousands of mostly young people, many wearing a pair of hero briefs outside their pants. In addition to the national rally in DC, there were also many local rally's taking place in cities across the country. Lady Gaga took the stage and sang two songs, "Imagine" by John Lennon and then "America the Beautiful," followed by several hip-hop artists, including Jay-Z. Next a succession of politicians, celebrities, and everyday citizens took to the podium to express their support for the movement and its principles. Then came the main address.

Justice, nervous and ecstatic at the same time, thought about her grandfather Bill and his notebook as she took the podium.

The crowd begins to chant, "JUSTICE IS THE ONLY WAY, THAT IS WHY WE'RE HERE TODAY! JUSTICE IS THE ONLY WAY, THAT IS WHY WE'RE HERE TODAY!"

She raises her hands to quiet the crowd. "One small step for man, one giant leap for mankind! That's what this is all about. We, the people of Whole Earth Justice, along with our many partners around the world seeking environmental sustainability and social justice, are taking small steps individually so that humanity can be preserved and thrive into the future.

"History shows us that our ability to bring change upon this planet is great. We've conquered mountain ranges, oceans, and outer space. We've survived challenges from despots, diseases, and natural disasters. We've enacted change incrementally, and we've done it through violent revolutions. Our powers to create and impose our will upon this world are great indeed.

"But today we face a new type of challenge. A challenge that doesn't simply reside out there, external to ourselves, but rather a challenge that contains both internal and external dimensions that cannot be separated.

"Our challenge is to speak with a single interdependent human voice and to act with compassion and respect for the whole living body of life upon this planet. But that challenge is great indeed. Today, we live in a world filled with isolation, alienation, and hopelessness. A society where idealism is foolish, greed is good, and seeking advantage at the expense of others is no hindrance to public adoration. A society where creeping nihilism and a deficit of caring threatens our ability to act as one. But if we cannot free ourselves of our internal prejudices and insecurities enough to care about the 'others,' then we cannot come together enough to solve the external threats we face.

"Can we learn to believe and trust in each other enough to cooperate? Particularly with people who are different from ourselves? Can we train ourselves to see the cooperative benefits of 'we' as easily as we see the individualized benefits of 'I'?

"Anything short of this, and we are simply running out the clock. But we should not feel unprepared for this moment. Our evolutionary path was set in motion ten thousand generations ago, when we emerged in the savannas of East Africa with our unique gifts. It was inevitable from the very first moments, that we would come to dominate this planet. It was inevitable that our population would grow. It was inevitable that our plunder of the Earth's finite resources would grow as well. And it was inevitable that we would find ourselves one day, with a set of global crises incompatible with our future. That day has arrived! But we should not cower at the arrival of this long-destined moment.

"Our history has taught us that our powers to create and shape our world are great, particularly when we act together. Our accumulation of knowledge over two hundred thousand years has given us tools with which to fight. And the existential nature of the crisis provides adequate motivations. The time is at hand, but we are neither lost nor unprepared.

"We were born to be here. And the choices are simple—we must learn to live together, or we should prepare to die separately. Today, we live in a world in which the strategic resources are scarce and shrinking rapidly. A world with weapons so powerful that every conflict carries the possibility of ending the human story. A world in which the actions of one group of people, in one part of the planet, will have significant consequences on all other groups of people on all other parts of the planet. This means we—"

An eruption of applause and cheers broke out across the National Mall, overwhelming her words.

"Let me repeat that: we are living in a world in which the actions of one group of people, living in one part of the planet, will have significant consequences on all other groups of people on all other parts of the planet.

"This means, we are all in this together. None shall survive, without the cooperation of the others. If our cultural heritage of competition, isolation, and advantage seeking at the expense of others has left us with a learning disability that prevents us from connecting with the others among us, then we are near the end of our journey.

"Some would have us waste time blaming each other for these problems. But we did not come to this moment, through willful disregard for known consequences but rather as a result of evolutionary destiny. Rather than fight among ourselves we must do what we have done numerous times before—assess the damage, accept the lessons gained, and adjust our ways, which is what Whole Earth Justice is about!"

Applause!

"Look around, we are the people we've been waiting for. This is our moment, and Whole Earth Justice is our cause."

Applause!

"How did we evolve the democratic ideals from 'one person, one vote' to a system where corporations, who are not citizens except in the eyes of the Supreme Court, are able to control the levers of government? How did 'one person, one vote' become one dollar one vote? Why do the interests of polluters, weapons manufacturers, drug companies, and oil companies matter more than the rest of us? How can our country, or indeed the whole world, succeed when we waste the talent and potential of so many of our people in the form of educational disenfranchisement, economic disadvantage, and criminally inadequate health care?"

Another tumultuous wave of approval from the crowd.

"This situation is socially unjust, economically insane, and morally bankrupt. It also ensures our eventual demise. Because cooperation is essential to battling our way out of the current crises. We need the insight and ingenuity of everyone. And true cooperation cannot be sustained in an unjust world. Now is the historic moment...

"As the human population nears an unimaginable eight billion people...When it's becoming clear that many of our development methods are destroying the natural systems upon which our survival depends...When we finally realize that lifestyles based on isolation from one another, massive consumption of material goods, immediate gratification, and distraction have left us less secure and more unaware of our true nature..."

"Now is the moment to pause, take a good look at ourselves, learn the lessons our amazing past provides us, and act as only humans can act, with the unique powers bestowed only upon us to create a world in which we love the whole of creation as much as the Creator herself, himself, themselves. Now is the moment to turn away from a society in which greed is good, isolation a virtue, and love a conditional and limited resource. Now is the moment for innovators to shift their focus from 'me' to 'we.' Now is the moment for antisocial profiteers and advantage seekers to become cooperative social entrepreneurs. Now is the moment for self-destructive polluters to transform themselves into heroic stewards. Now is the moment for us all to reach out to someone different from us—a different race, religion, nationality, economic background, or cultural perspective. Now is the historical moment when our choices are stark in their contrast. And large in their scope. And difficult to implement.

"But we have the comfort and inspiration of knowing our history. Knowing what we have accomplished in the past. Knowing what we're capable of. And knowing the direction we need to head. We may feel afraid, or selfish, or even lazy…but we are not lost. Because we are the place in the world where vision and foresight reside. Vision to see the past and vision to see the future.

"It is no coincidence that after thousands of years of development, we find ourselves with a set of problems that are global in nature. Problems that transcend national, ethnic, or economic boundaries. Problems whose solutions render our tribal instincts and prejudices obsolete. Problems that by their very nature require us, all of us, to work together to save ourselves."

The crowd responds, "Justice is the only way, that is why we're here today! Justice is the only way, that is why we're here today!"

"We should not feel surprised at the revelation of this truth. The instruction to build an inclusive civilization of life has been at the center of our faith traditions for many millennia: Do unto others as you would have them do unto you! Love thy neighbor as thyself!

"The same sentiment is expressed in all the world's major religious traditions, and in every language stretching back to the earliest written traditions. Do unto others, as you would have them do unto you—so simple, so profound, so important! It is more than a slogan, it is the key to our survival upon this planet. It is the operating system of civilization and the only path capable of ensuring our survival.

"Given our interdependent world and the multiple existential global crises we face, a new interpretation might read as follows: To save ourselves, we must save the others. To save the others, we must free ourselves. This means freeing ourselves of the prejudices and the selfish disregard for the whole of life. We cannot live alone. There is no living me only a living we!

"To that end, we embark on this great journey to restore and realign the constitution with the demands of this time and the intentions of its framers.

"First, that 'one person, one vote' be restored to our democracy and that noncitizen organizations and special interests not be allowed to continue to distort and disrupt the governance of this country.

"Second, health care and education, being of critical importance to the success and survival of the nation, shall be deemed rights of citizenship, not able to be rationed based on wealth or income.

"Third, to those who have benefited the most from the inheritance of public commons or equities we all own together, a return on investment shall be owned back to the nation upon the transfer from one generation to the next.

"These amendments are fair, they are aligned with the intentions of the framers of this government, and they are necessary to insure our survival in these difficult times.

"Lastly, let me say this about our journey—forethought, reason, and creativity are the essential characteristics of human beings. And those unique qualities ensured our dominance of this planet, but they are not enough to ensure our survival. For that, we will need to evolve a new trait, one that is not available to us as a matter of involuntary inheritance but rather is only accessible to us as a matter of will. We are the people we've been waiting for. This is our time to step up to our destiny and move human civilization forward. Not just for ourselves, but for the sake of future generations of people, as well as for the protection of the entire body of life upon this planet. Thank you."

"JUSTICE IS THE ONLY WAY, THAT IS WHY WE'RE HERE TODAY! JUSTICE IS THE ONLY WAY, THAT IS WHY WE'RE HERE TODAY!"

Chapter 26

TEN OF CLUBS

Ten of Clubs

In the months that followed the Washington rally, the campaign to push congress to pass the three new amendments got off to a raucous start. The speaker of the house and the senate majority leader both refused to bring the proposed amendments to the floor for a vote. But a midterm election was coming up, offering an opening to change leadership in both houses.

The amendments enjoyed generally more support in blue states than in red states, but that's not the whole story. As an initiative from outside the usual political channels, the proposal disrupted some longstanding political alliances, especially among conservatives. Blue-collar workers and "family values" voters split off from other conservatives with more libertarian views about the economy and the role government. The amendments scrambled the deck because less well-off Republicans and those calling themselves conservative because of social rather than economic beliefs supported the provisions for providing all Americans with better education and health care benefits. A lot of them figured that folks making millions of dollars a year could afford to help out people like them. This was a particularly pronounced attitude among women in the group. These voters also supported the campaign finance amendment as well. They knew they were being sold down the river by their own elected officials

234

who catered to moneyed interests. They were attracted to the idea of constitutional amendments being proposed by citizens because it felt like the people taking control away from the elected politicians who they saw as selling them out. While the pro-LGBTQ and abortion sentiments of most on the "yes" side made some social conservatives uneasy, those issues were not touched upon in the amendments.

There was lots of money pumped into the debate on both sides. In addition to money generated by small donations and branding deals, the WEJ movement had a few billionaires of their own, mostly from the entertainment and high-tech fields along with some activist heirs. But most wealthy people and business executives lined up with the "no" side. They didn't like the fair compensation "estate tax" amendment but the bigger motivator was the campaign finance amendment. This would drastically reduce their influence in setting economic policies. Among the public as a whole, the "yes" side had a younger feel because the movement had been launched by college students and many Americans under forty were burdened by college debt.

In the run up to the first midterm election since the start of the amendment fight, each side employed nontraditional messaging campaigns. The Whole Earth Justice and "yes" side deployed a series of media ads that focused on some of America's accomplishments. It showed Neil Armstrong stepping off the lunar lander, the celebration of the 1980 Olympic hockey team after winning the gold medal, Yellowstone being preserved as the world's first national park, construction of the Golden Gate Bridge, and Jimi Hendrix showcasing the great art form of rock 'n' roll—with the screen going black and the word "WE" appearing. The other side went with a different tactic. Using hastily formed organizations with names like the Freedom for American Democracy Institute or the American History Project, they circulated a raft of fake studies showing how environmental regulations, government services, and changing demographics were betraying the core tenets of America.

The "yes" campaign seemed to be working surprisingly well in southern states, many which are home to large numbers of people of color as well as blue-collar voters. There was also some movement in the white male blue-collar vote in the rest of the country.

By mid-October, a number of conservative incumbents in tight races announced they would support the "yes" vote. Election night brought a decisive change of leadership in both the house and the senate, meaning that the amendments would get a vote but probably not win the supermajority required in each house (certainly not the senate) that would, then pass the measure on to states to approve.

It's 2:00 a.m. and Justice is sound asleep. The phone rings. She wakes up and answers, "Hello."

"Justice, it's the ten of clubs!"

"Lana, are you okay?"

"Yes, yes, I'm just calling to congratulate you and set up our celebration!"

"Well, I'm glad you're okay, Lana, I'm going to hang up now."

"Justice, don't hang up."

"It's 3:00 a.m. here, Lana."

"I'm sorry, listen, I'm sending a plane for you tomorrow. Bring a friend and let's get together and celebrate."

"Where?" Justice says.

"I'll have you back in less than forty-eight hours, I promise," Lana says. "Bring your passport and a swimsuit."

"Lana…Well…it's not—" Justice says.

Lana interrupts, "It's the weekend, whatever it is, you can reschedule it."

Lana hears Justice say, "She's sending a plane for us, can you come. She says she will have us back in forty-eight hours."

"Who are you talking to?" Lana inquires.

"My boyfriend, Neal. He's on the wisdom council also."

"Great, it's going to be fun to see you," Lana says.

"Yes, I think so. Can I get back to sleep now?"

"Sure, ten of clubs signing off."

When Justice wakes up, she wonders whether she had dreamed about the call. Justice gets up, puts on her bathrobe brushes her teeth, and heads downstairs.

Neal is at the table drinking coffee and reading the paper. "Doesn't that girl ever sleep?" Neal asks.

"Good question, I'd say the evidence is lopsidedly no!"

"Well, here's the thing, she's sending a plane to pick us up in a couple of hours so we can celebrate the election results," Justice says.

"Do you know where we're going?" Neal asks.

"No, our only clues are the passports and swimsuits."

"Perfect!" Neal says with a laugh.

Justice asks, "Does your phone have international service?"

"Yes, it does," Neal responds.

Early that afternoon, Justice and Neal arrive at the small charter terminal at the airport. They go to the charter desk as instructed and show their IDs. A pilot comes over and introduces himself as Jim Peterson and says, "He will be taking them to their destination today."

"Where are we going?" Justice asks Jim.

"Vancouver, BC," he says.

Then Jim says, "Okay, I need to trade these phones with you," producing two cellphones.

"I don't understand, why," Neal says.

"These are untraceable," Jim responds. "I'll take your phones and put them in this locker." He opens them and shows them the locker key. "You should write down several numbers from your phone book that you could call if need be." Jim places the two phones in the locker, locks it, and gives the key to Neal. "When you get back, you can collect them."

In the time it takes them to buckle up, the plane is taxiing down the runway. After they land in Vancouver, they taxi to a stop and the door opens. Justice catches Lana running over to greet them. They embrace, and jumping up and down, Lana says, "Congratulations, I'm so happy! I'm so excited by what happened."

"It is great," Justice says, "but we didn't win yet!"

"Yes, but we made tremendous progress and we're not dead yet," Lana responds.

"Why would we be dead," Neal says with a curious, concerned voice.

"Sometimes that's what happens when you piss off the beast," Lana responds.

Justice looks at Neal and says, "Putin!"

"Vladimir Putin," Neal says. "We pissed off Vladimir Putin?"

"Yep, we kicked the beast right in the balls," Lana exclaims.

"Oh man, this trip just took quite a turn," Neal says.

Lana puts her arm around Neal and says, "No worries, you're safe here. Come on, let's have some dinner and a couple of drinks and we can talk about the campaign," Lana says.

The three of them get into an SUV with a driver. The car heads up the mountain toward Whistler ski resort. They pull into a private driveway and the car pulls up in front of a giant ski chalet-type house.

"Wow, do you own this place?" Neal says.

"Ha, no, I don't own much of anything," Lana responds. "Any real assets I have, which isn't much, are in a trust for the benefit of my son," Lana says.

"Your son," Justice responds. "I didn't know you had a son."

"Well, yes, I do. He lives with a relative in another country. Not Russia. He's five years old," Lana says. I had him just before the protests that sent me to prison."

"I'm still just reeling from the idea that we kicked Putin in the balls!" Neal says.

"You really must kick him because he's not tall enough to knee in the balls," Lana says, laughing.

"I know how you kicked Putin in the balls, but I'm a little unclear how I managed to do it?"

"Oh, simple," Lana says. "First, you must realize that Putin has plans and ambitions that include the whole world. They only pretend to be nationalists to gain and maintain power. He foments nationalism and bigotry in other countries as well because he thinks it will create more opportunities for him to have influence over these countries. It's just as it says in Justice's class Futurama 2.0, we can either go forward into interdependence or back words into greater dependence on thugs like Putin."

"Hey, you took my class," Justice says.

"Yes, I enjoyed it very much."

"Okay, let's stay on topic here. Let's get to the part where I kick Putin in the balls," Neal says.

"The beast is smart,' Lana says. "He understands this and is doing everything in his power to bring about a more dependent society all over the world. And the WEJ movement is the only real movement toward a more interdependent world. My guess is, he will be much more active in your next presidential election trying to stop the WEJ movement from taking hold."

"Wow," Neal says, "we really kicked the beast in the balls."

For the next few hours, Justice, Neal, and Lana sat on the deck, drank, laughed, ordered food to be delivered, and then dipped in the hot tub. They talked late into the night about what was to come in the months ahead.

At one point Neal says, "Sometimes I think we should take a more incremental approach."

"What do you mean?" Justice asks.

"Well, I mean we can take time to build our membership and let people change over time. It doesn't need to be a revolution," he says.

"I think you're wrong about that," Lana says. "If we don't push and win, the forces seeking to destroy the movement will gain the upper hand and win."

Neal looks at Justice, and she says, "I agree with Lana on this. Bigger is better. We need to keep the momentum and keep challenging. That's where our members are coming from. We slow down and they slow down. We speed up and attack harder and they speed up and attack harder."

Neal starts to talk, and then pauses for a full ten seconds, finally saying, "But these amendments don't really solve the problems directly. Maybe we should focus on the actual issues, like climate change for example!"

"It's too late for that," Lana says. "I know these people, they're going to try and destroy the movement no matter what we do. Our only chance is if we succeed to the point, they cannot turn back the clock."

Neal responds with a little frustration in his voice, "Look, I'm committed to winning! I've changed the course of my life too, I'm in for the cause, I just don't think 'all or nothing' is the only way, or even the best way to play the game. We've apparently made some powerful enemies. They've threatened you, Lana, they've infiltrated and tried to destroy my business, and we're meeting in secret hideouts. I just don't think we should blindly go on without recognizing the situation. We need to consider and explore all the possible paths forward.

"You're right Neal," Justice says. "We need to stay aware and vigilant and look at all our options and not take unnecessary risks. We need to be smart about it, but I think Lana is also right, it's too late to back off. Our enemies are going to try and destroy us. I think our best strategy is to move aggressively forward. Dash for the finish line.

Finally, as Justice and Neal fight off sleep, Lana holds her glass high, and toasts, "To the world we want to live in!"

Upon arriving back at the charter terminal, Neal takes the key given to him by the pilot and opens the locker and retrieves their phones. Justice checks her massages and sees that Miguel has called several times and left a voice mail. She retrieves the message: "Justice, it's Miguel. I'm assuming you've heard the news about Hogwood and Dahl? Call me back as soon as you can."

Justice returns the call. "Miguel, how are you? What news about Hogwood and Dahl? I've been out of the country and didn't get your message."

"Hi, Justice, well, they've both resigned."

"What, you're kidding, why?"

"Apparently, a congressional oversight committee launched an investigation into corrupt practices, and they became targets. Rumors are that Hogwood has maybe flipped and is cooperating with investigators against Dahltech," Miguel says.

"Oh my god!" Justice exclaims.

"Yeah, and Dahltech is suing everybody and trying to make the case they're being set up."

"Wow, that's so interesting, somebody must have talked," Justice says.

"Listen, I've got to run right now, but let's stay in touch on this," Miguel says.

"Yes, for sure," Justice replies. "I'll let you know if I hear anything."

Chapter 27

THE CAMPAIGN

The Presidential Election

To move the amendments out of congress and send them to the states for ratification, Whole Earth Justice will need to collect 67 of 100 senate votes, and 288 out of 435 house votes, plus a presidential signature. Then 38 legislatures of the 50 states must ratify the amendments. A tall order for any proposition—and even more in an era of deep pollical polarization. The last proposed amendment to pass and become part of the US Constitution (twenty-seventh) was ratified by the required number of states in 1992—after 202 years of trying. Many amendments are proposed every congressional session. Very few ever make it out of congressional committees and onto the floor for a vote, much less generate the supermajority support needed to pass congress and land on the president's desk.

Three weeks after the midterm election the top people from each of the state's WEJ movement met for a strategy meeting in a hotel in Denver, Colorado. Zip Dodson was hired by WEJ to help with strategy for the campaign. During the first joint meeting with people from every state in attendance, Zip was on hand to lead the participants through an analysis of where they were and what had happened in the midterms.

"Well, I'll say this for you," Zip says, walking out on stage. "You've successfully gotten the establishment's attention."

Cheers ring out through the hall.

"The bad news is, WEJ leadership has informed me that they want us to do more! They tell me that they intend for us to change the world, for the better. The good news is, they are highly confident we can do it, thanks to your efforts, and we are all to dedicate whatever resources it's going to take, for as long as it's going to take to get the job done. We're going to change the world!" Zip shouts.

An eruption of clapping yelling and the stomping of thousands of feet.

"While I'm confident of our eventual success," Zip continues, "we will need to be realistic in our expectations and strategies. To that end, we've done a lot of number crunching since the election three weeks ago and the results are both encouraging and the task in front of us daunting. As you will see from the materials you were handed upon entering the room, we are going to split you into several groups.

"The first are what we're calling 'yes, yes' states. These are states where the population polled significantly 'yes' and the state's congressional delegation is a majority 'yes.' The second, group are the 'yes, no' states, where the people say yes, but the delegation says no or is mixed. Third are the 'no, yes' states, where politicians are out in front of the voters. And fourth are the 'no, no' states, where the population and the delegations were both no.

"A different set of strategies is appropriate for each category of state. You'll get specific plans for your state in the breakout sessions but in general the strategy remains the same, change the constituency, and get the politicians to follow them, or replace them. The math is clear," Zip says. "To win we need to deliver 80 percent of the delegation votes in group one, the 'yes, yes' states. In group 2, we need 70 percent. In group 3, we need 60 percent. And in group 4, we need 50 percent of the delegation's votes, and the election is now just over twenty-three months away. A tall order indeed. But we're going to do it, because we have to, the world needs changing now!"

Then they broke up into the corresponding groups from the states they were from. Each group had a discussion facilitator to help keep the discussion going down productive paths. They shared insights about their states seeking to uncover common issues and solutions as well as identify differences. They had analysis of every congressional district and of the congressman or woman in that seat and what their positions were.

In between breakout sessions, they have meetings where everybody is together to hear a speaker during a meal. Justice is standing outside the main ballroom where lunch is being served, and she's checking messages on her phone. A young woman walks up to her and waits patiently.

Justice says, "Hi, can I help you?"

She extends her hand and says, "My name is Wren, and I was a student in your Futurama class at Northrop that was almost shut down by the police."

"Oh, nice to meet you," she said, shaking her hand.

"I don't remember you, were you registered?"

"No, I audited the class so I'm not in the official rolls."

"You actually know me by another name," Wren says.

"Oh, what name?" Justice says curiously.

"You know me as Whistle-Blower!"

Now she has Justice's full attention.

"I tried to encourage you to contact me," Justice says.

"Yes, I know, and I understood the message, but I was afraid."

"Afraid of Jack Dahl?"

"Well, yes, but it's a little more complicated than that. You see I'm implicated as well," Wren says.

"What do you mean?"

"I worked in the lab and was in a position to know what was going on. I was offered and took a high-paying job at Dahltech. Anyway, over time I came to regret my silence. I convinced myself that because I wasn't directly involved in any wrongdoing, I was okay. Then I had a baby girl, and I became a member of WEJ, and I came to realize that I had a responsibility to the rest of society. We have a duty to participate in creating the world we want to live in. I want that world for myself and for my daughter. So eventually I contacted my congresswoman, who happens to sit on the House Oversight Committee and spilled the beans."

"I understand both Hogwood and Dahl have left the university and are gearing up to defend themselves in court, so it must have worked," Justice says.

"Yeah, but I'm not very proud of myself."

"Listen, we all make mistakes. The real test is doing what you're doing, correcting them," Justice says. Then she reaches into her purse and pulls out a business card and writes her personal number on it and says, "Do you have a lawyer?" Justice asks. "WEJ would like to help you if we can."

"No, I don't have a lawyer," Wren answers.

"Well, my guess is, you should. Guys like Jack Dahl will fight hard to preserve his power and he's probably not playing under the same ethical standards you are, so it could get bumpy," Justice advises.

Wren takes the card and says, "Thank you, Justice."

"You're welcome and be sure and let me know how we can help you," Justice exclaims.

At one of the consolidated lunch meetings, a speaker who was an operative during the LGBT movement spoke. He is introduced as James Camp.

"You probably don't know me," he said. "I operate in the background. I'm a lawyer and I was a member of a team during the gender orientation justice campaigns that would be called in to deal with problems that arose. Problems like disinformation campaigns. Problems like charges or allegations being leveled at operations people or candidates. False flag operations and worse. I can tell you that I know the people working behind the scenes on the other side, and they will not go down without a fight—a dirty fight. You will be surprised at the direct and blatant lying. Don't be. You will be surprised at the sophistication and efforts they put into disinformation. Don't be. You will be surprised at the cruelty and utter disregard they show toward people that are in their way. Don't be. We're here to win, and we're going to win, but the task of winning isn't made any easier by naivete. We need to be prepared and we need to act. The best way to do that is to work closely with my special operations team. We want to know about curious phone calls and suspicious meetings. We want you to get in the habit of journaling what happened during the day and recording meeting notes. And we want you to take another person with you to meetings. And above all, keep us involved. We're here to protect you. Now, I know that many of you already knew all of that and are experienced, but it bares reviewing it. Thank you."

If those messages sounded a little overly paranoid in the meeting that day, less than a day later, they seemed prophetic.

The CEO of a large American oil and gas company was leaving after giving testimony at a house oversight committee in Washington, DC, when a group of people wearing Pussy Riot ski masks and underwear on the outside that said "Pussy Riot" on them attacked the target's bodyguards and kidnapped the executive. The whole incident was caught on cellphone cameras of people nearby. Two hours later several members of the press corps received text messages from burner phones telling them where they could find the victim, who they claimed was safely restrained. The reporters informed the police and proceeded to the location designated. It was a warehouse and inside was the victim bound and gagged but otherwise healthy with a note pinned to his chest. The handwritten note said, "Vote Yes!"

A short time later a Whole Earth Justice spokesperson and Lana hold a press conference. Lana denies any involvement by Pussy Riot. "Our people are under strict instructions to never engage in violence or crimes beyond civil disobedience. If you see someone doing that as Pussy Riot activists, they are opposition forces doing false flag operations. Don't fall for it. We do not operate that way. We are a nonviolent organization that educates the public about people's bad behavior." The problem with these kinds of incidents is that they work to a degree. The people who are already supportive of the movement believe in the denial, and the people who are against tend to not believe, but there are always a few undecideds in the middle who can be moved either way.

In this case the special operations forces with the WEJ movement track down who had supplied the videotape to the media and police. While they say they are just there by coincidence, they have extensive ties to people on the "No" campaign. It is clearly a false flag operation run by the "No" campaign special operations people. The "Yes" campaign gathers the evidence and feed it to a reporter to do a story about, which they did. Despite the clear evidence it is a false flag operation, the damage has been done. To prevent it from happening again, the Pussy Riot people create a photo and identification directory of every member and gives the police and FBI access to it. They also develop and present an information campaign talking about the Pussy Riot rules. No hats, directories, and IDs and every action is filmed by Pussy Riot themselves.

In March, with about eight months to go before the next election the president is being primaried from within his own party, as well as being challenged from the democratic opposition, congressional hearings are called to investigate the kidnapping of the oil executive and the WEJ movement's activities as well as that of the opposition. In addition to their efforts to impede the WEJ progress within state delegations, the opposition's overall strategy has become clear to Justice and the rest of the movement's managers: to create chaos and discord in every way possible. Associate the yes side with that chaos and then present the no side as the reasonable adults. That strategy places Whole Earth Justice in a very vulnerable position and makes Pussy Riot a potential huge liability for them. Regardless of whether it is deserved or not, Pussy Riot has a reputation as disrupters and that feeds into the narrative being promoted by the opposition. And the Russian origins of Pussy Riot doesn't help either. The congressional hearings have become a battle ground for both sides with angry pro and con speeches being made on each side of the issue.

Lana from Pussy Riot is called to testify at the hearings. She is such a controversial figure that her performance is seen as critical to both sides in the debate. If she comes off as an anarchist, she will do tremendous damage to the WEJ movement, Justice thought. On the other hand, if she comes off as a smart and courageous change agent seeking justice who stood up to Putin, she might benefit the cause. Some within the WEJ movement are putting pressure on Justice to denounce and distance herself and the movement from Pussy Riot and Lana. Neal is among the voices who caution Justice and suggest she should distance herself from Lana. Justice is the kind of person that once she's decided, additional pressure just makes her more intrenched and resistant. In one angry exchange, Justice asks

Neal if he will someday abandon her when it becomes expedient! Immediately upon saying it, Justice realizes it is unfair and regrets saying it, but the damage has been done.

The congressional hearings have become a daily prime time event. Coverage is wall to wall, including live telecasts of some of the more controversial witnesses. So far, the hearings have mostly produced grand standing speeches by congressmen on both sides of the issues. The media have played up the potential testimony of Lana, even though congress have very little leverage to compel her testimony. She isn't a US citizen and doesn't live in the country. Despite that, the opposition feels it is worthwhile to invite her to testify. If she shows, they feel they could make her look like a foreign subversive and they can paint the whole WEJ movement with the same brush. If she fails to show, they will claim the same thing and say she is afraid to show and be exposed. Justice and Lana have several conversations in which they both decide that it will be best if Lana does not testify and instead put out a press release reinforcing Pussy Riot's nonviolent message and policy and then stay out of site for a while. As a result, it is a total surprise when Lana suddenly appears at the hearing chamber and says she wants to testify.

"Ms. Kazakov," the congressman starts, "thank you for coming to testify today."

"Yes, you're welcome," Lana says.

"You are one of the leaders of an activist group called Pussy Riot, isn't that correct?" the congressman says.

"Yes, that correct," Lana responds.

"Do you have a statement to present to this committee before asking you some questions?"

"Yes, I do, Congressman," Lana says in a calm voice.

"Please proceed," the congressman says.

She looks for a moment like she's confused, then she pulls an eight-by-ten photo from her papers and holds it up to the camera.

"This boy is six years old. His name is Victor Andreaeve, and he is my son. He lives in London at 167 Downing Street with his caregiver, Salena Guyevski. They are at this moment being held hostage by forces aligned with Vladimir Putin to compel testimony from me

at this hearing, that Pussy Riot and the Whole Earth Justice organizations have conspired to terrorize and disrupt the nation to get
these amendments passed. That is not the case. My son's father has
already been killed and I believe my testimony here today could very
likely result in my own murder as well. If my son and his caregiver are
found dead or missing, you will know who the opposition is. If they
are alive, I am asking officials in London to immediately take my son
and his caregiver into protective custody."

The hearing room explodes with noise as reporters scramble
in the back of the room. The chairman pounds the gavel. "Order,
order, come to order!" The room quiets and the chairman asks Lana
a question. "Ms. Kazakov, when you refer to the opposition of these
amendments, who are you referring to?"

"It's a petrol cartel made up of large oil interests, including some
oil-producing countries as well as some large international petroleum
companies and individuals," Lana says.

"And Vladimir Putin is part of this group?" the congressman
asks.

"Yes," Lana says.

"And why would he do such a thing, Ms. Kazakov?"

"Because his power and that of the others is maintained through
oil and gas revenues," Lana responds.

"And how do these amendments relate to the oil and gas industry?" the congressman asks.

"If these amendments pass, the petrol cartel will lose their ability to control oil and gas policies in the US and around the world."

The chairman of the committee then looks around at his colleagues and sees no one interested in asking questions. "Ms. Kazakov,
thank you for your testimony, we have no further questions at this
time. Committee adjourned," the congressman says.

Immediately after her testimony, Lana goes directly from the
hearing room to the British Consulate in Washington, DC, and asks
for asylum and to be placed under protective custody by the British
government. Within thirty minutes of her testimony before the committee, there is video of the British authorities taking the young boy
and his caregiver into custody. There is no sign that they were being

held by anyone. A short time later Vladimir Putin does a press conference and announces that there is no petrol cartel working in opposition to American amendment proposals. That they have not been involved in any killings or hostage taking or activities of any kind as was alleged. Lastly, that Russia considers Svetlana Kazakov a terrorist and anarchist and that the British government has an obligation to prosecute her for her crimes against civilization, but Russia is not involved. The whole incident was shocking and very dramatic TV. Polls several days after the incident reveal that the incident changes few minds, but that it has the effect of hardening people's preincident positions.

Speculation about Lana and the kidnapping allegations are international news for days. Talk shows in the UK and the United States are filled with people speculating and giving their opinions on the incident. Some people of course think that Lana made the whole thing up. Others thought she is right, and the Russians stand down and call off the kidnapping because of the testimony. About ten days after the incident, the police in the UK announce they have discovered sophisticated surveillance equipment in the apartment where the boy and his nanny live.

Justice apologizes to Neal for her angry outburst during the debate about how to handle Lana, and Neal says he understands, but things have definitely cooled off in their relationship.

About six weeks after the congressional testimony incident, Justice receives another message from Father Dimitri at the church, asking if she can stop by again. Wanting to engage with Neal, she asks him to walk down to the church with her.

"Neal, Justice, how are you?" Father Dimitri says.

Neal says, "Fine."

Justice says, "I'm stubborn and demanding and hard to work with and I regularly alienate those closest to me!"

Father Dimitri and Neal would be shocked except they've both seen this kind of confession from Justice before. They all just sit silently, not knowing how to react.

Then Father Dimitri says, "Neal, do you agree with what Justice says?"

Neal waits a moment and then says, "Yes, but it isn't the way she thinks."

Neal faces Justice and says, "It's like being in love with a base jumper or a mountain climber who insists on going without a safety harness. Everything is about right or wrong, black or white with you. Well, most of us don't get to live in that world. Most of us see lots of gray and lots of risk. Many of us, including people who love you, live in a more complicated world than you do, and it's hard for us to watch you."

"Thank you for telling me," Justice says. I will try and do a better job of seeing the nuance and listening to other points of view, but," she says, pausing, "maybe some of your own ambiguity comes from your own aversion to making commitments that would close out other options. Sometimes you must decide, or you risk losing everything."

Neal says, "Nothing," but reaches over and gives her a hug and says, "It will work out."

"Thank you, Father," Neal says as they head for the door.

"Oh, Justice, I almost forgot, I asked you to come for a reason."

"What is it, Father?"

He reaches into his robe pocket and pulls out a ten of clubs and hands it to her. On the back side, he's written an international phone number. Then Father Dimitri says, "You can get a burner phone and call her at this number."

"But how…" Justice is shocked.

"Remember, get a burner phone," Father Dimitri says.

"Thank you," Justice responds.

"Yes, thank you, Father," Neal says.

Justice and Neal walk home. "Thank you for saying what you said, Neal, and I meant what I said. I'm going to be more…ah… deliberative and more open!"

Neal laughs and says, "I know you'll try, Justice, thank you."

When they get home, Justice jumps on her bike and heads to the store to buy a burner phone and call Lana.

She dials the number and a voice she doesn't recognize answers, "Hello."

"Ah, this is Justice Miller I'm calling—"

Hang on please.

"Justice, is that you?"

"Yes, Lana, how are you? Oh my gosh, are you and your son safe?"

"Yes, we are guests of the United Kingdom secret service for now."

"How did this all happen?" Justice asks.

"Well, I wasn't going to testify as we had decided, then two nights before the committee hearing, I get a call from a Russian agent. He told me that I should testify and say that WEJ and Pussy Riot were involved with terrorist activities. He then told me where my son and his nanny live."

"Oh my, Lana."

"So I had no choice but to go and testify. They clearly had my son under surveillance. But in thinking about it, I decided that if I disclosed and asked for the UK government to intervene, that might produce the best chance for my son. So that's what I did. We are safe for now, but I don't know how or when this will end."

"Well, you probably saved your son and WEJ," Justice says.

"Well, but we might be trapped here forever though too," Lana says.

"I'm sure things will change in time," Justice says, "and in the meantime, you're safe."

"Yes," Lana acknowledges.

"Will I be able to visit you or call again?" Justice says.

"I don't know. I guess it's all up to intelligence security people, I guess. I'm sure we will need to contact you and give you instructions like this time."

"Yeah, speaking of that, you know Father Dimitri."

"Who? No, I don't think so," Lana responds.

"Well, he's where I got the number and the ten of clubs," Justice says.

"No, I don't think I know him. He must be connected to foreign intelligence or something?"

"Amazing," Justice says.

"Well, take care, Lana, and let me know when we can talk again, or if I can help in any way."

"Thank you, Justice, ten of clubs out."

Chapter 28

NEW COALITIONS

Things seem to settle into a more typical campaign for a while. The WEJ committee continually updates their information on each candidate, particularly the candidates or congressional districts they consider swing or on the bubble. Their research suggests they have a ways to go but are within striking distance if things go well in the upcoming election cycle. WEJ endorses the Democratic front-runner for president who came out for the amendments. On the Republican side there is a dramatic primary challenge to the first-term Republican president. The challenger has come out in favor of the amendments and the president was a definitive NO! The WEJ would have been willing to endorse the Republican challenger in the primary, but the candidate asked that they not do so.

With six weeks to go before the election, as they approach the October surprise season, the WEJ movement is feeling guardedly optimistic. The polls indicate the WEJ movement and the yes side was up slightly nationally, as well as taking the lead in a number of critical state delegations. The subject of the amendments and the politician's positions on them are being discussed in town hall meetings and in election debates all over the country. The amendments have caused the entire electorate to be scrambled. It no longer means anything to describe constituents with the old labels of progressive or conservative. There is a sizable faction of the conservative base that is pro-amendments and a part of the traditional progressive base that was opposed to them.

Polling suggests that the conservative base is being reshaped because less educated social conservatives are splitting from the establishment financial conservatives. This group of social conservatives sees the health care and education amendment as positive developments and they generally think the campaign finance amendment is positive too. These blue-collar social conservatives have always felt the system is rigged against them; they just don't like the idea of siding with abortionists, or homosexuals, or social engineers, or second amendment deniers to get there. Lastly, the arguments made by the Just Compensation amendment designed to get a fair return on public investments also resonated. It speaks directly to this idea that the system is rigged against them. It's one thing to say we need to take money from one group and give it to another; it feels unfair; in fact, it feels like social engineering which they hate because from their perspective those types of policies give groups of "others'" advantages at their expense. Affirmative action being a classic and clear example. But the Just Compensation amendment says something different from other attempts at wealth redistribution. The Just Compensation amendment affirms something they already believe, that they are being ripped off by the elite establishment that is stealing resources owned by all of us and not paying a fair price for them. The amendments confirm that the system is rigged against them, do something about it, and don't touch on any of the hot-button social issues that motivate them. They also like the amendment process itself; it feels like grassroots action or a revolution, and it's carried out at the expense of the establishment, which they love.

This coalition scramble is taking place on the progressive side as well. The traditional progressive coalition includes a lot of very successful people. Limousine liberals, they used to be called. This group is progressive on the same social issues that motivated the blue-collar social conservatives, but in the opposite way. They think gay people should have all the same rights as straight people. They think abortion is a moral judgment that should be made by the mother and her doctors and counselors, and they feel embarrassed at the level of gun violence in our society. They have lots of money and they don't mind paying taxes provided it gets spent wisely, but they don't like that the amendments take away their ability to influence the system with campaign finance reforms, and they don't like the idea of a greatly increased estate tax that prevents them from passing on nearly all their wealth.

Another interesting divergence from orthodoxy is women. Women of all ages, all backgrounds, all races, all geographic distinctions, both urban and suburban. Women universally like the idea that the WEJ movement is led by women and the amendments are based on improving government and making it more responsive to a broad constituency rather than deferring to establishment interests.

In the end, the amendments campaign is uniting constituency groups who have been successfully separated through years of derisive politics. For the first time in years, blue-collar northeast union liberals find themselves in league with white southern blue-collar social conservatives. What the amendments campaign is effectively doing is carving out a new coalition consisting of lower- and middle-class people from both coalitions and putting them in conflict with wealthy interests from both the progressive and conservative coalitions.

The WEJ team's analysis show that they are close to getting the percentages they needed from the state delegation groups—80 percent from the "yes, yes" group, 70 percent from the "yes, no" group, 60 percent from the "no, yes" group, and 50 percent from the "no, no" group. Most of the politicians who are holding out against a pro-amendment constituency have drawn tough opponents and are fighting to keep their jobs.

Among the toughest states are the oil states of Texas and Oklahoma. One of the key senate races is in Texas where a long-time senator, who has traditionally taken a lot of money from big oil, has switched his position and come out in favor of the amendments. Big oil turns on him immediately and fields both a Republican primary challenger and supports a Democratic challenger for the general election. They are also running relentless negative ads trying to unseat the senator. The WEJ side doesn't cower, however; they step in with their own institutional ads supporting the amendments and the incumbent. It is one of the few races where the pro-amendment side is supporting a Republican incumbent over a Democratic challenger who has declared himself to be anti-amendment. As a result of the weird party splitting, the race has become national news. It becomes even more so when the challenger accuses the incumbent of campaign finance violations within a debate. With ten days to go before the election, the Texas population is running at about 55 percent pro-amendment and 45 percent against. The senate race is about the same with the pro-amendment Republican incumbent with a tiny amount of momentum and polling at 51 percent. Then the unthinkable happened, the senator's small plane flies into a storm and goes down on his way to a campaign rally. Three people in the plane die and two remain in critical condition in the hospital. The senator is among the dead. The whole country is shocked. A memorial service is quickly organized and broadcast live. One of the survivors is the copilot of the plane and from his hospital bed claims they had told the senator's staff they shouldn't fly because of weather conditions, and the campaign staff had insisted that they go.

The Republican Party quickly fields a retired former governor to run in the senator's place who is anti-amendments, but it is too late. As a gesture to reach out to a shocked electorate, the Democratic challenger agrees to revisit the amendment issues once he is in office. That statement along with very effusive statements about the deceased senator seals his election. Election Day goes smoothly all over the country with one exception. Charges of voter suppression efforts designed to restrict the voting rights of blue-collar and middle-class voters in both parties are charged. Many people from both parties show up at the polls to vote and discover that they have been expunged from the voter rolls for some unknown reason and will need to reregister and vote with a provisional ballet. The president is defeated and becomes a one-term administration, and the post-election analysis shows the pro-amendment side prevails and likely has enough to pass the amendments out of congress and on to the states for ratification.

The votes on the amendments are scheduled as one of the first acts of the new congress after they are sworn in and seated. The vote takes place at the very end of January in both houses and goes to the president's desk. The new president signs it in front of a large press pool at the White House, the first week in February. It is a historic occasion. The WEJ movement quickly organizes a national celebration of the accomplishment and a kickoff for the campaign ahead to get the amendments ratified by 75 percent of the states. The celebration is scheduled for early June in Washington, DC, and will include entertainment provided by many famous entertainers and speeches on the mall. After the February signing by the president, several states want to be the first state in the union to ratify the amendments. Minnesota wins the competition and becomes the first state in the union to ratify the amendments. In the four-plus months between signing by the president and the celebration in Washington, DC, twenty states ratify the amendments, leaving just eighteen to go to reach the 75 percent threshold to have the Constitution of the United States amended.

The mood that day in early June is ecstatic across the country at big rallies in all fifty states—75,000 people in Cheyenne; 175,000 in Lincoln, Nebraska; 350,000 in Birmingham; 550,000 in Indianapolis; and even bigger crowds in some traditionally blue states. The amendment struggle has taken on a historic feel. Everybody knows about it and everybody has opinions. As a result, there are concerts broadcast from all over the country. It has a New Year's Eve kind of vibe as the cable coverage bounces from city to city, watching entertainers perform and being interviewed by TV news personalities. The themes people expressed are many and varied, but they all echo similar themes—the future, the environment, the dignity of humanity.

As the celebration moves toward completion, Justice takes the stage. But this time rather than deliver the speech herself, she introduces Karen as a member of the wisdom council and a great friend of Whole Earth Justice. Karen delivers the address.

To paraphrase President Ronald Reagan, Karen begins,

You can go to France to live, but you cannot become a Frenchman. You can go to live in Germany or Turkey, but you won't become a German or a Turk. But anybody, from any corner of the world, can come to America to live and become an American. Because America, at its core, is an ideal.

"America is an ideal!

"It was certainly an ideal for our founding fathers. A group of mostly successful, middle-aged men who put everything they had, including their lives on the line for an idealistic idea—liberty to pursue one's own happiness, equality before the law, and the democratic principle of one man, one vote.

"They certainly heard the taunts and fears from concerned friends and family: Idealism opens you up to risks and makes you vulnerable! Idealism is not your responsibility! The path to success is not assured. Idealism is foolish! They did not expect the path to be easy, and it wasn't. But they had faith that their ideals were right. They were just. They were worth fighting for. And they had faith that providence could be counted on.

"The messages, experiences, and resources supporting the enlightenment had been building within society for a long time, and the timing was right. Our forefathers did not cower at the challenge presented by their ideals. They did not hedge their bets. They chose to be vulnerable idealists. They chose to accept the yoke of history and not pass the responsibility on to another generation. They chose idealism in the belief of democracy. And they did so without the ability to predict the events that would be required to succeed.

"Today we live in a similar time of great choices. Choices between idealism and fears. Between idealism and progress, and life for humanity into the future or safety and conflict avoidance for a few of us today. Our choice, like that of the founders of this great nation, turns on the very definition of who and what we are.

"If we are but individuals, living a life defined by our physiological boundaries, it is one answer. But if we are in fact part of something greater than ourselves, as our forefathers decided we were, something that transcends our time and singular nature, then it could be another choice. An idealistic choice. A choice to do what is right, over what is expedient.

"Today the amendments we seek, to this glorious Constitution, will not solve climate change. They will not cure our racial or social divisions. They will not make the world an equitable place. But they will give us and future generations the tools and opportunities we need to make those things manifest, if we so choose, and the events of providence continue to shine upon us.

"So when concerned friends and family tell you that your being foolish to be idealistic, when they say your opening yourself up unnecessarily to risks and it's not your responsibility, and when they tell you that you cannot afford to trust, and that the game is played by seeking advantages over others, you will share something with our founding fathers, a choice between idealism and fear. Between a broad and narrow definition of humanity.

"No, idealism is not foolish, it's necessary, and it's mine and your responsibility now! Now let's get these amendments ratified and change the world!

"Thank you and God bless America!"

Chapter 29

POISON

The day of the Whole Earth Justice rally in Washington, DC, is a long one for Justice. After Karen's speech receives a thunderous response, Neal gives Justice a hug and kiss.

"You did a great thing by sharing the stage with Karen today."

"Well, thank you, but this whole thing has never been about me," Justice says.

Both Justice and Neal snake through the crowd shaking hands and receiving high-fives. Many receptions, celebrations and meetings with key public officials and funders are on tap for the evening, so Neal and Justice split up to cover more ground. As WEJ's leading spokesperson, Justice is in high demand. She dashes from event to event, making a few remarks, thanking people for their support, emphasizing the need for humanity to work together for a brighter future and then closing with "Do unto others as you would have them do unto you!" and its modern interpretation "To save ourselves, we must save the others. To save the others, we must free ourselves!"

Neal, on the other hand, is wrapped up in a series of strategy sessions about how to translate today's success in the streets across America to votes in state legislatures.

As Justice scoots out of the final party at the AFL-CIO headquarters, she calls Neal, "Where are you, babe?"

"I'm just finishing up here at the Hilton, I think it's the Hilton. How about if I meet you back at the room in about forty-five minutes?"

"Okay, that sounds good, I'll see you there, I'm on my way over there now."

Twenty minutes later, Neal springs into the room he calls out, "Sweetheart, you won't believe who I just heard from…"

Justice is lying on the carpet and appears to be unconscious.

"OMG! Justice! Justice!"

No response. He quickly calls 911 and throws open the door of the room and yells, "Help!"

The emergency dispatcher's voice comes on the phone and directs in a calm but pressing voice, "See if she's breathing."

"Yes, I think so."

"Is there any sign of trauma, blood or anything?"

"No."

Neal is cradling her head and trying to rouse her. "Justice, wake up, please wake up!"

People begin to gather at the doorway.

Soon the emergency team arrives. They check her vital signs and lift her onto a gurney for transport to the hospital. She still has not awoken.

In the ambulance, the paramedics quiz Neal as they monitor Justice's condition.

"Do you know how long it's been since she has eaten?"

"No, I wasn't with her."

"Is she allergic to anything?"

"No, not that I know of."

She is quickly admitted to the hospital, where they administer a stream of tests to try to understand what's going on.

"Did she have a stroke or something?" Neal asks.

"She appears responsive but we don't know anything yet," answers one of the ER nurses. "You're the boyfriend, right?"

"Yes."

"But you weren't with her when this happened?"

"No, I found her on the floor when I arrived."

"Do you have any idea how long before you discovered her?"

"I talked to her on the phone about forty-five minutes before I arrived."

"It would be helpful if you would wait in the waiting area," the nurse says. "We will let you know the second we know something."

About fifteen minutes later, a doctor comes into the waiting area and says, "She appears to have been poisoned."

"Poisoned, by what?"

"We don't know but we've called in experts from the CDC as well as the Pentagon," she says.

"The Pentagon," Neal says in shock.

"Yes, this has some of the characteristics of a chemical weapons attack of some kind. Come with me, you're going to have to be quarantined until we can know for certain you're not infected as well. It's for your own protection. Until we find the source and understand what this is, we must be very careful." Then the doctor asks, "Was she in conflict with anyone, any arguments or major disagreements?"

Neal looks at the doctor, a short Asian woman, trying to process what the doctor is asking him.

"Yes," Neal says in a weary voice.

"Who?" the doctor responds.

"Well, we have lots of enemies, we're part of a movement called Whole Earth Justice."

"And who are the enemies, you're speaking of?"

"I mean potentially, oil and gas or coal companies, big business executives, Russia, Middle Eastern petrol states, right- or left-wing fanatics. I think it could be a long list."

"Have you been threatened by anyone?"

"Not directly as far as I know."

"Okay, well, we're going to do tests on you. You will need to remain in a clean environment and isolated from other people. I will be needing to go through the same thing until I am cleared as well. And so will the paramedics and the people who were standing in the hotel hallway."

"Can I sit with Justice again, just for a minute?"

"Not now, I would guess it's going to take a while."

"Doctor, is she going to make it?"

She grasps his hand. "I hope so. We are going to do everything we can."

That was the last conversation Neal had with someone not in a hazmat suit for about twelve hours. And none of them seemed to know much about Justice, except that she was still alive and that the medical team was hopeful.

Early afternoon the next day a doctor comes in for the first time without a hazmat and says, "I'm Dr. Walters with the CDC. You've been cleared."

"Thank you, Doctor, is Justice still unconscious?"

"Yes, but her scans are coming back well. She has brain functions. Dr. Yeung is monitoring her case from the CDC. She's an expert in poisoning, and she's optimistic about Justice's recovery."

"Do they have any idea what this is?"

"Well, they do have an idea. They believe she was attacked with a chemical weapon. It's in a class of weapons that disables and often kills the victim by shutting down the nervous system. We have administered a serum designed to mitigate the effects of the toxin."

"When do they expect her to wake up?"

"They don't know, it could be soon, or it could last quite a while."

"And will she be okay?"

"We think so. She appears to be functioning normally, but really won't know for sure until she wakes up and we can do an evaluation. It's a good thing you found her as soon as you did. Time is of the essence in this kind of situation."

"Thank you, Doctor, when can I see her?"

"Hopefully later on today. In the meantime, there are some military investigators here that want to ask you a few questions."

Two men and a woman dressed in olive-green scrubs introduce themselves as doctors who work in military intelligence specializing in chemical weapons. They get right to the heart of the matter.

"Do you have any contact with people from a former Soviet state? Russia, Ukraine, Belarus, etc."

"Yes, we're friends with Svetlana Kazakov. She's a member of the dissident Russian group called Pussy Riot. She has powerful enemies in Russia. We may have many enemies there as well. We are both connected with a group called Whole Earth Justice."

They look at each other, and then one explains, "The chemical agent that appears to have been used is similar to a nerve gas from the WWI era. It is still manufactured in organized crime labs in Russia and perhaps in North Korea and other places. It's still used because it's easy to manufacture and transport in small amounts."

"Do you know how she was exposed to it?"

"No, we've swept the whole hotel and found no trace."

"We've also tracked down her Uber driver from last night and discussed what happened and searched his car for any trace of it. There can also be a delay in symptoms depending on dose and method of attack."

"Well, before she got home, she was with hundreds of thousands of people."

"Yes, we know."

"And no one else has shown up with symptoms?" Neal asks.

"No, not yet."

"Can I go to be with Justice now?"

"Yes, the quarantine has been lifted. We just needed to make sure there wasn't still an ongoing threat of transmission."

"I understand," Neal says.

Neal walks into Justice's room and sits down on the chair next to the bed.

He grabs her hand and says "I love you" to her but sees no reaction.

A few minutes later Justice's parents walk into the room, dragging suitcases. They've come directly from the airport.

Neal jumps up and throws his arms around Matt and Emma at the same time.

"How is she?" they ask.

"She seems to have brain function, the doctor says, so they're hoping she will just spontaneously come out of the coma, but they have no idea when that could be. The doctor who first saw her is an expert on chemical poisoning and is in constant contact with the care team."

"What happened? Matt asks.

"We don't know for sure. But they think there is a possibility that it was a deliberate chemical weapon attack on her."

"Oh my god, who would do such a thing?" Matt says.

"Because of the particular poison used. They're focused on people connected to Russia."

"Russia, but why?" Matt asks.

"They don't know but speculation is that it's an enemy of the WEJ movement, maybe a Russian oil company or even Putin's government."

Neal notices that Justice's father is carrying a tattered copy of a book called *The Dandelion Insurrection*.

Everyone sits down, and after a few minutes of silence, Matt says, "We are so proud of the work, Justice, and you are doing. It was such a great speech Karen gave."

Neal smiles for the first time in what seems like forever and says, "Yes, she was. Justice was supposed to give the speech, but she gave it to Karen. I'll tell you something, she did a lot for internal politics at WEJ by doing that," Neal says.

Matt and Emma tell Neal that they're going to go check into the hotel. "We've been up all night," Matt adds. "Camera crews were camped out on our front lawn, hoping that we had some news about Justice. Washington Police hustled us out of National Airport before the reporters could get us, and we rode here in a squad car with siren blaring."

"We will be back soon to spell you, Neal," Emma says.

"Sure, come back when you can, but I'm planning on staying right here," Neal says.

"I understand," Matt says. "Neal, did you ever hear the story about this book?"

"No, I don't think so," Neal responds.

Matt says, "Well, as you know, there were lots of complications with the pregnancy and Justice was born very premature. But before she was born, we spent about ten days in the hospital trying to hold off the birth as long as possible before they had to go in and fix a brain aneurysm that had developed in Emma. It was a very dicey situation because if E's aneurysm burst, it would threaten them both. Justice was right on the edge of viability, and they wanted to hold off as long as possible, before doing the Cesarean birth. Those were tough days waiting, and Bill, my dad, suggested that I read to Justice in utero while we were all waiting for her. It was probably more for my own good than hers, but I got this book down at the bookstore and started reading to her. I felt a little silly reading to my wife's stomach, but I did it anyway. The book happened to be about a grassroots movement for social justice, and a funny thing happened. When I read to her the nurses would notice changes in her activity level. So when she was finally born, I continued the practice of reading to her, particularly books about social justice. She seemed to be calmed down by it, and it made her a little stronger. So I read book after book to her staying with the social justice theme. So we named her Justice."

"Thanks, Matt, she never told me that story. But I can see the book made a lasting impression on her. Do you mind if I look at it?" Neal asks.

Matt hands the book to Neal and he reads the back cover.

After Matt and E leave, Neal remembers that he had grabbed Justice's purse when they wheeled her out of the hotel room, thinking he might need an ID or cellphone or insurance card or something. It was sitting in the corner of her hospital room. Neal gets up and opens it and looks inside. There was a big paperback with a picture of a beefcake type of guy on a horse. Obviously, a romantic novel of some type.

Well, if that's what she wants to be reading these days, who am I to judge? he thinks. *She might need a break from social justice.* So over the course of the next ten days, Neal stays at Justice's side reading romantic novels. He sleeps in the big recliner in the room and only leaves long enough to eat and take a shower.

And then it just happened. Neal was seated at the side of the bed in the middle of the night reading about a knight and a princess embracing in the middle of a deep forest when she opens her eyes and looks at him. He stops reading, looks deeply into her face to make sure this is not a hallucination, and says, "I love you, Justice. Will you marry me?"

Justice smiles and nods, signaling yes.

Neal gets up and walks over to his bag and pulls out a small decorative sack from a jewelry store. In it are two boxes. He opens one and produces a diamond engagement ring. A simple gold band with a large brilliant diamond. He places it on her finger. Justice is unable to speak, but her eyes are large and wet with emotion and her chin quivers. Neal then opens the second box. In it is a custom-designed bracelet.

"It's a representation of the golden rule," he tells her. "On one side is a single bead representing ourselves as individuals," Neal explains. "On the other side is a group of brightly colored beads representing the others."

In between are two sterling silver metal plates. On one it says, "To save ourselves, we must save the others." On the other it says, "To save the others, we must free ourselves."

"It represents your grandfather Bill's journey as well as your own, and the aspirations and solutions for humanity," Neal explains as he places it on her wrist.

Chapter 30

THE BEGINNING

Finally, alone in her hotel room after a long day of campaign stops, Justice collapses into a large chair, puts her feet up on the ottoman, and kicks off her shoes. She feels physically and mentally exhausted but spiritually energized and grateful. As she often does, Justice thinks about her grandfather Bill. How her grandparents and her parents and many others along the way guided her along the path she's now following. On the table is a WEJ-branded backpack, and inside is a new copy of Bill's "My Big TOE" notebook, which was just published for the first time. Justice reaches over to pull out the book and opens it to the closing section, which she has read countless times since age twenty-two:

> **What I Believe (So Far)**
> Sometimes people ask me if I believe in God. I always give the same answer. I have never attempted to prove or disprove the existence of God, because I have always believed in God. Through my life I have sought to gain a greater understanding of humanity and human civilization and those studies—along with the totality of my experience in life—has informed my perceptions as to the nature of reality and the intentions

of God. As I am in the final chapter of my life, I look forward to learning more soon.

Justice looks out the window at the trees budding and feels a wave of contentment, which is not a very frequent feeling for her. She continues reading.

> I find that my own speculations resonate with the pantheist community, who follow in the tradition of the great Jewish Dutch philosopher Baruch Spinoza (1632–1677), who viewed God and nature as two names for the same fundamental reality that underlies all existence. I also find myself echoing the teachings of the Jesuit priest Pierre Teilhard de Chardin (1881–1955), who perceives a direction and maturation of the human spirit toward a universal consciousness, or what he called the Cosmic Christ. De Chardin wrote of the unique human quality to apply synergy, which is our ability to add new energy to things, to counteract entropy, the natural state of decline and disorder. This quality makes us cocreators of our own reality.
>
> Through such pantheist ideas, I find it possible to reinterpret a great many of our wisdom traditions: For example, it is said repeatedly that Christ will return to judge the living and the dead. Maybe this is true by virtue of our own journey toward embodying the Cosmic Christ?
>
> Maybe the last supper and the Christian sacraments were not a promise from a deity to stay with his followers but instead a message of interdependence and a oneness to come?
>
> Maybe "do unto others, as you would have them do unto you" is more than just an ethic between individuals and reflects an underlying

reality in which "we" and the "others" are one in the same.

Perfect Oneness

If we look at the edges of Einstein's relativity theory, we see timelessness and infinite mass and power. *Perfect oneness.* If we look at the edge of *quantum mechanics,* we see all possibilities existing simultaneously. *Perfect oneness.* If we look at the construction of the universe itself, we see interconnected organization, in which each layer is made up of the materials from the layer beneath. *Perfect oneness.*

My Big TOE Is One

Perfect oneness is the who and the why we are. One gives context and meaning to God's love. One means all of us in unity. All of us in unity means love. Love means God, and God means one.

I remember thinking as a child, after I first observed the similarities between the seemingly endless scale of the universe and its design, with the design and scale of the atomic and subatomic worlds, both being made up of rotating orbs of various descriptions, *What if the whole universe existed within the Big TOE of God?*

Love, Bill Miller

After rereading Bill's final thoughts in the "My Big TOE" notebook, Justice grabs the "TOE 2" notebook from her bag and a pen from the dresser, turns the page to a blank sheet at the end, and begins to write:

Modern humans emerged from our predecessors two hundred thousand years ago. Based on our unique abilities and character, it was predictable that humanity would become the dominant species upon this planet. It was predictable that the human population would grow and flourish and consume greater and greater portions of the planet's bounty, placing increasing pressure on all other living species. So it's no surprise that our actions would someday tax the capability of the Earth to provide for us, and our very existence would be threatened. Nature is a self-regulating system that balances itself through boom-and-bust cycles of growth and destruction. To some, the existential nature of this story requires a spiritual context to have meaning. Often this idea is accompanied by feelings of guilt and unworthiness, with our survival dependent upon the grace of a loving God. But this is not the only way to understand our story.

Contrary to popular assertions, humanity is neither hopelessly selfish, irredeemably biased, or guilty of willful indifference. We have acted out our story with all the drama and courage and ineptitude and folly the path of our journey would allow, including incredible heights and unspeakable depths. Along the way we have learned that the entire universe, including life itself, is an interdependent construction. We've learned that dominion within an interdependent context is meaningless without stewardship and caring. We've learned we're capable of remarkable transformative change, when we act together and are motivated. We've learned that our most intractable problems require cooperation and greater interdependence to solve. We've learned that cooperation cannot happen without a sense of justice. We've learned that contrary to popular belief, forgiveness and love and care are innate to our nature.

God and Opportunity

I personally see God in quantum physics that requires a conscious observer before reality can transcend probability and manifest in a singular objective truth.

I see God in the values generated within the voids. Mozart's music is more than an inventory of notes; it's their arrangement within the void that gives the notes meaning. The same is true of Da Vinci's *Mona Lisa*—and everything else humans produce. It's not an inventory of elements; it's their arrangement within the void that gives the production meaning.

I see God in the notion that the big bang is not yet over. We, along with all reality is a product of and element in, that ongoing big bang explosion which is now some 13.7 billion years into its life. Since time and space are also products of that same ongoing event, we cannot be "other" to the singularity that the universe emanated from.

I see God in the enemies and forces of resistance that stimulate action and organization and commitment. It is through their actions that the forces of entropy are deferred and the meaningful struggle pursued. Easter is dependent upon Good Friday, Christ is dependent upon Judas, and a civilization's evolution into an interdependent whole is dependent upon the existential global threats that have brought us to this moment and to this choice—to live together or to die separately. The problems we face are not foreign, or mistimed, or impossibly difficult to deal with; they're the required elements in a journey that is asking us, all of us, to set aside our adolescent ways and mature into an interdependent body of life upon this planet. This is the time, we are the people, the path of our journey is clear.

I also see opportunity for those willing to embrace the power and values intrinsic to interdependence. Think for example of the economic values and wealth generation associated with the move to independence. The economic value of the development of the Americas. The economic values associated with all the outputs of the Industrial Revolutions and the values associated with all the democracies around the world and the innovation and creativity generated through enlightened self-interest. Add all that value up over five hundred years, and it is, but a small fraction of the potential represented by going from independence to interdependence. Would you except vastly greater wealth, if the only cost was that everyone else got it too?

It is the time in our story to overcome our fears and transcend our bigotries. Time to heal our injuries and forgive and care about the others. Interdependence is not impossible, overly optimistic, or foolish. It's the construction method underlying our reality and the destiny of humankind. Humanity can survive and even thrive but only as an interdependent member of the body of life upon this planet.

Due onto others, as you would have them due onto you—the golden rule.

To save ourselves, we must save the others; to save the others we must free ourselves—an interpretation of the golden rule for our time.

APPENDICES

Pope Francis's Encyclical Excerpts
Obama's Sustainable Development Goals speech at UN
Neal's Creed
Resources

The following passages are excerpts from Pope Francis's 2015 encyclical letter on ecology.

The earth herself, burdened and laid waste, is among the most abandoned and maltreated of our poor (2)

The pace of consumption, waste and environmental change has so stretched the planet's capacity that our contemporary lifestyle, unsustainable as it is, can only precipitate catastrophes, such as those which even now periodically occur in different areas of the world. (161)

True statecraft is manifest when, in difficult times, we uphold high principles and think of the long-term common good. (178)

Living our vocation to be protectors of God's handiwork is essential to a life of virtue; it is not an optional or a secondary aspect of our Christian experience. (217)

A great cultural, spiritual and educational challenge stands before us, and it will demand that we set out on the long path of renewal. (202)

The climate is a common good, belonging to all and meant for all. (23)

A very solid scientific consensus indicates that we are presently witnessing a disturbing warming of the climatic system. In recent decades this warming has been accompanied by a constant rise in the sea level and, it would appear, by an increase of extreme weather events, even if a scientifically determinable cause cannot be assigned to each particular phenomenon. Humanity is called to recognize the need for changes of lifestyle, production and consumption, in order to combat this warming or at least the human causes which produce or aggravate it. (23)

There is a nobility in the duty to care for creation through little daily actions (211)

Along with the importance of little everyday gestures, social love moves us to devise larger strategies to halt environmental degradation and to encourage a "culture of care" which permeates all of society. (231)

Clearly, the Bible has no place for a tyrannical anthropocentrism unconcerned for other creatures. (68)

Creation is of the order of love. (77)

A fragile world, entrusted by God to human care, challenges us to devise intelligent ways of directing, developing, and limiting our power. (78)

All of us are linked by unseen bonds and together form a kind of universal family, a sublime communion which fills us with a sacred, affectionate and humble respect. (89)

Everything is related, and we human beings are united as brothers and sisters on a wonderful pilgrimage, woven together by the love God has for each of his creatures and which also unites us in fond affection with brother sun, sister moon, brother river and mother earth. (92)

Encountering God does not mean fleeing from this world or turning our back on nature. (235)

We have to realize that a true ecological approach always becomes a social approach; it must integrate questions of justice in debates on the environment, so as to hear both the cry of the earth and the cry of the poor. (49)

Every ecological approach needs to incorporate a social perspective which takes into account the fundamental rights of the poor and the underprivileged. (93)

We are not faced with two separate crises, one environmental and the other social, but rather one complex crisis which is both social and environmental. Strategies for a solution demand an integrated approach to combating poverty, restoring dignity to the underprivileged, and at the same time protecting nature. (139)

The emptier a person's heart is, the more he or she needs things to buy, own and consume. (204)

Obsession with a consumerist lifestyle, above all when few people are capable of maintaining it, can only lead to violence and mutual destruction. (205)

The principle of the maximization of profits, frequently isolated from other considerations, reflects a misunderstanding of the very nature of the economy. As long as production is increased, little concern is shown about whether it is at the cost of future resources or the health of the environment; as long as the clearing of a forest increases production, no one calculates the losses entailed in the desertification of the land, the harm done to biodiversity or the increased pollution. In a word, businesses profit by calculating and paying only a fraction of the costs involved. (195)

Each community can take from the bounty of the earth whatever it needs for subsistence, but it also has the duty to protect the earth and to ensure its fruitfulness for coming generations. (67)

Intergenerational solidarity is not optional, but rather a basic question of justice, since the world we have received also belongs to those who will follow us. (159)

The following is the text of a speech given by President Obama to the United Nations General Assembly upon the passing of the Sustainable Development Goals, September 27, 2015.

General Assembly Hall
United Nations
New York, New York
3:04 p.m. EDT

PRESIDENT OBAMA: Good afternoon. Mr. Secretary General, fellow delegates, ladies and gentlemen. It is a great honor to be here to address the topic of sustainable development.

In many of our nations, especially developed countries, there is among our general population a genuine compassion towards those in need. There is a recognition of the grinding poverty that so many experience every day around the world. And yet sometimes it's said that our efforts to combat poverty and disease do not and cannot work, that there are some places beyond hope, that certain people and regions are condemned to an endless cycle of suffering. Here, today, we put those myths to rest. Today, we set aside the skepticism, and we lift up the hope that is available to us through collective action.

Because the world came together in an unprecedented effort, the global hunger rate has already been slashed. Tens of millions of more boys and girls are today in school. Prevention and treatment of measles and malaria and tuberculosis have saved nearly 60 million lives. HIV/AIDS infections and deaths have plummeted. And more than one billion people have lifted themselves up from extreme poverty—one billion.

The entire world can take enormous pride in these historic achievements. And so let the skeptics and cynics know development works. Investing in public health works. We can break the cycle of poverty. People and nations can rise into prosperity. Despite the cruelties of our world and the ravages of disease, millions of lives can be saved if we are focused, and if we work together. Cynicism is our enemy. A belief, a capacity in the dignity of every individual, and a recognition that we, each of us, can play a small part to play in lifting up people all around the world—that is the message that we are sending here today. And because of the work of so many who are assembled here today, we can point to past success. And yet, we are also here today because we understand that our work is nowhere near done. We can take pride in what we've accomplished, but we cannot be complacent.

When eleven boys and girls die every single minute from preventable causes, we know we have more work to do. When hundreds of women die every single day just from having a baby, we know we have more work to do. When tens of millions of children are still not in school, when hundreds of millions of people have no clean water, no toilets, we have so much more to do.

Right now, some 800 million men, women and children are scraping by on less than $1.25 a day. Imagine that. Gripped by the ache of an empty stomach. Billions of our fellow human beings are at risk of dying from diseases that we know how to prevent. Many children are just one mosquito bite away from death. And that is a moral outrage. It is a profound injustice. It is literally a matter of life and death, and now the world must act. We cannot leave people behind.

And so, today, we commit ourselves to new Sustainable Development Goals, including our goal of ending extreme poverty in our world. We do so understanding how difficult the task may be. We suffer no illusions of the challenges ahead. But we understand this is something that we must commit ourselves to. Because in doing so, we recognize that our most basic bond—our common humanity—compels us to act. An impoverished child in a distant slum or a neighborhood not that far from here is just as equal, just as worthy, as any of our children, as any of us, as any head of government or leader in this great hall.

We reaffirm that supporting development is not charity, but is instead one of the smartest investments we can make in our own future. After all, it is a lack of development—when people have no education, and no jobs, and no hope, a feeling that their basic human dignity is being violated—that helps fuel so much of the tensions and conflict and instability in our world.

And I profoundly believe that many of the conflicts, the refugee crises, the military interventions over the years might have been avoided if nations had truly invested in the lives of their people, and if the wealthiest nations on Earth were better partners in working with those that are trying to lift themselves up. (Applause.)

As one of the founders of the United Nations, Ralph Bunche once said, "Peace is no mere matter of men fighting or not fighting. Peace, to have meaning...must be translated into bread or rice, shelter, health, and education."

I'm here to say that in this work, the United States will continue to be your partner. Five years ago, I pledged here that America would remain the global leader in development, and the United States government, in fact, remains the single largest donor of development assistance, including in global health. In times of crisis—from Ebola to Syria—we are the largest provider of humanitarian aid. In times of disaster and crisis, the world can count on the friendship and generosity of the American people.

The question before us, though, as an international community, is how do we meet these new goals that we've set today? How can we do our work better? How can we stretch our resources and our funding more effectively? How can donor countries be smarter, and how can recipient countries do more with what they receive? We have to learn from the past—to see where we succeeded so that we can duplicate that success, and to understand where we've fallen short and correct those shortcomings.

And we start by understanding that this next chapter of development cannot fall victim to the old divides between developed nations and developing ones. Poverty, growing inequality exists in all of our nations, and all of our nations have work to do. And that includes here in the United States.

That's why, after a terrible recession, my administration has worked to keep millions of families from falling into poverty. That's why we've brought quality, affordable health care to more than 17 million Americans. Here in this country, the wealthiest nation on Earth, we're still working every day to perfect our union, and to be more equal and more just, and to treat the most vulnerable members of our society with value and concern.

That's why, today, I am committing the United States to achieving the Sustainable Development Goals. (Applause.) And as long as I am President, and well after I'm done being President, I will keep fighting for the education and housing and health care and jobs that reduce inequality and create opportunity here in the United States and around the world. (Applause.) Because this is not just the job of politicians; this is work for all of us.

This next chapter of development cannot just be about what governments spend, it has to harness the unprecedented resources of our interconnected world. In just a few short years—in the areas of health, and food security, and energy—my administration has committed and helped mobilize more than $100 billion to promote development and save lives. More than $100 billion. And guided by the new consensus we reached in Addis, I'm calling on others to join us. More governments, more institutions, more businesses, more philanthropies, more NGOs, more faith communities, more citizens—we all need to step up with the will and the resources and the coordination to achieve our goals. This must be the work of the world.

At the same time, this next chapter of development must focus not simply on the dollars we spend, but on the results that we achieve. And this demands new technologies and approaches, accountability, data, behavioral science—understanding that there's lessons that we have learned, best practices on how people actually live so that we can dramatically improve outcomes. It means breaking cycles of dependence by helping people become more self-sufficient—not just giving people fish, but teaching them how to fish. That's the purpose of development.

Rather than just sending food during famine—although we have to do that to avert starvation—we also have to bring new techniques and new seeds and new technologies to more farmers so they can boost their yields and increase their incomes, feed more people and lift countless millions out of poverty. Rather than just respond to outbreaks like Ebola—although we have to do that, and we have—let's also strengthen public health systems and advance global health security to prevent epidemics in the first place.

As more countries take ownership of their HIV/AIDS programs, the United States is setting two new bold goals. Over the next two years, we'll increase the number of people that our funding reaches—so that nearly 13 million people with HIV/AIDS get lifesaving treatment—and we'll invest $300 million to help achieve a 40 percent reduction in new HIV infections among young women and girls in the hardest-hit areas of sub-Saharan Africa. (Applause.) And I believe we can do that—the first AIDS-free generation. (Applause.)

This next chapter of development must also unleash economic growth—not just for a few at the top, but inclusive, sustainable growth that lifts up the fortunes of the many. We know the ingredients for creating jobs and opportunity—they are not a secret. So let's embrace reforms that attract trade and investment to areas that are in need of investment and in need of trade. Let's trade and build more together, make it easier for developing countries to sell more of their goods around the world. And let's invest in our greatest resource—our people—their education, their skills. Let's invest in innovative entrepreneurs, the striving young people who embrace new technology and are starting businesses and can ignite new industries that change the world. I have met young people on every continent, and they can lead the way if we give them the tools they need.

Our new development goals are ambitious. But thanks to the good work of many of you, they are achievable—if we work together; if we meet our responsibilities to each other. I believe that. The progress of recent years gives us hope. We know what works. We know how to do this. But perhaps because this is now my seventh year of addressing the General Assembly, I tend to be more blunt. Along with the gray hair, I'm becoming more likely to speak my mind. (Laughter.) So indulge me when I say that we will never achieve our goals if we do not squarely confront several insidious threats to the dignity and well-being of people around the world. No matter how much hard work is done by development agencies, no matter how large the donations and commitments that are made by donor countries, if we don't take care of some other elements of development, we will not meet the goals that we've set.

Number one, development is threatened by bad governance. Today, we affirm what we know to be true from decades of experience—development and economic growth that is truly sustainable and inclusive depends on governments and institutions that care about their people, that are accountable, that respect human rights and deliver justice for everybody and not just some.

So, in the face of corruption that siphons billions away from schools and hospitals and infrastructure into foreign bank accounts, governments have to embrace transparency and open government and rule of law. And combating illicit finance must be a global effort because it is part of our development effort. And citizens and civil society groups must be free to organize and speak their mind and work for progress, because that's how countries develop; that's how countries succeed.

Development is also threatened by inequality. And this is a political debate that we have in this country, so I just want to be clear, this is not something from which the United States is immune to. Every country has to grapple with this issue. The wealthiest and most powerful in our societies oftentimes like to keep things as they are, and they often have disproportionate political influences. When poor children are more likely to get sick and die than children in wealthier neighborhoods just across town; when rural families are more likely to go without clean water; when ethnic and religious minorities, or people with disabilities, or people of different sexual orientations are discriminated against or can't access education and opportunity—that holds all of us back. And so, in all of our countries, we have to invest in the interventions that allow us to reach more people—because no one should be left behind just because of where they live or what they look like.

Development is threatened by old attitudes, especially those that deny rights and opportunity to women. In too many places, girls are less likely to be in school than boys. Globally, women are less likely to have a job than men and are more likely to live in poverty. I've said this before and I will keep repeating it—one of the best indicators of whether a country will succeed is how it treats its women. (Applause.) When women have an education, when women have a job, their children are more likely to get an education, their families are healthier and more prosperous. Their communities and countries do better, as well. So every nation—all of our nations—must invest in the education and health and skills of our women and girls.

And I have to say I do not have patience for the excuse of, well, we have our own ways of doing things. (Applause.) We understand that there is a long tradition in every society of discriminating against women. But that's not an excuse for taking a new path in order to make sure that everyone in a society has opportunity.

Development is threatened if we do not recognize the incredible dynamism and opportunity of today's Africa. Hundreds of millions of Africans still struggle in the face of grinding poverty and deadly diseases, daily assaults on their lives and dignity. But I visited Africa recently, and what I saw gave me hope and I know should give you hope, because that continent has made impressive gains in health and education. It is one of the fastest-growing regions of the world, with a rising middle class.

And during my travels, Africans—especially young Africans—tell me they don't just want aid, they want trade. They want businesses. They want investment. So I call on the world to join us as we mobilize billions of dollars in new trade and investment and development in Africa—and that includes Power Africa, our initiative to bring electricity and greater opportunity to more than 60 million African homes and businesses. If we get Africa fulfilling its full potential, that will help the entire global economy. Everyone here will be helped. It's not a zero-sum game. We are invested in their success. (Applause.)

Development is threatened by war. This should be a simple proposition, but it bears repeating. It is no coincidence that half of the people living in extreme poverty around the world live in places afflicted by chronic violence and conflict. Today, some 60 million men, women and children have been forced from their homes, many by conflicts in the Middle East and in Africa. These are humanitarian crises and refugees that we cannot ignore, and we have to deliver the urgent aid that is needed right now. And those countries that can must do more to accommodate refugees, recognizing that those children are just like ours. But our efforts must be matched by the hard work of diplomacy and reconciliation to end conflicts that so often tear societies apart.

And as I said earlier, war and conflict is more likely to arise where we have bad governance, and we have high inequality, and we have discrimination against minority groups and ethnic groups, and we have low educational levels. So these things are all related.

And finally, development is threatened by climate change. And I want to thank the Secretary General for the extraordinary leadership and work that he's done on this issue. (Applause.)

All of our countries will be affected by a changing climate. But the world's poorest people will bear the heaviest burden—from rising seas and more intense droughts, shortages of water and food. We will be seeing climate change refugees. As His Holiness Pope Francis has rightly implored the world, this is a moral calling.

In just two months, the world has an opportunity to unite around a strong global agreement. I saw President Hollande walk in a few moments ago—we are going to be converging in Paris. With his leadership, and the leadership of every world leader, we need to establish the tools and financing to help developing nations embrace clean energy, adapt to climate change, and ensure that there's not a false choice between economic development and the best practices that can save our planet. We can do the same at the same time. And the communities and lives of billions of people depend on the work that we do. (Applause.)

Future generations of young people watching today and tomorrow will judge us by the choices we make in the months and years ahead. And one of those young people is Eva Tolage. Eva lives in a village in Tanzania. She's 15 years old, and she wrote me a letter. Some of you know I get 10 letters a day, mostly from inside the United States, but sometimes international letters. I get 40,000 a day, but I read 10. (Laughter.)

And so Eva told me about her parents—farmers who struggle to provide for their seven children. And this young 15-year-old girl—a girl the age of my daughters—she dreams of going to college, but with little food to eat, she explained how it's hard for her sometimes to concentrate in school. She explained that her house doesn't have electricity, so it's hard for her to study at night.

It's not because her parents don't love her and don't have ambitions for her. Her father works incredibly hard in the fields to pay for her education. But they just need a little help. "I won't let him down," Eva said. "I'll do whatever it takes," she said in her letter. And then, knowing that we would be gathered at this summit to help lift up families like hers, she asked me a question that could be asked of all of our nations—"What will you commit to doing…?" What will you do?

And there are billions of boys and girls just like Eva. They're just like our children. They have as much talent and as much hope for the future. And they're willing to work hard, and their parents love them just as much as we love ours. And just by the accident of birth, it's so much more difficult for them to achieve their dreams as it is for our children. But in the eyes of God, they are the same children. They're just as important.

And for Eva, and all those just trying to survive another day in conditions that many of us can barely imagine, it can sometimes seem as if the world is blind to their struggles and their dreams. And so today, I say to Eva and hundreds of millions—billions—like her: We see you. We hear you. I've read your letter. And we commit ourselves—as nations, as one world—to the urgent work that must be done. To standing with families like Eva's as they work and strive for a better life. To ending the injustice of extreme poverty. To upholding the inherent dignity of every human being. Whatever it takes. We can't let them down. And with your help, we won't.

Thank you very much. (Applause.)

Neal's Creed

I believe there is a spirit world underlying all existence, living and inanimate.

I believe separateness and independence are an illusion and wholeness and interdependence are the reality.

I believe Jesus was inspired of the spirit world and a great teacher whose message was one of inclusion and love and against exclusion and isolation.

I believe injustice against other people, particularly those we have power over, diminishes us.

I believe we have an obligation to respect all life and be loving stewards of the natural world. Not doing so diminishes us.

I believe in love and equity and justice and sustainability.

I believe the people and all living creatures of the future have rights today and we have an obligation to respect their rights.

I believe all religions, teachings, metaphors, or philosophies that serve to bring people to these values are inspired of the spirit and legitimate.

I believe in an undefined and mysterious afterlife.

I believe in the human capacity to act in this world and the unencumbered human spirit free of spiritual debt.

I believe in the golden rule: do unto others as you would have others do unto you.

I believe unacted-upon beliefs are hollow and of little value.

I believe intentions matter, common intentions are powerful, and universal intentions are miraculous.

Resources

Please visit us at
www.wholeearthjustice.com

ABOUT THE AUTHOR

 After receiving his baccalaureate from the University of Minnesota, Gene worked in the Twin Cities as a commercial real estate broker who specialized in urban redevelopment. Gene is also a backyard inventor with two patents to his credit and an Impressionist artist who has had numerous shows at galleries around the Twin Cities. He is also an entrepreneur who became passionate about sustainable living strategies. In 2015 Gene founded a Minnesota nonprofit organization called CarFreeLife Inc., which is dedicated to promoting and facilitating car-light living. Among the products offered by CarFreeLife is a car ownership sharing program called Neighborcar. CarFreeLife can be reached at carfreelife.org and neighborcar.com.

www.wholeearthjustice.com

CPSIA information can be obtained
at www.ICGtesting.com
Printed in the USA
JSHW010748140220
4228JS00003B/16